# American Women

# A Concise History

D1253965

## About the Cover

*American modernist painter Florine Stettheimer (1871–1944) painted this exuberantly detailed scene of Asbury Park South, a well known resort in New Jersey, in 1920. Even though the sea-shore had designated areas for white and Black beachgoers, Stettheimer portrayed an integrated social gath-ering, filled with individuals, couples and families on the boardwalk, pier, and beach. The canvas is arranged like a stage, its space filled with small, humorous scenes. The use of careful-ly crafted miniaturization and vivid primary colors characterized much of Stettheimer's work.*

# American Women

## A CONCISE HISTORY

Susan Ware

New York  Oxford
OXFORD UNIVERSITY PRESS

Oxford University Press is a department of the University of Oxford.
It furthers the University's objective of excellence in research, scholarship,
and education by publishing worldwide. Oxford is a registered trademark of
Oxford University Press in the UK and certain other countries.

Published in the United States of America by Oxford University Press,
198 Madison Avenue, New York, NY 10016, United States of America.

© 2022 by Oxford University Press

For titles covered by Section 112 of the US Higher Education Opportunity
Act, please visit www.oup.com/us/he for the latest information about
pricing and alternate formats.

All rights reserved. No part of this publication may be reproduced, stored in
a retrieval system, or transmitted, in any form or by any means, without the
prior permission in writing of Oxford University Press, or as expressly permitted
by law, by license, or under terms agreed with the appropriate reproduction
rights organization. Inquiries concerning reproduction outside the scope of the
above should be sent to the Rights Department, Oxford University Press,
at the address above.

You must not circulate this work in any other form
and you must impose this same condition on any acquirer.

**Library of Congress Cataloging-in-Publication Data**

Names: Ware, Susan, 1950– author.
Title: American women: a concise history/Susan Ware.
Description: New York: Oxford University Press, 2021.|Includes
bibliographical references and index.|Summary: "American Women: A
Concise History offers the most accessible and engaging introduction to
the history of American women"—Provided by publisher.
Identifiers: LCCN 2021002008 (print)|LCCN 2021002009 (ebook)|ISBN
9780197522349 (paperback)|ISBN 9780197522370 (spiral bound)|ISBN
9780197522356 (epub)|ISBN 9780197522363 (pdf)
Subjects: LCSH: Women—United States—History—Sources.|Women social
reformers—United States—History.|Women civic leaders—United
States—History.
Classification: LCC HQ1410 .A445 2021 (print)|LCC HQ1410 (ebook)|DDC
305.40973—dc23
LC record available at https://lccn.loc.gov/2021002008
LC ebook record available at https://lccn.loc.gov/2021002009

Printing number: 9 8 7 6 5 4 3 2 1
Printed by Quad/Mexico, Mexico

# BRIEF CONTENTS

# CONTENTS

CHAPTER **three**

CHAPTER **four**

CHAPTER **seven**

Feminism and Its Discontents,
**1960–1992**   179

CHAPTER **eight**

Our Bodies, Our Politics, **1992–2020**   207

# LIST OF MAPS AND FIGURES

# INTRODUCTION

"Always ask what did the women do while the men were doing what the textbook tells us was important," historian Gerda Lerner provocatively challenged in 1981. This book answers that charge, documenting the diversity of American women's lives and experiences by drawing on the explosion of scholarship in women's and gender history to which Lerner herself was a leading contributor and theorist.

Few fields of American history have grown as dramatically as women, gender, and sexuality studies over the past several decades. Courses in women's history taught by specialists are now standard in most colleges and universities, as are interdisciplinary courses on women, gender, and sexuality. Historians, writers, and biographers produce a wide range of literature on issues related to women and gender. Textbooks now include full discussions of major topics and viewpoints in women's history as an integrated part of their general narrative.

Gender is now recognized as an extremely important tool for the study of history, especially women's history. Historians first began to engage with the concept in response to Joan Scott's pathbreaking article "Gender: A Useful Category of Analysis" which appeared in 1986. Because all historical actors have a gender, practically any historical question, from diplomacy to leisure to state policy, can be subjected to a gender analysis.

In its most common formulation, gender refers to the historical and cultural constructions of roles assigned to the biological differences and attributes of women and men. While sex differences are often presumed to be unchanging and innate, gender differences are subject to wide variations historically and across cultures, precisely because they are socially constructed. In other words, what it means to be a woman—or a man—changes over time. And those definitions can interact with and legitimize other hierarchical relations of power, such as race and heterosexuality.

But we need to be far more flexible than that, realizing that not all people inhabit a simple two-sex model. In fact they (the use of this pronoun here is deliberate) often affirmatively choose to live outside the male/female binary. Alongside those who were assigned the female sex at birth and continue to identify themselves as cisgender, the narrative includes individuals assigned male at birth who lived as women. It also includes those we would now call non-binary or gender non-conforming.

As feminist scholarship has amply demonstrated, the category of women is difficult to generalize about. Another challenge in providing an overview of the history of women is foregrounding which women are being discussed and not simply allowing the better documented experiences of white middle-class women to stand in for the rest. Therefore, this narrative highlights the diversity of American women's experiences as continually shaped by factors such as race, class, religion, geographical location, age, sexual identity and gender expression, among others. It also highlights the moments when differences between women, such as white slaveholding women and Black enslaved females, call out for contrasting perspectives. Think of this project as a giant balancing act, with multiple balls in the air at once.

As its overarching theme, this survey presents "woman as force in history." Paying homage to historian Mary Ritter Beard's pathbreaking scholarship from the 1930s and 1940s, this conceptual framework highlights the contributions, recognized and unrecognized, that women have made to the American experience. Without downplaying the historical constraints and barriers blocking women's advancement, the story emphasizes women as active agents rather than passive victims in a variety of contexts throughout U.S. history. Along with that goes a commitment to see America through women's eyes.

What is this America we will be exploring through women's eyes? That term, like women, needs to be contextualized and explained historically. At the beginning of the narrative the scope of the story encompasses a broad geographical sweep including both North America and Central America and their indigenous inhabitants. As indigenous peoples interacted with waves of colonizing European settlers from the seventeenth century on, our focus shrinks somewhat to encompass the future physical boundaries of what will become the continental United States—what political scientist Benedict Anderson has called the "logo map." But as the United States built an overseas empire starting in the late nineteenth century, acquiring far flung possessions around the world such as the Philippines, Guam, and Samoa, the focus expands outward again. By the end of the narrative the United States is fully embedded in an interconnected global economy. All these stages are part of an expansive definition of what comprises American history.

The goal of the text is familiarity with the main currents and themes of American history through engagement with the specific history of its women. This dual focus is necessary because it is impossible to write about women in isolation from men or unaffected by broader events and trends. And yet women's stories link to larger themes at the same time they often challenge them. For example, traditional markers such as the American Revolution, the Civil War, and World War II are not necessarily the most useful concepts for organizing women's history. With women's stories fully integrated into the broader national story, the end result will be a richer understanding of American history in all its complexity, including its transnational and global dimensions.

While gender analysis has been enormously important to the fields of women's history and women, gender, and sexuality studies, we must never lose sight of the "real" women who make American history happen. These flesh-and-blood historical actors propel the story that follows, enriching and complicating traditional historical narratives while confirming that women have been central to American history from the start. To quote Gerda Lerner again: "What we have to offer, for consciousness, is a correct analysis of what the world is like. Up to now we have had a partial analysis. Everything that explains the world has in fact explained a world that does not exist, a world in which men are at the center of the human enterprise and women are at the margin 'helping' them. Men and women have built society and have built the world. Women have been central to it. This revolutionary insight is itself a force, a force that liberates and transforms." Knowledge is power, Lerner reminds us, and history matters, especially for women who for so long were denied theirs.

# ACKNOWLEDGMENTS

When I took over as general editor of the *American National Biography* in 2012, I became part of the Oxford University Press family. That connection brought me in contact with Nancy Toff, who recruited me to write a Very Short Introduction (VSI) on American women's history which was published in 2015. Charles Cavaliere of Oxford's Higher Education Group, who remembered me knitting during meetings for an earlier textbook project we collaborated on, pitched the idea of turning my VSI into a concise women's history textbook and then enthusiastically supported the project every step of the way. Assistant editor Katie Tunkavige's help and good cheer were much appreciated as the manuscript moved through production, as were editorial assistant Danica Donovan's contributions to photo research and other tasks. As always, it has been a pleasure working with the dedicated professionals on the OUP team.

I would also like to acknowledge the extremely generous comments of reviewers who helped me identify what aspects of the VSI needed to be expanded and updated and pointed me to scholarship that would enhance the manuscript. Along with the reviewers who wished to remain anonymous, warm thanks to the following:

Elaine S. Abelson, The New School
Brittany Adams, Irvine Valley College
Neeka Aguirre, Mendocino Community College
Sara Alpern, Texas A&M University
Hilary Aquino, Albright College
Dorothea Browder, Western Kentucky University
Amy Canfield, Lewis-Clark State College
Karen Dunak, Muskingum University
Miriam Forman-Brunell, University of Missouri–Kansas City
Jennifer L. Gross, Jacksonville State University
Christopher Hayashida-Knight, California State University–Chico
Lindsay Keiter, Penn State University–Altoona
Katherine Marino, University of California–Los Angeles
Louise Newman, University of Florida
Kimberley Reilly, University of Wisconsin–Green Bay
Nina Silber, Boston University
Jan Wilson, University of Tulsa

A special shout-out to Katherine Marino, who has been an enthusiastic supporter of the project from the very start. I first met Katherine when she took an undergraduate class on feminist biography I taught at Harvard in 2002. What fun to stay in touch with her over the years and watch her become a respected historian in her own right.

In 2020 I participated in many public programs surrounding the centennial of the Nineteenth Amendment and I would often end my talks by reminding audiences that when they voted, they were standing on the shoulders of the suffragists. I feel the same way about the contributions of several generations of scholars who built women, gender, and sexuality studies into the thriving field that it is. I too am standing on shoulders, and I gratefully acknowledge that debt.

# ABOUT THE AUTHOR

**Susan Ware** is the author and editor of numerous books on twentieth-century U.S. history and biography. Educated at Wellesley College and Harvard University, she has taught at New York University and Harvard, where she served as editor of the biographical dictionary *Notable American Women: Completing the Twentieth Century* (2004). Ware has long been associated with the Schlesinger Library at the Radcliffe Institute for Advanced Study where she currently is the Honorary Women's Suffrage Centennial Historian. Since 2012, she has served as the general editor of the *American National Biography*, published by Oxford University Press under the auspices of the American Council of Learned Societies. She divides her time between Cambridge, Massachusetts, and Hopkinton, New Hampshire.

# American
# Women
## A Concise History

MATOAKA ALS REBECCA FILIA POTENTISS : PRINC : POWHATANI IMP : VIRGINIÆ.

Ætatis suæ 21. A. 1616

Matoaks als Rebecka daughter to the mighty Prince
Powhatan Emperour of Attanoughskomouck als virginia
converted and baptized in the Christian faith, and
wife to the wor.ᵗ Mr. Joh Rolff.

i.Paß: sculp:          Compton Holland excuₐ

# one

# In the Beginning: North America's Women TO 1750

## CHAPTER OUTLINE

This portrait of Pocahontas, done in London in 1616, references her multiple identities as Matoaka (her birth name) and Rebecca (her English name), as well as her status as the daughter of a Powhatan chief and the wife of John Rolfe. All those signifiers prompt the question: who was she really, and what was she feeling when she sat for this portrait so far from her native land?

Pocahontas is one of the best-known stock characters in the history of the founding of the United States. The young Powhatan girl who supposedly saved British explorer John Smith from execution and then later journeyed to England as the wife of John Rolfe has been reduced to a conventional (and convenient) stereotype: noble Indian princess who helps white European men and thus by extension gives Indians' blessing to all that comes after.

Walt Disney made Pocahontas into a love-struck teenager, but feminist scholars see her as a much more complex character. Think of all that happened to her in the barely twenty years she lived: she literally had her feet in two different cultures, the Powhatan world in which she was raised and the English world to which she converted. And yet even as she participated in English society, she never abandoned the Powhatan spirit world that nurtured her.

Pocahontas (a childhood nickname; her birth name was Matoaka) first encountered the newly arrived English settlers from Jamestown in 1607, when John Smith was brought to her village as a captive. She was a girl of twelve, he a middle-aged man, a shaky foundation for the fateful (and likely fanciful) story of her dramatic intervention to save his life. Several years later Pocahontas herself was kidnapped and held hostage by English captors for almost a year. In part to cement Powhatan-English relations, she agreed to marry John Rolfe in what was arguably North America's first mixed-race marriage. In 1616 the couple and their young son made the difficult sea journey to England, where Pocahontas, now known by the English name Rebecca, was treated like a celebrity. Alas, British hospitality also meant exposure to British disease, against which she had no immunity, and she died as she prepared to sail home. Instead of returning to her ancestral birthplace, she was buried on English soil.

Pocahontas was an adventurer who straddled the two cultures whose interaction determined much of the early history of colonial North America: indigenous cultures, usually referred to as Native or Indian, and the cultures of the European settlers (Spanish, English, French, and Dutch), exported in the surge of exploration and colonization set in motion by Christopher Columbus's 1492 journey of discovery. European explorers often conceived of the North American continent as "virgin land," sparsely inhabited and still largely untouched by human settlement. In fact, North America was home to a range of vibrant and complex Native American cultures that did not simply disappear once European colonizers stepped ashore.

The contact between these two cultures involved war, upheaval, disease, and sexual violence, as well as interaction, negotiation, and adaptation, and gender was central to the story. Whether you were male or female affected your life just as much as whether you were Native or European. The contrast between gender roles in Indian societies and European ones demonstrates the malleability of the concept of gender, as well as showing how deeply invested European settlers were in their own conceptions of the way that relationships between the sexes should be ordered.

There is no simple or linear progression in women's status over the course of the seventeenth and eighteenth centuries, either for European women or their Indian counterparts. Some things changed for the better, others worsened, not necessarily at the same time or the same rate for each group. By 1750, however, a vibrant colonial culture was flourishing along the Eastern seaboard, bringing prosperity and wealth to colonists who actively participated in the thriving Atlantic commercial culture. And Native societies continued to adapt and persist in the midst of this changing landscape.

Many older and more traditional American history texts begin with the settlements at Jamestown in 1607 or the landing of the Pilgrims at Plymouth in 1620, which gives the impression that the story only starts when the white folks arrive. Instead we will start our story with the peoples who were already there.

1.1: Sir Walter Raleigh commissioned artist John White to document the plants, animals, and indigenous people he encountered during his time in Roanoke, Virginia, in the 1580s. This drawing, entitled "Theire sitting at meate," depicts a Native American couple as they prepare to eat a meal, most likely prepared by the woman by boiling the corn to remove the hulls.

# ORIGIN STORIES

"Is it a bow or a sifter?" That is how the Cherokees assigned a male or female gender to a newborn infant. Bows were used in hunting and fishing, connecting the male infant to his future life in the forest and streams. Sifters were used in making bread and processing corn, linking the female infant to her future in the world of agriculture, plants, and food production. The Iroquois conceptualized life along similarly gendered lines when they personified the forest as male and the village as female. Most human societies differentiate men's and women's roles in some form or another; the key factor is how those differences are valued and enforced. In general, Indian societies saw these demarcations as complementary, not a sign of the subordination of one sex to the other.

Not all Native people fit this gender binary, however. Spanish explorers and early missionaries noted (with astonishment tinged with disapproval) the existence of individuals who crossed gender lines, usually individuals assigned male at birth who took on female roles. As Cabeza de Vaca recorded about his explorations of Northern Mexico in the 1520s, "I saw one man married to another ... , and they go about dressed as women, and do women's tasks." Anthropologists later labeled these individuals "berdaches," a term that Natives found offensive. More recently they have been called **two-spirit**, although that term has also been criticized for reinforcing gender binaries. Whatever the label, such gender-nonconforming individuals were present in most Indian cultures. And while the most attention has focused on men who donned women's clothing, female-to-male crossing also occurred, although with much less flexibility to cross back and forth between genders than men who lived as women.

Women played vital and significant roles in Native cultures—larger, perhaps, than their European counterparts. Native women were especially important in the active spirit world, in part because of their close relationship to the production of food as well as their reproductive roles. Many creation stories, such as the Acoma Pueblo origin myth of Tsichtinako (Thought Woman) and the two sisters Iatiku (Mother of the Corn Clan) and Nautsiti (Mother of the Sun Clan), drew parallels between the origins of life and the germination of plant seeds, with human life emerging from the underworld like a sprout of maize pushing up through the soil. To honor this creation myth, all Pueblo infants received an ear of corn, a symbol of the Corn Mothers, who had given life not just to humans but to plants and animals as well.

The great majority of Indian tribes were organized in a **matrilineal** way—that is, inheritance passed through the mother's line. Sexual activity began at a comparatively early age and was not confined to marriage. On marriage men moved into their wives' extended family networks, which often included multiple generations living together; these women's kin groups, rather than the conjugal ties between husband and wife, served as the glue of social interaction. In Indian societies the community always took precedence over the individual.

These generalizations need to be tempered by the fact that indigenous peoples never collectively identified themselves as "Indian" or "Native American,"

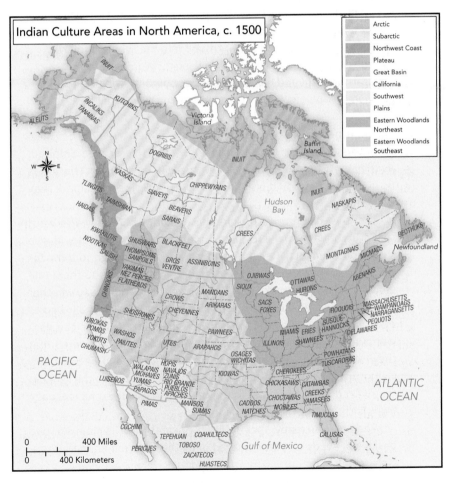

**MAP 1.1**

# The Origin Myth of the Acoma Pueblo

In this creation myth transcribed by anthropologist Matthew W. Stirling in 1928, the story unfolds not in a linear or chronological fashion, but cyclically. Two sisters emerge from the darkness of underground into the light and follow the instructions of Tsichtinako (Thought Woman) as they learn to plant and harvest corn, symbolically giving life to humans, plants, and all the creatures on the earth.

In the beginning two female human beings were born. These two children were born underground at a place called Shipapu. As they grew up, they began to be aware of each other. There was no light and they could only feel each other. Being in the dark they grew slowly.

After they had grown considerably, a Spirit whom they afterward called Tsichtinako spoke to them, and they found that it would give them nourishment. After they had grown large enough to think for themselves, they spoke to the Spirit when it had come to them one day and asked it to make itself known to them and to say whether it was male or female, but it replied only that it was not allowed to meet with them. They then asked why they were living in the dark without knowing each other by name, but the Spirit answered that they were nuk'timi (under the earth); but they were to be patient in waiting until everything was ready for them to go up into the light. So they waited a long time, and as they grew they learned their language from Tsichtinako.

When all was ready, they found a present from Tsichtinako, two baskets of seeds and little images of all the different animals (there were to be) in the world. The Spirit said they were sent by their father. They asked who was meant by their father, and Tsichtinako replied that his name was Uch'tsiti and that he wished them to take their baskets out into the light, when the time came.

...

The hole now let light into the place where the two sisters were, and Tsichtinako spoke to them, "Now is the time you are to go out. You are able to take your baskets with you. In them you will find pollen and sacred corn meal. When you reach the top, you will wait for the sun to come up and that direction will be called ha'nami (east). With the pollen and the sacred corn meal you will pray to the Sun. You will thank the Sun for bringing you to light, ask for a long life and happiness, and for success in the purpose for which you were created."

...

And as they waited to pray to the Sun, the girl on the right moved her best hand and was named Iatiku, which meant "bringing to life." Tsichtinako then told her to name her sister, but it took a long time. Finally Tsichtinako noticed that the other had more in her basket, so Tsichtinako told Iatiku to name her thus, and Iatiku called her Nautsiti, which meant "more of everything in the basket."

...

Tsichtinako next said to them, "Now that you have your names, you will pray with your names and your clan names so that the Sun will know you and recognize you." Tsichtinako asked Nautsiti which clan she wished to belong to. Nautsiti answered, "I wish to see the sun; that is the clan I will be." The spirit told Nautsiti to ask Iatiku what clan she wanted. Iatiku thought for a long time but finally she noticed that she had the seed from which sacred meal was made in her basket and no other kind of seeds. She thought, "With this name I shall be very proud, for it has been chosen for nourishment and it is sacred." So she said, "I will be Corn clan."

*SOURCE: Matthew W. Stirling, "Origin Myth of Acoma and Other Records,"* **Bureau of American Ethnology Bulletin 135 (1942), 1, 2–3, 4.**

which were terms only used by Europeans. Instead they aligned themselves with their individual tribes or the confederations to which their tribes belonged. Further belying any sense of collective Indian identity is the striking array of cultural diversity: linguists estimate that there were four hundred spoken languages in use when Europeans began showing up on the shores. There were also significant differences among various tribes, especially by region and geography. Acoma Pueblos in the Southwest practiced intensive agriculture based on the three crops of corn, squash, and beans, whereas tribes in the Northwest, such as the Nootkas, subsisted primarily by fishing. The tribes of the Great Plains, such as the Sioux, Comanche, and Blackfeet, were hunters: the bison the men shot were then skinned and prepared by the women. The Iroquois in New York were distinctive for the large roles women played in the tribe's governance.

On the eve of Columbus's arrival in 1492, the traditional jumping-off point for narratives of American history, the North American continent was already populated with a diverse range of Native peoples and cultures. Less than two hundred years later, 90 to 95 percent of that indigenous population had been wiped out, partly by warfare but mainly by the devastating array of diseases that Europeans brought with them to North America, especially smallpox, against which Native Americans had no immunity. But they did not vanish. As late as the 1770s, indigenous people were still a majority in the Americas.

 ## GENDER FRONTIERS

While recognizing the breadth and diversity of indigenous Native cultures, shared experiences often shaped their interactions with the new arrivals. Indians were far from passive victims at the hands of the colonizing Spanish in the Southwest and Mexico or the French, English, and Dutch settlers along the Atlantic coast and in the backcountry. Instead, one historian described them as diplomatic hosts to "unexpected European guests"—but then those guests confused the situation by deciding to stay! A "gender frontiers" approach looks at both sides of these encounters with special attention to cultural meanings of gender norms and sexuality.

At first it was the Europeans who did most of the accommodating, having to adapt to Native rules and customs in order to survive and hopefully prosper in this new environment. Most interaction revolved around trade: products such as beaver hides and deerskins were exchanged for European goods such as firearms, metal tools, gunpowder, tobacco, and alcohol. The impact of these new trading patterns, specifically the incorporation of European goods acquired through the Atlantic trade into Native daily life, was widely apparent as early as 1650.

Like Pocahontas, who first came in contact with English settlers as a child in Jamestown, women were central to these encounters. The extensive and complex trading relationships that increasingly linked Indians and European settlers were often mediated by Indian women, who acted as **cultural mediators** or "negotiators of change." Their services were needed, especially in the fur trade, because economic activity was conducted by families and communities, not individuals, and because Indian tribes and European settlers brought fundamentally different expectations to the table. For Natives, the act of exchanging goods and gifts represented a way to promote goodwill within and between communities, whereas their European counterparts tended to think of traded goods as tribute or profit. Very often it was Native women who supplied the social skills and local knowledge to bridge the cultural gap. Both Algonquian and Iroquoian women traded furs and deerskins directly with Dutch settlers in the seventeenth century.

The significance of kinship in Native communities explains the key role women played. European explorers and traders, whether they be Spanish, French, Dutch, or English, were all strangers when they showed up in a new location, but what really drew attention was the fact that they came without women. To Native societies structured around matrilineal kin relationships, this gender imbalance was almost unfathomable: there literally was no place in their worldview for men without wives. So in order to build the relationships they understood to be necessary for trading alliances, the strangers had to be incorporated into kinship networks, primarily through marriage to Native women or the informal arrangements that the French called *mariage a la facon du pays* (after the custom of the country). These were not casual or promiscuous relationships but solid family units that often included children adopted from the wife's previous relationships in addition to the couple's new biracial, bicultural offspring.

Such relationships were most prevalent in the French fur trade but were also common between the Spanish conquistadors and Native women in the Southwest, where intermarriage produced the mixed-raced offspring who were called *mestiza*. In contrast, intermarriage between English settlers in New England and Native women was rare, in large part because the sex ratio in that region was fairly equal, unlike the skewed male-female imbalance elsewhere, especially in the seventeenth century.

Malintzin (c.1501–c.1529) was one such Indian woman who straddled multiple cultures. Also known as La Malinche or Doña Marina, Malintzin served as a trusted translator to Spanish explorer Hernán Cortés. Sold as a child to Mayan slave traders, she was one of twenty women offered to Cortés by the Tabascan people as a gesture of goodwill and accommodation when

1.2: This contemporary Aztec drawing prominently features Doña Marina (Malintzin) as she translates an exchange between Hernán Cortés, whose back she literally has, and the Aztec emperor Montezuma II, at Tenochtitlan in November 1519. Visual artifacts confirm her place in history, even though she left no written records.

he showed up in 1519 on the Yucatán peninsula in the Gulf of Mexico. The Spaniards had no way of communicating with the indigenous peoples they were trying to conquer and subdue, and Malintzin, a gifted linguist, seized the opening to broker these interactions, quickly making herself indispensable. This was also a sexual relationship: Malintzin had a son with Cortés, whom he acknowledged as his progeny. She then cemented her position and that of her children by marrying another high-ranking Spanish official.

Malintzin's place in historical memory has been contested. Unlike Pocahantas, she has often been portrayed as a traitor for selling out indigenous peoples to the Spanish conquerors. Feminist scholars offer a different interpretation, recognizing her as a bridge between multiple cultures and a consummate survivor who made the best of her situation as a captive Indian in the face of the Spanish conquest.

Artifacts and archaeology tell us quite a lot about the lives of Indian women, with one glaring exception: we do not know how they felt about the middle ground they occupied between two cultures because no surviving written documents preserve their stories. Instead we have the accounts of European settlers and missionaries. Luckily these documents, when read carefully, can provide a wealth of information about Native life—and a window on European attitudes and prejudices.

European observers seemed genuinely flummoxed by Native gender roles, which were so different from their own. For example, in European cultures hunting and fishing were sporting pursuits of the upper class, so the large roles that Native American men played as hunters were dismissed as frivolous and nonessential. And agriculture, especially working in the fields, was men's work in Europe, whereas it was women's work in Native American communities, and therefore was immediately devalued by missionaries and government officials who thought men should be in charge. This cultural miscommunication was the foundation of the demeaning European image of the Indian squaw forced to work like a drudge because her lazy husband was off besporting himself in the woods. If there was ever any question about the power of gender preconceptions, the total inability of Europeans to understand that Indian cultures were organized around different and quite effective norms is a case in point.

 ## GENDER AND RACE IN THE EARLY SETTLEMENTS

Europeans did not come to North America to learn from Native cultures; they came to get rich. The first waves of migrants who began arriving in Virginia in 1607 were overwhelmingly male—basically a group of young men on the make who lacked good prospects back home—and totally unprepared for dealing with such necessities as surviving the winter or foraging for food. The Indians literally were their saviors.

In the early Chesapeake settlements, white women were a tiny minority and much sought after. Most white women came as **indentured servants**, contracting for a set number of years of service in return for their passage over; like men, they responded to the lure of starting a new life in a new country. Once their indenture was finished, they were all but assured of marriage because of a sex ratio that hovered around six to one. Despite numerous initiatives encouraging migration to Virginia, seventeenth-century Chesapeake society failed to develop strong communities based on stable families. Only in the eighteenth century did the sex ratio come more into balance.

Settlers hoped for gold to win quick fortunes, but tobacco (introduced in 1613) turned out to be the ticket to the future for Virginia, with strongly divergent outcomes for its population based on race and gender. In contrast to

DOCUMENTING AMERICAN WOMEN

# Bernal Díaz del Castillo Remembers Doña Marina

Bernal Díaz del Castillo marched and fought with the Spanish explorer Hernán Cortés in his conquest of Mexico between 1517 and 1521. Years later he wrote this account of the expedition, one of the most extensive descriptions of the importance of the translator Doña Marina (Malintzin) to the mission's success. Translators like Malintzin by definition moved back and forth between different worlds, acting not just as linguists but also as cultural intermediaries.

Before telling about the great Montezuma and his famous City of Mexico and the Mexicans, I wish to give some account of Doña Marina, who from her childhood had been the mistress and Cacica (chief or tribal leader) of towns and vassals. It happened this way:

Her father and mother were chiefs and Caciques of a town called Paynala, which had other towns subject to it, and stood about eight leagues from the town of Coatzacoalcos. Her father died while she was still a little child, and her mother married another Cacique, a young man, and bore him a son. It seems that the father and mother had a great affection for this son and it was agreed between them that he should succeed to their honours when their days were done. So that there should be no impediment to this, they gave the little girl, Doña Marina, to some Indians from Xicalango, and this they did by night so as to escape observation, and they then spread the report that she had died, and as it happened at this time that a child of one of their Indian slaves died they gave out that it was their daughter and the heiress who was dead.

The Indians of Xicalango gave the child to the people of Tabasco and the Tabasco people gave to her to Cortés. I myself knew her mother, and the old woman's son and her half-brother, when he was already grown up and ruled the town jointly with his mother, for the second husband of the old lady was dead. When they became Christians, the old lady was called Marta and the son Lázaro. I knew all this very well because in the year 1523 after the conquest of Mexico and the other provinces, when Crist'obal de Olid revolted in Honduras, and Cortés was on his way there, he passed through Coatzacoalcos and I and the greater number of the settlers of that town accompanied him on that expedition as I shall relate in the proper time and place. As Doña Marina proved herself such an excellent woman and good interpreter throughout the wars in New Spain, Tlaxcala and Mexico (as I shall show later on) Cortés always took her with him, and during that expedition she was married to a gentleman named Juan Jaramillo at the town of Orizabo.

Doña Marina was a person of the greatest importance and was obeyed without question by the Indians throughout New Spain.

...

Doña Marina knew the language of Coatzacoalcos, which is that common to Mexico, and she knew the language of Tabasco, as did also Jerónimo de Aguilar, who spoke the language of Yucatan and Tabasco, which is one and the same. So that these two could understand one another clearly, Aguilar translated into Castilian for Cortés.

This was the great beginning of our conquests and thus, thanks be to God, things prospered with us. I have made a point of explaining this matter, because without the help of Doña Marina we could not have understood the language of New Spain and Mexico.

*SOURCE: Bernal Díaz del Castillo,* The Discovery and Conquest of Mexico, *1517–1521, chapters 22–23 (1585), translated by A. P. Maudsley (New York: Noonday Press, 1965).*

the significant roles that Native women played in the fur trade, English men in the Chesapeake dominated the Atlantic tobacco trade.

Tobacco was an extremely labor-intensive crop, and labor was one thing the Chesapeake lacked. Increasingly, the Virginia tobacco growers bought slaves imported from the west coast of Africa to fill the void. The overall numbers of enslaved persons were still small in the mid-seventeenth century, but by the 1680s most plantations were relying for labor on enslaved Africans. Like the white settlers, the enslaved people in the seventeenth century were mostly men; among women overall, the number of enslaved women brought to the country far exceeded white European women who came voluntarily. (Before 1800 four out of every five female migrants to the Americas were Africans.). Slaves were scattered through the rest of the North American settlements, but never on the scale of the Southern colonies.

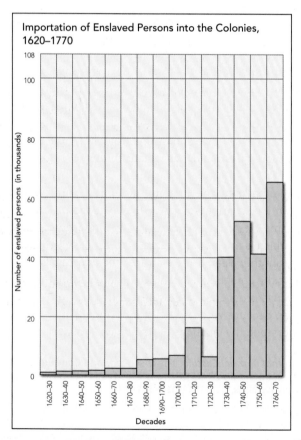

**Figure 1.1:** Importation of Enslaved Persons into the Colonies, 1620–1770 *Source:* Helen Hornbeck Tanner, *The Settling of North America* (New York: Macmillan, 1995), p. 51.

Historians continue to explore critically the roots of slavery on American soil, which developed very differently from the slave system in the Caribbean, with its heavy reliance on large-scale plantations and much higher numbers (100,000 enslaved people in the British West Indies alone in 1675). And yet the number of enslaved Africans in North America grew inexorably: from approximately 5,000 in 1675 to 13,000 by 1700, 53,000 by 1730, and 150,000 by 1750. Women and girls made up almost 40 percent of those sent involuntarily to the colonies between 1650 and 1750.

African Americans of both sexes shared the hardship of enslavement, but females bore the added responsibilities associated with child-rearing and domestic life. While there was some initial overlap in the tasks performed by enslaved and indentured workers, indentured women worked in the fields infrequently, while enslaved women did so regularly. White women who were not indentured never did. This divergence is one key to the development of slavery in the Americas: white slaveholders had to willfully ignore their cultural norms about gender in order to consign enslaved women to field work, including women who were pregnant or had recently borne children. Without Black women's bodies performing this agricultural work (a carryover from their West African roots), slavery would have failed to thrive, if not collapsed entirely.

Choosing to adopt the practices of the institution of slavery offered attractive opportunities for accruing status and power to white people in the increasingly stratified class structure. And enslaved Africans filled a labor shortage as the number of indentured white servants declined dramatically. Even when white laborers were available, plantation owners chose slave labor over free labor, allowing racist assumptions to create an enslaved class of laborers who were seen (by the white owners, that is) as more suited for such menial labor. Sexist assumptions were a factor too, specifically that Black women could toil ceaselessly in the fields because they were impervious to pain, including in childbirth. This racialized view linking savagery with sexuality positioned Black women as uniquely suited for both reproductive and productive labor.

Soon this cultural inferiority became coded as racial difference through the legal system. For example, a key 1662 statute in Virginia said that an enslaved woman's child inherited her unfree status. Now that slaveholders controlled not just the living people they enslaved but also their future progeny, it offered a route to pass along this "wealth" to their own children. And this focus on maternal succession basically absolved all fathers, including white fathers, from any paternal responsibility. More broadly, it meant that the entire institution of slavery was predicated on women's bodies. As historian Jennifer Morgan argues forcefully, "to write the history of racial ideology without gender is to omit the most fundamental reality of race as a trope: its heritability."

**DOCUMENTING AMERICAN WOMEN**

## The Legal Foundations of Slavery

This Virginia statute from 1662 shows how slave status was being codified into law in the mid-seventeenth century. More specifically, it gives slaveowners the legal right to claim children born to enslaved women as property, a cornerstone of the system of racial slavery and confirmation of the centrality of Black women's bodies to its perpetuation. The law also represents an early attempt to limit interracial sex between "Christians" (European settlers) and Africans.

WHEREAS some doubts have arisen whether children got by any Englishman upon a negro woman should be slave or free, Be it therefore enacted and declared by this present grand assembly, that all children born in this country shalbe held bond or free only according to the condition of the mother. And that if any Christian shall commit fornication with a negro man or woman, hee or shee soe offending shall pay double the fines imposed by the former act.

SOURCE: *"Laws of Virginia: 1662." In* The Statutes at Large, Being a Collection of All the Laws of Virginia, *ed. William Waller Hening (Charlottesville: University Press of Virginia, 1969), 2:270.*

New England patterns of settlement were quite different from those of the Chesapeake. New England settlers migrated as members of families, the sex ratio was fairly even, and a stable community life was present from the very start. These families proved remarkably fecund—women typically bore seven or eight children—causing explosive population growth that put pressure on the highly compact patterns of New England town settlement. In part because of a more hospitable climate than the disease-ridden South, seventeenth-century New England settlers also lived longer: 71.8 years for men and 70.8 for women, compared to their southern counterparts' 48 and 39 years, respectively.

Religion was also far more central to the New England experience than in the Chesapeake, for women as well as for men, with churches among the first institutions the settlers established in their new communities. Religious persecution had fueled many of the original migrations. Nearly 50,000 Puritans, dissenters from the established Church of England, left England between 1620 and 1640 for destinations such as Plymouth and Boston, including an eighteen-year-old bride named Anne Bradstreet, who confessed her heart "rose" (rebelled) at finding "a new world and new manners" but quickly submitted once she was convinced it was the will of God. While Puritan women could not become ministers or preach, they supplied a key constituency as church members. Religion functioned as an important solace for women as they struggled to establish new lives for themselves and their families under very primitive conditions.

White women's household labor was central to the success of the early colonies. The household was the key economic unit and the one where much of women's labor occurred. While seventeenth-century houses and farms were fairly simple, the profession of housewifery was highly skilled. Women's tasks involved a range of labor inside the home and in its surrounding gardens and outbuildings, such as cooking and baking, tending the fire, making clothes and candles, and slaughtering pigs and other farm animals. And yet New England households were far from self-sufficient. Just as Indians actively embraced the opportunities offered by trade with Europeans, so did colonial families seek out and embrace opportunities to buy certain goods and services and sell others rather than make everything themselves. Our picture of idyllic self-contained New England villages should instead portray them as very much linked to the world beyond their town boundaries, even in the seventeenth century.

A constant of daily life for all the colonists was interaction with Native Americans, often punctuated by bloody and devastating outcomes on both sides. At the basis of the conflict was an insatiable hunger on the part of the Europeans, especially the British, for land, driven in part by the population explosion of continued migration and family growth. And as the number of Europeans was growing, the number of Indians continued to drop, their tribes often decimated by disease and disruption. As a survival strategy, individual Indian tribes quickly learned to play colonial politics, pitting the French against the English or vice versa. For long stretches of time European and Indian cultures would manage something akin to peaceful coexistence, only to break out into periodic conflict and bitter warfare. Examples include Metacom's (also known as King Philip's) War in the 1670s and, looking ahead

PHILIP. *KING* of Mount Hope.

1.3: Paul Revere made a copper engraving of King Philip (also known as Metacom or Metacomet) in 1772, testimony to the Indian chief's historical importance for his role in King Philip's War in 1675–1678. No comparable image exists for Wetamoo, the powerful female Wampanoag chief who was Metacom's sister-in-law.

to the eighteenth century, the Seven Years War (also known as the French and Indian War) from 1756 to 1763.

Both Indian and white women were often caught in these skirmishes. In 1675 Mary Rowlandson, a minister's wife, was kidnapped from her home in Lancaster, Massachusetts, and taken hostage by the local Wampanoag Indians. Rowlandson spent twelve weeks in captivity, living as part of the community while constantly on the move. In her narrative of captivity, published in 1682 and one of the most widely read prose texts of its time, she styles herself as a "godly captive" who endured her trials as a test of her religious faith. When she was finally released after her husband paid a hefty ransom, she wanted nothing more to do with her Indian captors, whom she considered "murtherous wretches" and "ravenous beasts."

Mary Rowlandson's story looks very different when told from the perspective of another woman: Wetamoo, the Wampanoag diplomat and tribal leader under whose supervision Rowlandson was placed. Like the better known male leader Metacom, Wetamoo was concerned about protecting her fields and land from the encroachment of English settlers. (English pigs and cows were especially disruptive to Indians' subsistence farming.) Now she was saddled with a captive who was unused to heavy labor and terrified of being in what she considered the wilderness, even though the Indians navigated the forested landscape with ease and confidence. In her narrative Rowlandson clings doggedly to English gender norms, portraying Wetamoo as simply a wife and mistress of a household, not a powerful leader in her own right. Why? "If Rowlandson accepted Wetamoo's position," reasoned historian Lisa Brooks, "she might question her own in New England."

Few English men ever willingly crossed over to Indian life, being more likely to resist than adapt, but some kidnapped white women decided to stay with their Indian captors. Mary Jemison made this choice after being abducted by the Shawnee from her home in Adams County, Pennsylvania, and then being given to the Seneca, with whom she remained. Esther Wheelwright was captured in a Wabanaki raid in Maine in 1703 at age seven, joining a Native family that had been exposed to Catholicism and taught to pray. At age twelve she entered an Ursuline convent in Quebec where she stayed for the rest of her life, shunning efforts of her family of origin to bring her back home. In these cases white women affirmatively chose different lives than they would have lived had they not been taken captive.

## THE DAILY CONTOURS OF WOMEN'S LIVES

Despite regional differences between New England, the Chesapeake, and the Middle Colonies of Pennsylvania, New York, and New Jersey with their large representation of Dutch and Quaker settlers, the lives of white colonial women bore many broad similarities. Almost every woman could expect to be married at some point in her life, often more than once if she was widowed. Once married, her life would include productive and reproductive labor: household management and food production alongside childbirth and child-rearing. The word "spinster" comes from spinning, but there were few unattached females in the colonies because the marriage rate for white native-born women was so high.

By law and custom, married women's lives in European coastal settlements followed a patriarchal model, with the husband as the head of the family and his wife and children his subordinates. That was also the model for the state, with the monarch playing the role of patriarch over his subordinate subjects. Indeed under the British common law doctrine of *feme covert* (a legal term for a married woman who was covered or protected by her husband), women lost the ability to act independently at law when they married, the assumption being (as English jurist William Blackstone famously put it) that "by marriage, the husband and wife are one person in law." And yet there were certain familial situations where wives willingly took on roles usually assigned to men. Women married to sea captains or fur traders, who were often away for months at a time, or women whose husbands were conscripted to fight in the various Indian wars, in effect functioned as "deputy husbands." As always, there was a gap between what prescriptive literature said women *ought* to be doing and the actual realities of their daily lives, which were often more fluid and complex.

Certain disorderly women pushed the boundaries even further by failing to conform to the values of wifely submission, general subordination to men, and religious modesty. "You have stept out of your place, you have rather bine a Husband than a Wife and a preacher than a Hearer; and a Magistrate

DOCUMENTING AMERICAN WOMEN

# Salem Witchcraft

In 1692 Cotton Mather described Mercy Short's possession by witchcraft in "A Brand Pluck'd out of the Burning," which included a verbatim transcription, excerpted here, of a "fit" she experienced while bewitched. Several years earlier, Short had been taken captive by Indians. She escaped, but her parents and several of her siblings were murdered, testimony to the fraught interaction between indigenous peoples and the colonial settlers whose farming practices and expansive population growth threatened Native patterns of land use and settlement.

Oh You horrid Wretch! You make my very Heart cold within mee. It is an Hell to mee, to hear You speak so! What? Are you *God*? No, bee gone, you Divel! Don't pester mee any more with such horrid Blasphemies!

...

Fine Promises! You'll bestow an Husband upon mee, if I'l bee your Servant. An Husband! What? A Divel! I shall then bee finely fitted with an Husband: No I hope the Blessed Lord Jesus Christ will marry my Soul

than a Subject." That was the judgment of Reverend Hugh Peters on Anne Hutchinson, an elite white woman in Massachusetts who challenged the religious authority of Puritan elders in the 1630s by holding meetings in her home where she discussed matters of theology and salvation with her followers. Hauled before the authorities, she was run out of town for her transgressions and relocated to Long Island, where she was killed in an Indian attack in 1643.

Mistress Margaret Brent of Maryland was more an extraordinary woman than a disorderly one, but she also rattled the status quo. An unmarried

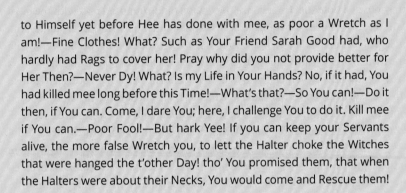

to Himself yet before Hee has done with mee, as poor a Wretch as I am!—Fine Clothes! What? Such as Your Friend Sarah Good had, who hardly had Rags to cover her! Pray why did you not provide better for Her Then?—Never Dy! What? Is my Life in Your Hands? No, if it had, You had killed mee long before this Time!—What's that?—So You can!—Do it then, if You can. Come, I dare You; here, I challenge You to do it. Kill mee if You can.—Poor Fool!—But hark Yee! If you can keep your Servants alive, the more false Wretch you, to lett the Halter choke the Witches that were hanged the t'other Day! tho' You promised them, that when the Halters were about their Necks, You would come and Rescue them!

...

What's that? Must the Younger Women, do yee say, hearken to the Elder?—They must bee another Sort of Elder Woman than You then! they must not bee Elder Witches, I am sure. Pray, do you for once Hearken to mee.—What a dreadful Sight are You! An Old Woman, an Old Servant of the Divel! You, that should instruct such poor, young, Foolish Creatures as I am, to serve the Lord Jesus Christ, come and urge mee to serve the Divel! Tis an horrible Thing!

SOURCE: Cotton Mather, *"A Brand Pluck'd out of the Burning," in* Narratives of the Witchcraft Cases 1648–1706, *ed. George Lincoln Burr (New York: Barnes and Noble, 1946), 267–72.*

woman of substantial property and standing, Brent further defied gender expectations when she was appointed the lord proprietor's attorney. Based on her appointment, she petitioned the colonial government in 1647 for the right to vote in Maryland's general assembly. Her request was turned down, but the fact of her application shows how in the 1640s, class and social status could trump gender, at least enough to frame this unusual request.

The most disorderly and disturbing women of this period were those accused of being witches. The best-known witch hunt is the one that occurred in

Salem in 1692, but that was just the culmination of a long history of outbreaks. Often these occurred at times when civil society was facing a crisis, such as deteriorating relationships with local Indians or conflicts over land distribution.

Witches were predominantly women, and they were also predominantly older women, often those on the fringes of their communities for various reasons: a scold, a meddler, a troublemaker, an angry neighbor. In other words, they posed a potential threat once they made their supposed pact with the devil but were also more vulnerable to accusation because of their outlier status. And in a generational twist, their accusers were often young girls, perhaps enjoying the thrill of being the center of attention as the accusations were hurled: "Whats that?" demanded seventeen-year-old Mercy Short. "Must the Younger Women, do yee say, hearken to the Elder?" At Salem, 115 local residents were accused of being witches, three-quarters of them women, and nineteen were executed. Only when religious and political leaders stepped in to quell the hysteria did it end. While there were a tiny number of witchcraft accusations after 1692, Salem basically represented the end of the line. It was almost as if the colonists decided to put aside the premodern beliefs in the supernatural that were common to rural agrarian communities in favor of a more secular approach to civic life.

 # TRANSATLANTIC CONNECTIONS

Another manifestation of changing mores was the onset of the **consumer revolution** beginning around 1700. Historians use this phrase to convey the new focus on buying and owning things for personal and domestic use—stuff, as it were—that accompanied rising prosperity and a move beyond subsistence and survival to a more vibrant mercantile economy as well as a society more stratified by class. Here is a simple illustration. In the seventeenth century, colonial houses were sparsely furnished. Life revolved around the hearth. Families ate dinner off of a table-board topped with several trenchers containing hollowed bowls to hold the food, which was eaten with spoons; beverages were drunk from a single flagon passed around the table. Colonists, especially children, often ate standing up because there were few chairs or stools. Cooking implements were utilitarian, as was clothing. Privacy was nonexistent. When guests came to stay, they often shared the family bed.

In the eighteenth century, households looked quite different, even at the lower end of the social strata. There were china plates and silver or pewter utensils for eating and chests of drawers for storing extra clothing and linens. Instead of guests being welcomed into the kitchen, they were now entertained in a formal parlor whose only function was for receiving visitors. Larger and more elaborate houses needed things to fill them up. So where did these material goods come from? The thriving Atlantic trade, which linked

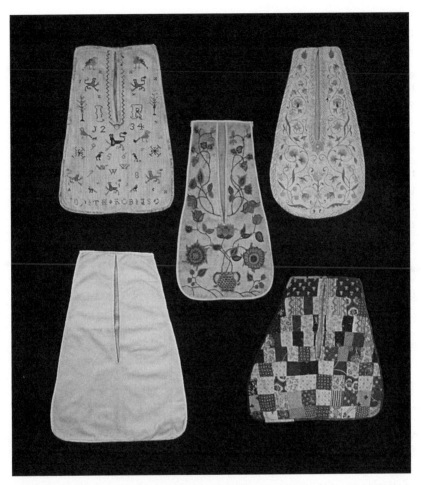

1.4: Pockets were the women's purses of the colonial era. Hand-sewn, often with embroidery or beadwork, pockets were tied around a woman's waist so as to be handy for carrying small objects. These examples date from the 1720s to the 1820s.

the American colonies to the markets of Europe and beyond. Instead of thinking of the colonies as isolated backwaters, think of them as active participants in a vibrant Atlantic culture that flourished on both sides of the ocean.

One of the most spectacular examples of this interconnected Atlantic world was the widespread dispersal and consumption of printed material. By the 1700s, colonists in Philadelphia, New York, and Boston were reading the same books and broadsides as their counterparts in London, Edinburgh, and Bath. They had access to newspapers with information and gossip from this wider world. They could follow new fashions and traffic in new ideas.

Some of the most enthusiastic consumers of this new Atlantic culture were white women, especially those who lived in the colonies' thriving

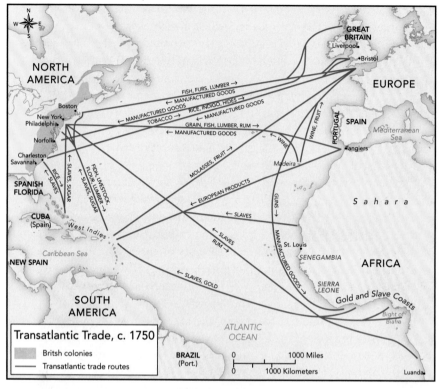

MAP 1.2

# Timeline

| | | |
|---|---|---|
| **1400–1500** | **1607** | **1647** |
| Between 7 and 12 million people live in the area that is now the United States | Pocahontas first encounters English settlers in Jamestown | Mistress Margaret Brent petitions colonial government for the right to vote in Maryland's general assembly |
| **1492** | **1613** | |
| Christopher Columbus arrives in the "New World" | Introduction of tobacco in America | **1650–1750** |
| **1519** | **1620–1640** | Women and girls make up almost 40 percent of those sent involuntarily to the colonies |
| Malintzin is offered to Cortés as a slave upon his arrival to the Yucatan peninsula in the Gulf of Mexico | Nearly fifty thousand Puritans leave England for destinations such as Plymouth and Boston | |

merchant centers. Women bought the china and then used it to serve tea (the quintessential consumer product, which quickly went from luxury to necessity) to their guests in their elaborately decorated parlors while wearing the newest fashions from London or Paris. While sipping their tea, they discussed the news from abroad or books they had recently read, such as Samuel Richardson's epistolary novels *Pamela: Or, Virtue Rewarded* (1740) and *Clarissa: Or the History of a Young Lady* (1748). Things had come a long way from the harsh and primitive conditions that had greeted white settlers when they first arrived in the early 1600s. The American colonies were definitely coming of age by 1750.

Midcentury is also an important mark for changing attitudes about white women's roles in colonial society. In the seventeenth century women's lives were defined by their roles as wives, daughters, and widows within a patriarchal family and state. A **women's sphere** did not exist, because women were not necessarily thought of as a separate category or entity from men. To be sure, women's lives were profoundly shaped by their gender (as were Native American women's lives) but they were primarily seen as members of communities or families rather than a group apart.

By 1750, especially in the transatlantic literature that colonists were reading, it is possible to see the inklings of a new view of women: "'Tis woman's sphere to mind / Their Children and their House," wrote an eighteenth-century poet. Instead of hearty colonial housewives slaughtering livestock or fending off Indian attacks, white women were now referred to as "the fair sex," increasingly associated with the family, and less involved, at least in theory, with the broader public world.

| 1662 | 1675–1750 | 1756–1763 |
|---|---|---|
| Statute in Virginia institutes that a slave woman's child inherits her unfree status | The number of enslaved Africans in North America grows from 5,000 to 150,000 | Seven Years War |
| | | **C. 1700** |
| | | Beginning of the "consumer revolution" |
| **1675** | **1688** | |
| Mary Rowlandson is taken hostage by the local Wampanoag Indians | Glorious Revolution in England | |
| | **1692** | |
| | Salem Witch Trials | |

1.5: This fireplace at the Burrough-Steelman House in Pennsauken, New Jersey, shows the tools and utensils available to a mid-eighteenth-century housewife. The most essential item was probably the large copper or pewter pot for cooking and heating water.

This growing split between the public and the private assigned a higher priority to motherhood as a specific role for women, with women now given large responsibilities for the moral and intellectual growth of their children, a role that previously had been assigned to patriarchal fathers. A loving conjugal relation between husband and wife also became more important, with the choice of a mate now one of the most significant decisions a woman could make. And in terms of religion, women increasingly filled the pews of eighteenth-century churches and would continue to do so in the nineteenth. As congregations became predominantly female, piety became even more associated with women.

It is easier to document these emerging trends than to explain why they happened, but the changes were obviously linked to broader historical developments. The explosive growth of commercial capitalism and an active mercantile economy spanning the globe spread goods and ideas far and wide. The thriving slave trade also spread its tentacles between West Africa, the Caribbean, and North America. The **Glorious Revolution** in England in 1688 transformed the relationship between monarchs and their subjects, as did the rise of Enlightenment thought, such as John Locke's *Two Treatises on Government* (1690), which proposed that political authority came from "social compacts," not divine right. Finally, a new understanding of biology and physiology after 1700 encouraged the division of humans into a two-sex model, rather than women being seen simply as lesser or inadequate versions of men. This new emphasis on difference grounded in fixed biological categories encouraged the view that women as a group were fundamentally different from men.

This new focus on women's sphere can be seen as diminishing women's extensive colonial roles, narrowing their lives to primarily home and family. This mindset clearly applied more to privileged white women than to enslaved women or Native women, whose lives continued to be shaped by different patterns of productive and reproductive work. And yet by introducing a new concept of womanhood, the ideology fostered a sense of sisterhood that encouraged women to think of themselves as a common group. Indeed that very gender solidarity eventually became the rationale for the birth of an aggressive nineteenth-century women's rights movement, which challenged and eventually overturned the very notion of limiting women to a restricted sphere. The emerging ideology thus opened the door for future generations of American women to take a larger role in affairs far beyond the domestic realm. This ongoing expansion of opportunities, seized by different groups of women at different times, characterizes American women's history from the eighteenth century all the way to the present.

## KEY TERMS

| | | |
|---|---|---|
| consumer revolution | Glorious Revolution | two-spirit |
| cultural mediators | indentured servant | women's sphere |
| *feme covert* | matrilineal | |

## Suggested Readings

Allen, Paula Gunn. *Pocahantas: Medicine Woman, Spy, Entrepreneur, Diplomat* (2003).

Brooks, Lisa. *Our Beloved Kin: A New History of King Philip's War* (2018).

Guttierez, Ramon. *When Jesus Came, the Corn Mothers Went Away: Marriage, Sexuality, and Power in New Mexico, 1500–1846* (1991).

Morgan, Jennifer Lyle. *Laboring Women: Reproduction and Gender in New World Slavery* (2004).

Perdue, Theda, ed. *Sifters: Native American Women's Lives* (2001).

Townsend, Camilla. *Malintzin's Choices: An Indian Woman in the Conquest of Mexico* (2006).

Learn more with this chapter's digital tools at http://www.oup.com/he/ware1e.

# A PHILOSOPHIC COCK

Tis not a set of features or Complexion
Or tincture of a Skin that I admire

# two

# Independence Gained and Lost in an Expanding Republic, 1750–1850

## CHAPTER OUTLINE

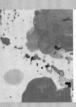

**Revolutionary Legacies**

**Populating a Continent That Was Already Populated**

**The Broad Shadow of Slavery**

This political caricature by Philadelphia engraver James Akin depicts Thomas Jefferson as a large strutting rooster, and an enslaved Black woman, presumably Sally Hemings, as an adoring hen. Even during Jefferson's presidency, rumors circulated about their relationship.

In 1787 a fourteen-year-old African American enslaved girl named Sally Hemings journeyed to Paris as a servant in the household of Thomas Jefferson, then serving as the ambassador to France from the newly established United States of America. When she returned to Virginia in 1789, she was pregnant. That child did not survive, but four other children did. Confirming generations of rumors, DNA evidence establishes that Thomas Jefferson was the father of Sally Hemings's children.

Despite being born into slavery, Sally Hemings's mixed-race identity tied her intricately to the white world. Her mother, Betty, an enslaved woman on the Virginia plantation of John Wayles, had a sexual relationship with her owner that produced several children, including Sally. When Wayles died in 1773, Betty and her children became the property of Thomas Jefferson, who had married Wayles's daughter, Martha, the year before. Martha Jefferson, worn out after bearing six children in less than ten years, died at the young age of thirty-four in 1782. Thomas Jefferson never remarried, an unusual choice for a man of his age and standing. One possible reason was his long-standing relationship with Sally Hemings, who was actually Jefferson's deceased wife's half-sister. The ties of slavery and bondage were intricate and complicated indeed.

Sally Hemings never spoke publicly about her situation or engaged in overt political acts, but she still was a significant historical figure for the role she played in the life of Thomas Jefferson, the country's third president. Her relationship with Jefferson was something of an open secret, in part because Sally's extremely light-skinned children bore an uncanny resemblance to the master of Monticello. Gossip about their relationship even played a role in the 1800 presidential campaign, yet it took almost 200 years for the truth to be confirmed.

As a human being who lived as a slave, Sally Hemings stands at the uneasy juxtaposition of slavery and freedom that was the legacy of the American Revolution. Her owner and the father of her children helped to conceive the new democratic experiment that became the United States of America at the same time he acquiesced in (indeed, profited from) the institution of slavery. As an enslaved American woman, Sally Hemings's life story mocks the Declaration of Independence's notion that all men were created equal. Combining race and gender (two strikes against her), her life allows us to ask what democracy meant for women, white and Black. Further, what would it take to win the freedom of both slaves and women, and who would plead their cause?

While the American Revolution did not dramatically reshape women's lives, it did set in motion a range of other changes that affected the early history of the country and its female inhabitants. One of the most significant was the resumption of an expansive westward thrust after the cessation of hostilities. The original colonies, now organized as a federation of states, filled up the backcountry, burst over the Appalachian mountains, and then just kept going; a similar surge happened after the Civil War. Yet this land was already inhabited by Native American tribes as well as by Spanish, Tejano, and Mexican settlers, who increasingly were seen as major impediments to land acquisition and permanent Euro-American settlement. No one asked why the space could not just continue to be shared.

# REVOLUTIONARY LEGACIES

What did the American Revolution mean to the new nation's women? In part it depends on which women. Enslaved women and Native American women saw little change in their status, despite the lofty rhetoric about liberty and equality contained in the Declaration of Independence. More broadly, the American Revolution did not radically change women's political rights and legal status. And yet it provided openings, especially for elite white women, to play larger roles in the new democracy. In 1798 playwright and poet Judith

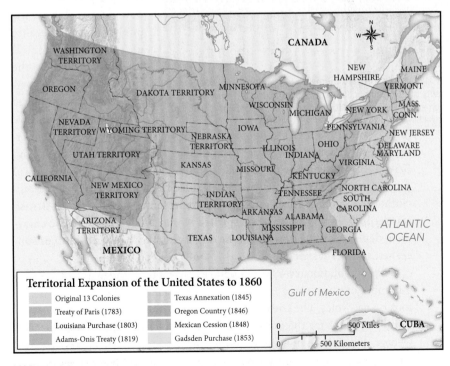

**Territorial Expansion of the United States to 1860**

| | |
|---|---|
| Original 13 Colonies | Texas Annexation (1845) |
| Treaty of Paris (1783) | Oregon Country (1846) |
| Louisiana Purchase (1803) | Mexican Cession (1848) |
| Adams-Onis Treaty (1819) | Gadsden Purchase (1853) |

0    500 Miles
0    500 Kilometers

**MAP 2.1**

A SOCIETY of PATRIOTIC LADIES,
AT
EDENTON in NORTH CAROLINA

Plate V.

2.1: This 1775 British cartoon makes fun of the revolutionary sentiments of the "patriotic ladies" of Edenton, North Carolina. Nobody seems to notice the dog lifting his leg in the lower right corner.

Sargent Murray predicted the dawn of "a new era of female history," and these changes in consciousness would play themselves out for decades to come.

Despite a prevailing ideology that defined women in terms of their homes and families, women could not have remained aloof from events leading up to the break with Great Britain even if they had wanted to. Embedded in a civil war that raged all around them and forced everyone to take sides, women tentatively began to forge a new relationship to the public realm. Because of housewives' central roles as consumers, the calls to boycott imported British goods like tea and cloth would have failed without women's support. Think of these boycotts as the politicization of the household, where a simple decision about whether to drink British tea or buy a book from a British publisher took on major political dimensions. Similarly, when women decided to make their own homespun cloth, their collaborative spinning bees represented a pointed anti-British stance. In Mercy Otis Warren's spirited words, "As every domestic enjoyment depends on the decision of the mighty contest, who can be an unconcerned and silent spectator?"

The Revolutionary War temporarily disrupted gender expectations in a number of ways. Once the war officially began in 1776, patriotic women took on new roles. The **Ladies Association of Philadelphia** was so successful in raising funds for the army that it earned a commendation from General George Washington himself for its "female patriotism." Women whose husbands went off to war or served in the new government had to cope on their own; Abigail Adams's famous entreaty to her husband John to "Remember the Ladies" was written during one of his lengthy absences.

Women married to Loyalist men, who sided with the British, saw their lives totally upended, especially if they did not agree with their husbands' decisions. After the war ended, their efforts to use legal recourse to regain confiscated property highlighted the limits of women's independent legal standing.

Some women actually fought in the war. Deborah Sampson, who had developed a variety of skills as an indentured servant in her home state of Massachusetts, enlisted in the Continental Army in 1781 under the assumed name of Robert Shurtliff. Donning men's clothing, she served for seventeen months and was wounded in a battle outside Tarrytown, New York. After being honorably discharged, she returned to living as a woman, marrying and bearing children. Decades later Congress awarded her a veteran's pension for her military service. Sampson/Shurtliff was unusual. More typical of women's participation in the war effort were the camp followers: wives and other women who trailed along with the ragtag colonial army and helped with the cooking, laundry, and other traditional female chores. Their domestic labor was just as essential to the prosecution of war as that of soldiers wielding a rifle.

Mohawk clan leader Molly Brant, who provided significant support to the British cause, adds another dimension to the roles that women played in the Revolutionary conflict. Reinforcing the role of kinship in gaining legitimacy and political power, Brant gained stature within both Mohawk and British circles by marrying William Johnson, the British official in charge of northern Indian affairs. After his death in 1774, she took an active role in gathering information for the British and served as an intermediary between British interests and those of the larger Iroquois Confederacy. Her wartime contributions built on the traditional roles that Native women played as mediators between two cultures.

Probably the largest gains for white women during the Revolutionary era were changes in consciousness epitomized by the concept of **republican motherhood**. In a new democratic country, the mothers of the republic were tasked with instilling in their sons the qualities of virtue, piety, and patriotism necessary to the young country's future. And in order to do this properly, they themselves needed more access to newspapers and knowledge of current events and books. While such a role was a long way from full participation in political life, it was an opening wedge.

As a corollary, the emphasis on republican motherhood encouraged a pragmatic new interest in education for women. Granted, expanding access to education was mainly to make women better wives and mothers, but linking erudition to republican ideals made it less threatening. (Previously, too much

## DOCUMENTING AMERICAN WOMEN

# Abigail Adams's Revolutionary Call

While her husband, John, served as a delegate to the Continental Congress in Philadelphia, Abigail Adams ran the farm and managed the family household in Braintree, Massachusetts. She was also an inveterate and witty correspondent (if inconsistent speller) who more than held her own with her husband, who would serve as the nation's second president. Two months after this exchange, the colonies declared their independence from Britain but failed to grant political or legal equality either to women or African Americans.

Abigail Adams to John Adams                    Braintree March 31 1776

. . .

. . . I long to hear that you have declared an independancy—and by the way in the new Code of Laws which I suppose it will be necessary for you to make I desire you would Remember the Ladies, and be more generous and favourable to them than your ancestors. Do not put such unlimited power into the hands of the Husbands. Remember all Men would be tyrants if they could. If perticuliar care and attention is not paid to the Laidies we are determined to foment a Rebelion, and will not hold ourselves bound by any Laws in which we have no voice, or Representation.

That your Sex are Naturally Tyrannical is a Truth so thoroughly established as to admit of no dispute, but such of you as wish to be happy willingly give up the harsh title of Master for the more tender and endearing one of Friend. Why then, not put it out of the power of the vicious and the Lawless to use us with cruelty and indignity with impunity. Men of Sense in all Ages abhor those customs which treat us only as the vassals of your Sex. Regard us then as Beings placed by providence under your protection and in immitation of the Supreem Being make use of that power only for our happiness.

. . .

John Adams to Abigail Adams                                    Ap. 14. 1776

. . .

As to your extraordinary Code of Laws, I cannot but laugh. We have been told that our Struggle has loosened the bands of Government every where. That Children and Apprentices were disobedient—that schools and Colledges were grown turbulent—that Indians slighted their Guardians and Negroes grew insolent to their Masters. But your Letter was the first Intimation that another Tribe more numerous and powerfull than all the rest were grown discontented.—This is rather too coarse a Compliment but you are so saucy, I wont blot it out.

Depend upon it, We know better than to repeal our Masculine systems. Altho they are in full Force, you know they are little more than Theory. We dare not exert our Power in its full Latitude. We are obliged to go fair, and softly, and in Practice you know We are the subjects. . . .

Abigail Adams to John Adams                         B[raintre]e May 7 1776

. . .

I can not say that I think you very generous to the Ladies, for whilst you are proclaiming peace and good will to Men, Emancipating all Nations, you insist upon retaining an absolute power over Wives. But you must remember that Arbitary power is like most other things which are very hard, very liable to be broken—and notwithstanding all your wise Laws and Maxims we have it our power not only to free ourselves but to subdue our Masters, and without violence throw both your natural and legal authority at our feet—

"Charm by accepting, by submitting sway

Yet have our Humour most when we obey."

. . .

*SOURCE: Abigail Adams and John Adams, "Letters" (March 31–April 5, 1776; April 14, 1776; May 7–9, 1776), The Adams Family Correspondence, volume 1, L. H. Butterfield, ed. (Cambridge, MA: Belknap Press, 1963), 369–71, 381–83, and 401–403.*

Publifhed according to Act of Parliament. Sept.ˢ¹.1773 by Archᵈ Bell, Bookfeller Nᵒ8 near the Saracens Head Aldgate.

2.2: Phillis Wheatley's "Poems on Various Subjects, Religious and Moral" was published in London in 1773. Wheatley was enslaved by a wealthy family in Boston, who taught her to read and write and freed her soon after the volume of her poetry was published. She married a free Black grocer but died in poverty and obscurity in 1784 at the age of thirty-one.

learning had been thought to unsex women, making them unfit for marriage and domestic duties.) In the early years of the republic, the topic of women's education received wide discussion, starting with the publication of Dr. Benjamin Rush's pamphlet "Thoughts on Female Education" in 1787. Soon a range of finishing schools and female academies sprang up; Emma Willard's founding of her eponymous school in Troy, New York, in 1819 exemplifies this trend. Other female seminaries followed, although confined mainly to the Northeast. As a byproduct, women found new opportunities as teachers in the expanding public and private school systems; by midcentury, a quarter of the nation's teachers were women, although the figure was much higher (four-fifths) in Massachusetts, a harbinger of the future. With a few notable exceptions, however, such as the founding of coeducational Oberlin College in 1833, the expansion of collegiate education for women would have to wait until after the Civil War.

 ## POPULATING A CONTINENT THAT WAS ALREADY POPULATED

When the **Treaty of Paris** officially ended the American Revolution in 1783, the idea that the new United States would someday stretch from "sea to shining sea" (as Katharine Lee Bates put it in the 1895 poem that became the basis for the song "America the Beautiful") would have seemed like a pipe dream. In the first place, Native Americans controlled most of the land, giving them (in the words of one historian) "a home field advantage." Secondly, even though the British no longer claimed the colonies as part of their overseas empire, both France and Spain continued to exert their own claims in the hinterlands.

That situation changed dramatically over the next few decades, as France sold a huge swath of land to the United States in the **Louisiana Purchase** of 1803 and Mexico won its independence from Spain in 1821, only to cede a major chunk of its territory to the United States in the **Treaty of Guadalupe Hidalgo** in 1848 after the Mexican-American War. The adage "we didn't cross the border, the border crossed us" applied both to **Californios** and Mexicans alike, who now found themselves part of the expanding United States empire.

As eager American settlers colonized land they conveniently rationalized was theirs for the taking just by showing up, Native Americans were steadily, almost inexorably pushed out of the way or displaced. According to historian Tiya Miles, "If slavery is the monumental tragedy of African American experience and the trauma of continual return in the memory of Black people, then removal plays the same role in American Indian experience."

The **Cherokee** are a case in point. The traditional Cherokee way of life had already undergone significant changes after contact with European settlers in the seventeenth and eighteenth centuries, changes that also affected gender roles. Specifically, a larger emphasis on war and trade, especially in deerskins, elevated men's roles relative to women, who continued their traditional focus on farming and food production, especially corn. The aftermath of the American Revolution led to new pressures on their land, which was desired by white settlers in the new state of Georgia who self-servingly reasoned that since the Cherokee were not actively cultivating all their commonly held land, they did not have a right to it. At the same time, a focus on "civilizing" the Cherokee on the part of missionaries and elected officials attempted to remake them along European lines, which consisted of turning men into farmers (even though this had always been women's work in Cherokee culture) and encouraging women's subservience in domestic matters. This in turn led to a marked decline in women's political influence within tribal governance by the 1820s.

The Cherokee adapted the new ways selectively, but no matter what they did, they were in the end defenseless against an aggressive U.S. policy that mandated compulsory cession of tribal lands to white settlers and the relocation of the Cherokee to territory far beyond the boundaries of the United States at the time. Severing the deep spiritual relationship between Cherokee identity and nature, between 46,000 and 53,000 Indians were evicted from their ancestral land. Thus began the **Trail of Tears**, the forced removal of the Cherokee nation to Indian territory in the future state of Oklahoma in 1838–1839. Not only did they lose all their land, but disease and hardship decimated their population along the way.

Historians call the process of eliminating or removing indigenous populations and populating their conquered or forfeited lands with a mainly white and mainly Euro-American settler population **settler colonialism**.

DOCUMENTING AMERICAN WOMEN

# Cherokee Women's Petition, 1818

Cherokee women identified deeply with their ancestral land and they spoke out forcefully against the U.S. policy of removal and relocation of their tribes to new lands further west. This petition from 1818 affirms the Cherokee nation as the first settlers of the land in question and women's collective determination to see that principle upheld.

Beloved Children,

We have called a meeting among ourselves to consult on the different points now before the council, relating to our national affairs. We have heard with painful feelings that the bounds of the land we now possess are to be drawn into very narrow limits. The land was given to us by the Great Spirit above as our common right, to raise our children upon, & to make support for our rising generations. We therefore humbly petition our beloved children, the head men & warriors, to hold out to the last in support of our common rights, as the Cherokee nation have been the first settlers of this land; we therefore claim the right of the soil.

We will remember that our country was formerly very extensive, but by repeated sales it has become circumscribed to the very narrow limits we have at present.

This seemingly insatiable hunger for land had deleterious effects on whichever tribes were in the way of white settlement, whether they be the Choctaw in Mississippi, the Iroquois in upstate New York, or the Sauk in Wisconsin. The new federal policy increasingly consigned Native Americans to federal reservations, especially in Oklahoma, but also much further west in what became Arizona, New Mexico, and South Dakota, while opening

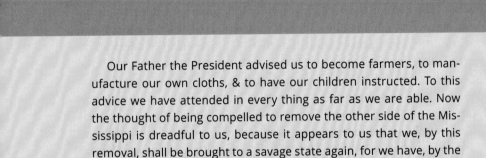

Our Father the President advised us to become farmers, to manufacture our own cloths, & to have our children instructed. To this advice we have attended in every thing as far as we are able. Now the thought of being compelled to remove the other side of the Mississippi is dreadful to us, because it appears to us that we, by this removal, shall be brought to a savage state again, for we have, by the endeavor of our Father the President, become too much enlightened to throw aside the privileges of a civilized life.

We therefore unanimously join in our meeting to hold our country in common as hitherto.

Some of our children have become Christians. We have missionary schools among us. We have heard the gospel in our nation. We have become civilized & enlightened, & are in hopes that in a few years our nation will be prepared for instruction in other branches of sciences & arts, which are both useful & necessary in civilized society.

There are some white men among us who have been raised in this country from their youth, are connected with us by marriage, & have considerable families, who are very active in encouraging the emigration of our nation. These ought to be our truest friends but prove our worst enemies. They seem to be only concerned how to increase their riches, but do not care what becomes of our Nation, nor even of their own wives and children.

*SOURCE: Andrew Jackson Presidential Papers microfilm, series 1, reel 22 (Washington, DC, 1961).*

large swaths of former Indian land to white settlement. And yet despite these geographical and cultural dislocations, Native tribes still demonstrated the cultural persistence that had characterized all encounters since the first contact with European settlers. The myth of the **disappearing Indian** was just that—a convenient fiction created by white settlers to justify their actions.

Similar patterns of contact, assimilation, and change were at work throughout the West. Actually "the West" is a bit of a misnomer: from the perspective of Mexico, which controlled much of this land until 1848, this same territory was "El Norte"—its northern frontier. Ever since initial contact, the dominant pattern in the borderlands with Mexico had been cultural interaction and accommodation interspersed with periods of violence and warfare. For example, during the Spanish and (after 1821 independence) Mexican occupations of what became New Mexico in 1848, an extensive system of captive exchange involved both Indian women and to a lesser degree Spanish and Mexican women, who literally crossed between cultures through capture, ransom, or sale. Then through adoption and marriage, many of these female captives stayed in their new culture, establishing families and being integrated into the community. More broadly, intermarriage between Mexican women and explorers, traders, and Natives occurred long before Anglos appeared on the scene—and continued afterward. In this fluid setting, women played critical roles as the cultural mediators between Mexican, Native, and Anglo cultures.

What historian Emma Perez calls a "decolonial imaginary" encourages us to move beyond the political and chronological narratives associated with westward expansion to imagine the perspectives of those who were subject to conquest and colonization, especially women. Even when Native, Spanish, and Mexican women encountered disruption of property and land, economic insecurity, sexual violence, and power loss at the hands of church and state, they continued to create new lives in the midst of changing contexts. Such a reimagining can occur without traditional written documents and serves to counter the negative stereotypes that settlers, male and female, left in their own written records.

While Anglo traders and trappers had been exploring and exploiting western lands for decades, the white presence took a significant leap forward in 1843 with the mapping of the **Overland Trail**. Over the next twenty years, more than 350,000 individuals made the arduous 2,000-mile trip from the Missouri River across the plains and the Rockies, with Oregon and California as their goal. Many of these migrants traveled in family groups, drawn by the prospect of new lives and fertile, bountiful land that was presented as waiting to be settled. Except, of course, that it was far from empty.

A mythic view of westward expansion and the frontier still holds a powerful sway on the popular imagination (especially where Hollywood is concerned), and gender is central to this story. In the traditional telling, heroic cowboys, Indians, miners, bandits, soldiers, and farmers battle nature and each other as they work to "tame" the West. The limitations of this view of the American West should be readily apparent. It focuses attention mainly on the relatively short period of Euro-American western expansion and ignores

2.3: This pictorial depiction from 1850 of an overland trip to California looks idyllic with its tidy family groups and well-ordered wagon train, but the mountains looming in the distance suggest the challenges and hardships ahead. Besides the many domestic chores that fell to women while in transit, mothers also had to watch their children closely to make sure they avoided trouble and injury along the way.

the ways the American West had long been a vibrant cultural crossroads. And it represents the archetypical Westerner as male. When women are mentioned at all, they fall into predictable stereotypes: the prostitute (with or without a heart of gold) and "the gentle tamer" who brings East Coast civilization to the wild and savage West solely by her presence. Native, Spanish, and Mexican women are summarily dismissed as racially inferior or otherwise rendered invisible and therefore not an essential part of the story.

Gender is central to telling the story of white settlers and westward migration. Usually it was men's decision, not women's, to seek a new life in the American West. "O let us not go," Mary A. Jones confided abjectly to her diary after her husband read a book about California and proposed relocating the family halfway across the continent. These hardy pioneers with their sunbonnets and sturdy boots made painful choices about what to take and what to leave behind as they loaded up a lifetime's worth of possessions onto Conestoga wagons. In many ways, women on the move had more to lose than men: their established homes, their female friends, their churches and associations, to say nothing of facing specifically female hardships on the trail, such as navigating pregnancy and childbirth while in transit. No doubt some unwilling pioneers rued their fates every step of the way. And yet other women, either single or in families, seized the opportunities for a new life less encumbered by traditions and constraints. Women schoolteachers were an especially hearty—and valued—bunch.

The experience of crossing the plains looks very different when told from the perspective of Native women. White women often confided their fears about being approached on the trail by groups of Indians in their letters and diaries. But what they saw as a potential attack was just as likely to be an attempt by local Native populations to reach out for food or supplies from the interlopers who were crossing their land and disrupting their traditional way of life. Given the numbers of emigrants involved, think how unsettling these encounters must have been. Sarah Winnemucca, a Paiute whose tribal lands were east of the Sierra Nevada, first came into contact with white emigrants as a child and never forgot the experience: "They came like a lion, yes, like a roaring lion, and have continued so ever since." She definitely got that last part right.

Whereas families traveled the Overland Trail, it was primarily single men who joined the **Gold Rush** that took off in California in 1849, causing a huge gender imbalance. Women made up only 8 percent of California's

2.4: Not just men prospected during the California Gold Rush, as this daguerreotype taken at the Auburn Ravine in 1850 confirms. Just years earlier this land had likely been under the stewardship of indigenous peoples, who were displaced by the rapid influx of white settlers in search of gold.

population in 1850, the year it became a state, and in 1860, men still outnumbered women two to one. In the boomtown, get-rich-quick atmosphere, it literally was a world upside down: without women to perform traditional services like cooking and cleaning, men had to learn to do these chores themselves or do without.

One thing men seemingly could not do without was sex. Prostitution was widespread in cities such as San Francisco and Sacramento and out in the mining camps, but prostitutes received few of the benefits associated with a Gold Rush economy. The sex trade was stratified among racial, ethnic, and class lines, with white males making up the vast majority of clients and women of color predominating among the sex workers. Because Indians initially made up the largest group of available women when the Gold Rush began, they were among the first prostitutes in the mining districts. They were soon joined by other equally poor and young women who turned to the trade in a desperate attempt to get by. The worst off by far were Chinese women, who were often sold to local brothel owners when they landed from China. Of the 681 Chinese women in San Francisco in 1860, 583 were listed as prostitutes.

In addition to the destabilizing effect of unequal sex ratios, California offered extraordinary demographic diversity. Its culture was influenced by its early Spanish roots, and later by dominion by Mexico. The vast majority of native Californians were of mestizo or Mexican background, but Anglo arrivals deployed the term "Spanish" or "Californio" to differentiate elite women belonging to landowning families who had married Europeans or Euro-Americans (the supposedly "good" women) from nonelite Mexican women, whom Anglos presumed to be immoral as well as racially impure. And yet even with the creation of this faux Spanish heritage, the racial and ethnic lines in California were never neatly drawn. María Amparo Ruiz de Burton later drew on her personal experiences to write a historical novel called *The Squatter and the Don* (1885), which detailed this liminal moment from the Mexican perspective.

California at midcentury also contained as many as 25,000 Chinese immigrants, almost exclusively men, who came as part of the Gold Rush, as well as a robust indigenous Native American population. Confirming a pattern that had occurred in the East and the Midwest, the relentless pressure of Anglo expansion and settlement and a new emphasis on mining and agriculture had deleterious effects on Native populations, such as the Miwok, whose traditional stewardship of the land was disrupted by the economic schemes of the newcomers. In addition, exposure to disease caused the Native population in California to drop from 150,000 in 1850 to 30,000 just ten years later. Anglo women as well as Anglo men reaped the rewards of the removal of Mexican and Indian populations from their ancestral lands.

## DOCUMENTING AMERICAN WOMEN

# Eulalia Perez Remembers Mexican California

Thomas Savage took this "testimonio" from Eulalia Perez at her home in San Isidro, California in 1877, a year before her death. At the time she was an aged woman, although her exact birth date is unknown. Married at fifteen to a Spanish army sergeant and later widowed, she remarried in 1832, becoming known as Eulalia Péres de Guillén Mariné. Her memories span California's Spanish, Mexican, and American periods, and show the importance of Catholic missions in shaping California history.

When I came to San Gabriel the last time, there were only two women in this part of California who knew how to cook [well]. One was María Luisa Cota, wife of Claudio López, superintendent of the mission; the other was María Ignacia Amador, wife of Francisco Javier Alvarado. She knew how to cook, sew, read and write and take care of the sick. She was a good healer. She did needlework and took care of the church vestments. She taught a few children to read and write in her home, but did not conduct a formal school.

On special holidays, such as the day of our patron saint, Easter, etc., the two women were called upon to prepare the feast and to make the meat dishes, sweets, etc.

The priests wanted to help me out because I was a widow burdened with a family. They looked for some way to give me work without offending the other women. Fathers Sánchez and Zalvidea conferred and decided that they would have first one woman, then the other and finally me, do the cooking, in order to determine who did it best, with the aim of putting the one who surpassed the others in charge of the Indian cooks so as to teach them how to cook. . . .

. . .

On the days agreed upon for the three dinners, they attended. No one told me anything regarding what it was all about, until one day Father Sánchez called me and said, "Look, Eulalia, tomorrow it is your turn to prepare dinner—because María Ignacia and Luisa have already done so. We shall see what kind of a dinner you will give us tomorrow."

The next day I went to prepare the food. I made several kinds of soup, a variety of meat dishes and whatever else happened to pop into my head that I knew how to prepare. The Indian cook, named Tomás, watched me attentively, as the missionary had told him to do.

At dinner time those mentioned came. When the meal was concluded, Father Sánchez asked for their opinions about it, beginning with the eldest, Don Ignacio Tenorio. This gentleman pondered awhile, saying that for many years he had not eaten the way he had eaten that day—that he doubted that they are any better at the King's table. The others also praised the dinner highly.

Then the missionary called Tomás and asked him which of the three women he liked best—which one of them knew the most about cooking. He answered that I did.

Because of all this, employment was provided for me at the mission. At first they assigned me two Indians so that I could show them how to cook, the one named Tomás and the other called "The Gentile." I taught them so well that I had the satisfaction of seeing them turn out to be very good cooks, perhaps the best in all this part of the country.

SOURCE: Carlos N. Hijar, Eulalia Pérez, and Agustin Escobar, Three Memoirs of Mexican California, recorded by Thomas Savage and translated by Vivien C. Fisher and others (University of California at Berkeley, 1988), 76–78.

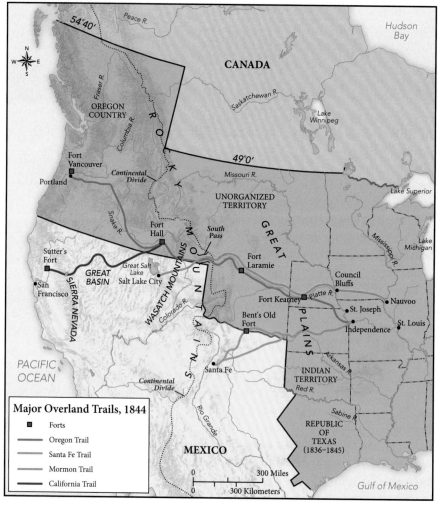

MAP 2.2

 # THE BROAD SHADOW OF SLAVERY

Slavery is generally presented through the lens of a Black-white binary, but Indians also have a long history of involvement in slavery, especially in the taking and selling of captives during wartime and using slavery to incorporate outsiders into tribal life. Indians were also periodically enslaved by foreign powers. During the early years of British settlement, between 30,000 and 50,000 Native Americans were enslaved by the British, with Native women being enslaved at a rate three to five times the rate of Native men. These enslaved Indians filled a labor vacuum created by the decline in indentured servants but before the numbers of Africans imported in the dreaded **Middle Passage** from Africa began its dramatic upswing.

The balance shifted again in 1808, when the United States officially stopped bringing enslaved people from Africa and began to rely on natural reproduction and an internal slave trade for its labor needs. Around the same time, the invention of the cotton gin in 1793 paved the way for a vast expansion of the cotton economy, a process that was intricately linked to Indian Removal. The states of Georgia, Mississippi, Alabama, and Arkansas and others in the Deep South where the plantation system thrived were the very areas that had seen the forced resettlement of Native peoples to land further west.

2.5: One of the most widely circulated images in nineteenth-century abolitionist circles was "Am I not a man and a brother?," which was based on a medallion designed by the English potter Josiah Wedgwood in 1787. In 1830 Elizabeth Margaret Chandler of Philadelphia adapted the iconography to feature an enslaved woman.

But the question of Indians and slavery is more complicated than that: a number of Indians enslaved African American people. In the Cherokee nation, for example, successful farmers and plantation owners affirmatively embraced the enslavement of African Americans as a way to demonstrate that they were "civilized" just like whites. Was Indian slavery any less horrific than the version practiced by white slaveholders in the South? Perhaps, mainly in the way that kinship ties could mitigate some of the harshest aspects by encouraging the acceptance of enslaved Afro-Cherokee as members of the community. Ironically, the Cherokee attempts to show how civilized they were failed to stop white settlers from taking their land with the strong backing of state and federal law enforcement. Meanwhile slavery tightened its grip on Southern society, with wide-ranging implications for both white and Black women.

White Southern women, whether they were members of a slave-owning family or not (about one-quarter of the region's free population enslaved African Americans), lived in an extremely patriarchal society that provided few outlets for participation in events and institutions beyond their homes and farming communities. Educational and cultural opportunities were limited, except in towns and cities, and churches and voluntary associations did not play the central role they did in Northern society. As the nineteenth century progressed, Southern society turned more defensive about the institution of slavery, making Southerners less willing to entertain challenges to traditional gender definitions either.

White Southern women of the slave-owning class lived side by side with the Black men and women their familes enslaved, their lives intertwined but profoundly different. The domestic realm was a site of power for the slave mistress, but also one of struggle and contestation. If a universal sisterhood united all women, one would expect to see solidarity between white mistresses and the females they enslaved. While scattered sentiments suggest that some white women were less invested in the slave system than their men ("Southern women are, I believe, all abolitionists at heart" said slave-owning Gertrude Ella Thomas of Georgia), most often these sentiments, penned privately, were directed more at the disagreeable aspects of managing conditions for the enslaved on farms and plantations rather than the institution of slavery itself. White women had far, far more in common with their menfolk on the basis of shared racial and class privilege than they did with enslaved women. Far from "passive bystanders," they were active "co-conspirators."

Some white Southern women, including married women, enslaved Black people on their own. Sometimes they had been gifted specific persons as children but other times they found ways to circumvent the laws

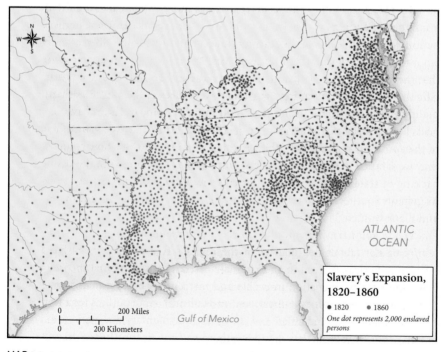

ATLANTIC
OCEAN

**Slavery's Expansion,
1820–1860**

● 1820   ● 1860
*One dot represents 2,000 enslaved
persons*

0        200 Miles
0      200 Kilometers

*Gulf of Mexico*

MAP 2.3

of coverture that limited married women's legal rights in order to own persons separately from their husbands. And with ownership went responsibilities for managing and disciplining their enslaved, which they took on willingly and without apology, including resorting to whippings and other forms of corporal punishment. But keeping enslaved people under control was not just a matter of brute force, and women slaveholders used psychological as well as physical forms of control. These "mistresses of the market" also showed no qualms about trading and selling the people they enslaved, either privately among friends and neighbors or more publicly by patronizing the slave auctions held in cities across the South. The bottom line is that for slaveholding women, just like slaveholding men, slavery was an economic investment on which they expected profit or return, a relation of property not a relation of emotion or feeling. As abolitionist Frederick Douglass, himself formerly enslaved, observed, "To talk of kindness entering into the relation of slave and slaveholder is most absurd, wicked, and preposterous."

Enslaved women's status—or more accurately, their economic value—was inextricably linked to their ability to reproduce the slave population. Most enslaved people were married (informally, that is, since these unions were not recognized by the law), but often to slaves on nearby plantations in what was called an abroad marriage. The ever-present threat defining enslaved women's lives was that they or a family member would be sold and forced to move far away. But that fact of life did not keep them from trying to build stable families within the institution of slavery.

With the official end of the slave trade in 1808, the main way to meet the labor needs of the expanding Southern cotton economy was through an internal slave trade; since men were more desirable as workers, they were sold to distant plantations in the Deep South at a higher rate, thereby breaking up the bonds they had formed in the slave quarters. As a result, the structure of many families of enslaved people was a loose extended family held together by the mother. Childbearing and childrearing could be both a great joy but also a terrible burden, because her children's fates were so completely governed by the institution of slavery. Toni Morrison's powerful novel *Beloved* (1987) captures those tensions and the often tragic outcomes they could lead to.

The daily life of enslaved women and girls was harsh. Only a few (no more than 5 percent, mainly on the largest plantations, and often the most light-skinned) worked as house servants. Instead most enslaved women of all ages toiled in the fields cultivating cotton, sugar, tobacco, and rice along with men, albeit usually in all-female work gangs; this demanding physical labor continued even during pregnancy and lactation. While enslaved men had some access to skilled work as artisans, the main skilled work open to enslaved women was serving as wet nurses to white babies. As historian Jennifer Morgan has detailed, the entire framework of slavery rested on women's bodies, which were forced to perform both reproductive and productive labor for their white owners.

Although all women faced the threat of sexual violence from men, Black women enjoyed far less control over their bodies than did white women. What this meant to the women who bore these violations is one of the great imponderables of slavery. Sexual coercion of enslaved women by white male slave owners was common, producing a range of mixed-race children who kept their mother's slave status at the same time they bore the patrilineage of the slave owner. Yet their existence was acknowledged only obliquely.

2.6: Harriet A. Jacobs published *Incidents in the Life of a Slave Girl* when she was in her forties, but the only known photograph of her is as a much older woman, three years before her death in 1897.

Southern slave owner Mary Boykin Chesnut captured the way white mistresses simultaneously knew what was going on while they looked the other way: "Any lady is able to tell who is the father of all the mulatto children in everybody's household but their own. Those she seems to think drop from the clouds."

The gripping story of Harriet Jacobs details the sexual exploitation experienced by enslaved women at the hands of their white owners and the complicity of white women in their husbands' behavior. *Incidents in the Life of a Slave Girl* was not published until 1861 under the pseudonym of Linda Brent, but the events took place in the 1830s and 1840s. Jacobs was enslaved in the Edenton, North Carolina, household of James and Mary Norcom, and her physician owner began making sexual overtures to her when she was sixteen, threatening that "he would kill me, if I was not silent as the grave." Because she was his property, "I must be subject to his will in all things," he told her repeatedly. When Mary Norcom learned of the relationship, divorce was not an option, so she took out her displeasure on Harriet, not her husband. Jacobs sought to escape Norcom's abusive behavior by entering into a relationship with another white man, with whom she had two children. She eventually ran away from the Norcom household and spent seven years living in the cramped attic of her grandmother, finally able to make her way to freedom in New York in 1842, where she was reunited with her children. In her published account, she refers only to verbal abuse but it is quite clear that she was sexually assaulted as well.

Let us return to Sally Hemings to put another human face on the complicated connections between sexuality and slavery, using the Hemings family as a window on Virginia plantation life and how circumstances were often beyond the control of even the most trusted (and intimate) enslaved people. Despite the meticulous accounts Thomas Jefferson kept of the workings of his plantation at Monticello, he was unable to keep his expenses in line with his income, so the estate began to rack up enormous debt. At one point he had to sell his cherished books to the Library of Congress to make ends meet.

When Jefferson died in 1826, Monticello was in a state of fiscal and physical disrepair. His will made no specific mention of Sally Hemings; such an inclusion would have been much too public an acknowledgment of what everyone suspected. But all four of her children slipped into freedom before and after Jefferson's death, taking advantage of their light skins to simply blend into the Virginia population. Sally herself moved to Charlottesville with her two sons, where she lived until her death in 1835. Others who were enslaved at Monticello did not fare so well: six months later at auction ("130 VALUABLE NEGROES" read the broadside), families were split up

## DOCUMENTING AMERICAN WOMEN

# Harriot Jacobs on "The Trials of Girlhood" for Enslaved Women

Harriet Jacobs's autobiography, *Incidents in the Life of a Slave Girl* (1861), forthrightly details the sexual abuse experienced by enslaved women like herself at the hands of white owners. Amy Post, a white Quaker abolitionist, urged Jacobs to write her narrative and another white abolitionist, Lydia Marie Child, helped arrange its publication.

During the first years of my service in Dr. Flint's family, I was accustomed to share some indulgences with the children of my mistress. Though this seemed to me no more than right, I was grateful for it, and tried to merit the kindness by the faithful discharge of my duties. But I now entered on my fifteenth year—a sad epoch in life of a slave girl. My master began to whisper foul words in my ear. Young as I was, I could not remain ignorant of their import. I tried to treat them with indifference or contempt. The master's age, my extreme youth, and the fear that his conduct would be reported to my grandmother, made him bear this treatment for many months. He was a crafty man, and resorted to many means to accomplish his purposes. Sometimes he had stormy, terrific ways, that made his victims tremble; sometimes he assumed a gentleness that he thought must surely subdue. Of the two, I preferred his stormy moods, although they left me trembling. He tried his utmost to corrupt the pure principles my grandmother had instilled. He peopled my young mind with unclean images, such as only a vile monster could think of. I turned from him with disgust and hatred. But he was my master. I was compelled to live under the same roof with him—where I saw a man forty years my senior daily violating the most sacred commandments of nature. He told me I was his property; that I must be subject to his will in all

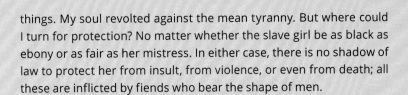

things. My soul revolted against the mean tyranny. But where could I turn for protection? No matter whether the slave girl be as black as ebony or as fair as her mistress. In either case, there is no shadow of law to protect her from insult, from violence, or even from death; all these are inflicted by fiends who bear the shape of men.

. . .

If God has bestowed beauty upon her, it will prove her greatest curse. That which commands admiration in the white woman only hastens the degradation of the female slave. I know that some are too much brutalized by slavery to feel the humiliation of their position; but many slaves feel it most acutely, and shrink from the memory of it. I cannot tell how much I suffered in the presence of these wrongs, nor how I am still pained by the retrospect. My master met me at every turn, reminding me that I belonged to him, and swearing by heaven and earth that he would compel me to submit to him. If I went out for a breath of fresh air, after a day of unwearied toil, his footsteps dogged me. If I knelt by my mother's grave, his dark shadow fell on me even there. The light heart which nature had given me became heavy with sad forebodings. The other slaves in my master's house noticed the change. Many of them pitied me; but none dared to ask the cause. They had no need to inquire. They knew too well the guilty practices under that roof; and they were aware that to speak of them was an offence that never went unpunished.

. . .

O, what days and nights of fear and sorrow that man caused me! Reader, it is not to awaken sympathy for myself that I am telling you truthfully what I suffered in slavery. I do it to kindle a flame of compassion in your hearts for my sisters who are still in bondage, suffering as I once suffered.

. . .

*SOURCE: Harriet Jacobs,* Incidents in the Life of a Slave Girl *(1861; Signet Classics, 2000), 26–27, 28, 29.*

## *Timeline*

**1774**

Molly Brant begins to serve as an intermediary between the British and the Iroquois Confederacy

**1775**

Revolutionary War begins

**1781**

Deborah Sampson enlists in the Continental Army under the name of Robert Shurtliff

**1783**

United States secures independence from Britain

**1787**

Fourteen-year-old Sally Hemings journeys to Paris as a servant to Thomas Jefferson

**1789**

Sally Hemings returns to the United States pregnant

**1793**

Invention of the cotton gin

**1798**

Judith Sargent Murray predicts the dawn of "a new era of female history"

**1803**

Louisiana Purchase

**1808**

United States bans the importation of slaves from Africa

and men, women, boys, and girls were scattered to near and distant plantations, their fates largely lost to history. Even with Thomas Jefferson as an owner, there was no such thing as enlightenment when it came to the institution of slavery.

## KEY TERMS

Californio
Cherokee
disappearing Indian
Gold Rush
Ladies Association of
    Philadelphia

Louisiana Purchase
Middle Passage
Overland Trail
republican motherhood
settler colonialism
Trail of Tears

Treaty of Guadalupe
    Hidalgo
Treaty of Paris

## Suggested Readings

Barr, Juliana. *Peace Came in the Form of a Woman: Indians and Spaniards on the Texas Borderlands* (2007).
Gordon-Reed, Annette. *The Hemingses of Monticello: An American Family* (2008).

**1819**

Emma Willard founds her school in Troy, New York

**1821**

Mexico wins its independence from Spain

**1826**

Thomas Jefferson dies and the majority of his slaves are sold at auction

**1833**

Founding of coeducational Oberlin College

**1838–1839**

Trail of Tears

**1842**

Harriot Jacobs finds her way to freedom

**1848**

Treaty of Guadalupe Hidalgo

**1849**

Gold Rush takes off in California

Hurtado, Albert L. *Intimate Frontiers: Sex, Gender, and Culture in Old California* (1999).

Hyde, Anne F. *Empires, Nations, and Families: A New History of the North American West, 1800–1860* (2012).

Miles, Tiya. *Ties that Bind: The Story of an Afro-Cherokee Family in Slavery and Freedom* (2005).

Perdue, Theda. *Cherokee Women: Gender and Culture Change, 1700–1835* (1998).

Learn more with this chapter's digital tools at http://www.oup.com/he/ware1e.

# three

# Freedom's Ferment,

## 1830–1865

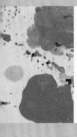

This photograph of the Beecher family, taken between 1858 and 1862, situates patriarch Lyman at the center, flanked by his four daughters (Harriet and Catharine to his left), with five of his sons standing behind them. Catharine Beecher and Harriet Beecher Stowe each became well known in their own right.

Few families exerted as much influence over nineteenth-century American life as the Beechers. The patriarch, Lyman Beecher, was one of the best-known evangelical preachers of his time, and his son Henry Ward Beecher followed in his path. The daughters in the family also excelled, each in her own distinctive fashion.

Catharine Beecher was the oldest of Lyman and Roxana Foote Beecher's nine children. When her mother died, she helped raise her siblings but then found herself at odds with her new stepmother as well as her father who pressed her to experience a religious conversion. Striking out on her own, Beecher founded the **Hartford Female Seminary** in 1823, a pioneering educational institution that aimed to move beyond teaching young women just embroidery and other ornamental skills. Later she took a leading role in promoting teacher training for women, combining her interests in raising women's status with fulfilling a critical need for schoolteachers in the country's expanding public school system. Beecher, who never married, also spoke and wrote widely about women's domestic duties and responsibilities.

Her younger sister Harriet subscribed to those domestic ideals, but took them in a different direction. A precocious child and avid reader, in 1836 she married Calvin Stowe, a biblical scholar and professor at the Lane Seminary in Cincinnati, and proceeded to bear seven children. Trying to raise a large family on a professor's salary was a challenge, and with Calvin's encouragement, Harriet supplemented their income by writing fiction and inspirational tracts. She enjoyed modest success until her breakout book, *Uncle Tom's Cabin; or, Life Among the Lowly*, was published in 1852. Written in response to the passage of the **Fugitive Slave Act of 1850**, the book thrust Stowe into the world of antislavery politics with its tale of Eliza, a woman who escaped enslavement by crossing the icy Ohio River to freedom, and Tom, who is sold away from his family and dies after a brutal beating. The fictional tropes of a sentimental novel helped make *Uncle Tom's Cabin* a national bestseller at the same time it became a factor in the events leading up to the Civil War. As Abraham Lincoln famously (if somewhat condescendingly) said in 1862 when Stowe visited the White House, "So you're the little woman who wrote the book that started this great war."

The lives of Catharine Beecher and Harriet Beecher Stowe encapsulate many of the themes of the antebellum period, including a heightened emphasis on a separate private sphere for women and the looming crisis over slavery that would lead to the Civil War. Beecher's emphasis on domesticity for elite white women also points to the dramatic changes underway in the world of women's work. Even as women were being told they belonged in the home, many women, by necessity or choice, were forging new lifestyles that took them far beyond its confines.

Often the story of **industrialization** in the North is presented as separate from that of slavery in the Old South, but just as democracy and slavery functioned as co-dependents in the early republic, so did slavery and the early Industrial Revolution. Slavery produced the cotton that was sent north to be woven into textiles by the young farm girls who flocked to the new mills in Lowell, Massachusetts; the Northern economy was just as dependent on raw materials from the South as the South was on Northern capital and credit. So let us not draw the contrasts between a free North and a slave South too starkly. Their histories—and the stories of their women—were deeply intertwined.

##  THE LADY AND THE MILL GIRL

A defining characteristic of the early republic, especially in the Northeast, was the remarkable range of benevolent, religious, and political associations founded to confront the ills of society. White women played a key role in this reform impulse, despite the prevailing ideology that relegated them to the private sphere of their homes and families. Stretching from religious benevolence to temperance to antislavery activism and even women's rights, women's participation in a broad range of activities reminds us that the line between public and private was quite porous indeed.

"Thine in the bonds of womanhood." Thus did Sarah Grimké sign a letter to a friend in the year 1838. This sense of sisterhood had its roots in the eighteenth century but came to fruition in the Northeast in the first half of the nineteenth in the concept of **separate spheres**, that is, the way in which women's lives were supposed to revolve around the familial and private, whereas men were expected to inhabit the wider world of politics, work, and public life.

As the dual meanings of Grimké's phrase suggested, the doctrine of separate spheres both recognized the oppression of women while simultaneously suggesting a path toward female autonomy and empowerment through shared consciousness. But as an actual description of nineteenth-century women's lives, the concept remains flawed, even for the white middle-class women who were its main constituency. Instead of occupying a separate sphere based on sex, many elite women were closely linked to comparable men by race and class. And many women—enslaved and free women of color, working-class women, and Native women, among others—were left outside this ideal entirely.

A **Cult of True Womanhood** defined by an emphasis on piety, purity, submission, and domesticity saturated early nineteenth-century prescriptive literature, specifically the women's magazines, books, and religious tracts dedicated to telling women how they ought to act. No one pushed this message more vigorously than Sarah Josepha Hale, the original editor of the *Ladies Magazine* (founded in 1828), who went on to spend forty years (1837–1877) as editor of *Godey's Lady's Book*. Filled with fiction, fashion, poetry, and (in the case of *Godey's*) individually hand-tinted illustrations, these periodicals both engaged and instructed the white middle-class women who were their target audiences. So, too, did some of the early housekeeping manuals, such as Lydia Maria Child's *The Frugal Housewife* (1829) and Catharine Beecher's widely read *Treatise on Domestic Economy* (1841).

FEBRUARY, 1855.

3.1: *Godey's Lady's Book* reached a wide audience in mid-nineteenth century America. Readers especially enjoyed the novelty of color fashion plates, which were individually tinted by hand because the technology did not yet exist to print color reproductions. This plate showing two fashionably dressed women appeared in an issue of *Godey's* from 1855.

If women wanted to escape from the demands of domesticity, they could turn to best-selling novels, many written by women, such as Catharine Sedgwick's *New-England Tale* (1827), Sarah Josepha Hale's *Northwood* (1827), Caroline Gilman's *Love's Progress; or Ruth Raymond* (1840), or Susan Warner's *The Wide, Wide World* (1850). In a class by itself was Harriet Beecher Stowe's *Uncle Tom's Cabin* (1852). According to *Harper's*, by the 1850s women made up an astounding four-fifths of the reading public.

An emerging middle class, with its rising incomes, expectations, and living standards, made this new lifestyle possible. Starting in the eighteenth century, the economy grew and diversified, giving an urban and market-oriented edge to what was still a predominantly agricultural country. American society had never been totally egalitarian—there were always rich and poor, even in the early colonial settlements—but the changes in the economy brought a more stratified class structure, especially in urban areas. At the center of this new system of exchange was cash: in the form of wages coming in for labor performed and goods sold, and money going out to buy a range of consumer goods and services that were no longer being produced in the household economy. Bostonian Abigail Lyman captured this shift perfectly when she exclaimed in 1797: "There is no way of living in this town without cash."

The story of domestic service, long the domain of women, exemplifies this growing class stratification. In the colonial and early Revolutionary eras, it was common for married women to have a local girl as "hired help," often a neighbor's unmarried daughter, who came into the household on a casual basis to help out with household chores like cleaning, laundry, or cooking. In other words, she was basically the same class as her mistress. By the mid-nineteenth century, the gap between mistress and maid had dramatically widened. The women who took jobs as domestic servants were increasingly recent immigrants, especially from Ireland, and they often lived in as permanent but poorly paid employees. Critical to the rising housekeeping requirements of nineteenth-century households, domestic servants performed more specialized tasks while allowing middle-class families to flaunt their ability to afford such help. Heaven forbid that a mistress answer the door when a servant could do it.

And yet even the hiring of domestic servants did not free middle-class women from the demands of running a household. It merely redistributed the responsibilities to involve more supervision and less physical work. For example, middle-class women now devoted far more time to the instruction, moral or otherwise, of their children, a task that was rarely farmed out to servants. Well-brought-up children were now one of the main products of a middle-class family.

The labor that women performed in their homes in the early nineteenth century paralleled the growth of the large-scale economic development that historians call industrialization. As men increasingly defined themselves and their roles by working for wages outside the home, labor became synonymous with wages, and wages became synonymous with male gender roles. However, women's domestic labor, which was not paid, was not considered comparable work. Since the wages men earned were often barely enough to support a family, it was up to women to supply the difference, either by bringing in additional cash for the family coffers or by substituting their own labor for something that would otherwise involve an outlay of cash. Such economic activities could add as much as $150 a year to a family budget, a hefty subvention. These contributions were not some abstract ideology of domesticity: these were real women doing real work. And yet because women's domestic work was generally unpaid and undervalued, it was practically invisible.

The insufficiency of men's wages was especially problematic for working-class women and their families living in urban areas. Urban poverty was different from rural poverty, and working-class women struggled to scrounge needed resources for their families. In addition to taking in boarders (which brought in cash but also made more work for women), they might go out scavenging on the city streets with their children, looking for cast-off goods and food with which to feed the family. Or women might take in piecework, earning pennies for work, such as sewing, that would later be consolidated in factories. Besides the precariousness of their existence, urban laboring women's lives lacked any sharp distinctions between public and private, with the urban neighborhood rather than the private home serving as the basis for working-class women's identity.

This focus on family and the household has implications beyond women's domestic roles. The economic contributions women made to their family survival in many ways allowed early capitalists to pay their male workers lower wages—and hence earn higher profits themselves. Thus housewives were central to the successful launching of industrialization. The home itself was also affected by the industrial transformation. New household technologies like central furnaces, cast-iron cookstoves, and sewing machines were beginning to reshape domestic chores and bring women's work more in line with the "time and task" routines characteristic of industrial labor.

Some women, mainly young farm girls from rural New England, played an even more direct role, flocking to the Lowell textile mills in the 1830s and 1840s. Women have always worked, but the Lowell experiment was the first

3.2: Lowell mill managers painted a sunny picture of good wages and healthy working conditions to attract young rural female workers, but this photograph of a textile mill circa 1850, with its poor lighting and no place to sit while workers tended the machines, suggests a different reality.

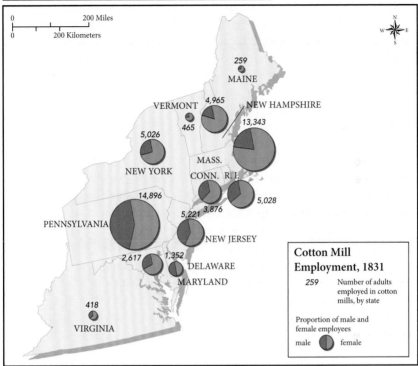

**Cotton Mill Employment and Textile Factory Strikes**

0    200 Miles
0    200 Kilometers

*259*
MAINE

VERMONT   *4,965*   NEW HAMPSHIRE

*465*   *13,343*

*5,026*

NEW YORK

MASS.

CONN.   R. I.

*14,896*   *5,028*

*5,221*   *3,876*

PENNSYLVANIA

NEW JERSEY

*2,617*   *1,352*

DELAWARE

MARYLAND

*418*

VIRGINIA

**Cotton Mill Employment, 1831**

*259*   Number of adults employed in cotton mills, by state

Proportion of male and female employees

male   female

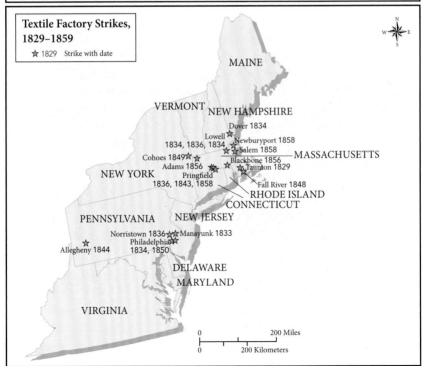

**Textile Factory Strikes, 1829–1859**

☆ 1829   Strike with date

MAINE

VERMONT   NEW HAMPSHIRE

Dover 1834

Lowell   Newburyport 1858
1834, 1836, 1834 ☆ ☆ Salem 1858

Cohoes 1849 ☆ ☆   Blackbone 1856   MASSACHUSETTS
Adams 1856 ☆☆   ☆ ☆ Taunton 1829

NEW YORK   Pringfield
1836, 1843, 1858   Fall River 1848

RHODE ISLAND
CONNECTICUT

PENNSYLVANIA   NEW JERSEY

Norristown 1836 ☆☆ Manayunk 1833
Philadelphia ☆☆
Allegheny 1844 ☆   1834, 1850

DELAWARE

MARYLAND

VIRGINIA

0   200 Miles
0   200 Kilometers

**MAP 3.1**

# Lowell Mill Girls

Mary Paul was a Vermont farm girl who starting at the age of fifteen embraced the opportunity to earn good wages in the textile mills of Lowell, Massachusetts. Here she describes her work as a doffer, which involves removing full bobbins of yarn from the spinning frames and replacing them with empty ones. Perhaps reflecting a newfound sense of self-reliance and independence, Mary Paul supported herself for twelve years before marrying in 1857.

Lowell Dec 21st 1845

Dear Father

I received your letter on Thursday the 14th with much pleasure. I am well which is one comfort. My life and health are spared while others are cut off. Last Thursday one girl fell down and broke her neck which caused instant death. She was going in or coming out of the mill and slipped down it being very icy. The same day a man was killed by the cars. Another had nearly all of his ribs broken. Another was nearly killed by falling down and having a bale of cotton fall on him. Last Tuesday we were paid. In all I had six dollars and sixty cents paid $4.68 for board. With the rest I got me a pair of rubbers and a pair of 50.cts shoes. Next payment I am to have a dollar a week beside

large-scale industrial undertaking whose owners welcomed, indeed relied on (cheap) female labor to make their products.

Adjusting to repetitive working conditions and twelve-hour days for six days a week was a challenge, but in many ways the excitement of living on their own in company boarding houses compensated for the poor conditions.

my board. We have not had much snow the deepest being not more than 4 inches. It has been very warm for winter. Perhaps you would like something about our regulations about going in and coming out of the mill. At 5 o'clock in the morning the bell rings for the folks to get up and get breakfast. At half past six it rings for the girls to get up and at seven they are called into the mill. At half past 12 we have dinner are called back again at one and stay till half past seven. I get along very well with my work. I can doff as fast as any girl in our room. I think I shall have frames before long. The usual time allowed for learning is six months but I think I shall have frames before I have been in three as I get along so fast. I think that the factory is the best place for me and if any girl wants employment I advise them to come to Lowell. Tell Harriet that though she does not hear from me she is not forgotten. I have little time to devote to writing that I cannot write all I want to. There are half a dozen letters which I ought to write to day but I have not time. Tell Harriet I send my love to her and all of the girls. Give my love to Mrs. Clement. Tell Henry this will answer for him and you too for this time.

This from
Mary S Paul

Bela Paul
Henry S Paul

*SOURCE: Thomas Dublin,* **Farm to Factory: Women's Letters, 1830–1860** *(New York: Columbia University Press, 1981), 103–104.*

"Don't I feel independent!" one mill worker wrote home to her sister in the 1840s. Kinship networks and cultural homogeneity also eased the transition to urban life. Confirming their sense of themselves as pioneers comparable to young men seeking their fortunes out West, Lowell mill girls contributed essays to the company-supported newspaper, the *Lowell Offering*, and later wrote books about their youthful experiences. Two of the best known are Lucy Larcom's *A New England Girlhood* (1889) and Harriet Hanson Robinson's *Loom and Spindle, or Life among the Early Mill Girls* (1898).

Alas, this heyday (if it ever was one) did not last. As early as the mid-1830s, female mill workers organized strikes to protest poor working conditions, long hours, and low pay; in the 1840s they formed labor unions. By then the owners of the mills had realized that New England farm girls were not the only cheap source of labor for their dramatically growing businesses: male and female immigrants from Ireland, then in the grip of a terrible famine, increasingly supplied the labor that ran the mills. And what of the Lowell mill girls? Even though they usually only worked in the mills for a few scant years, the experience had a lifelong impact. As a group, they tended to marry later and were more likely to stay in towns and cities rather than returning to rural farm life. Work outside the home was definitely a transformative experience for multiple generations of American women.

 ## THE FEMALE WORLD OF BENEVOLENCE AND REFORM

Just as transformative was participation in the gamut of religious, charitable, and reform societies that flourished in the first half of the nineteenth century, mainly in the Northeast but also in the recently settled Midwest. Even though women lacked access to traditional forms of political influence, such as the vote or participation in political parties, they were still very much involved in a range of political and cultural issues of their day. To put it another way, foregrounding women's reform and benevolent activities encourages a dramatic broadening of what constitutes political history. This insight applies to both Black and white women. So too do the class dimensions of this reform activism, which often featured middle-class women imposing their values and standards on working class women, who did not always welcome the intervention.

The starting point for understanding this burst of reform is religion, specifically women's central roles as members of churches. As English novelist Frances Trollope observed after living in the new nation for several years in the late 1820s, never had she seen a country "where religion had so strong a hold upon the women, or a slighter hold upon the men." But this religious fervor ebbed and flowed, subject to bursts of revivalism such as the Great Awakening, from the 1750s to the 1770s, and then the **Second Great Awakening** of the 1820s and 1830s that brought new converts, male and especially female, into the Protestant fold. All this religiosity needed an outlet beyond just going to church on Sundays, and **benevolent societies** and **voluntary associations** flowed naturally from new conversions. By one estimate, at least 10 percent of all the adult white women in the Northeast participated in some form of benevolent reform in these years.

Women's benevolent work covered a range of initiatives and interests. Maternal societies brought women together in their shared role as mothers. For example, the Dorchester (Massachusetts) Maternal Association was founded in 1816 by members who were "aware of our highly responsible situation as Mothers & as professing Christians" and wanted to "commend our dear offspring to God." In contrast, moral reform societies hoped to hold men and women to a single high standard of purity, the standard adhered to by women, who were presumed to be less interested in sexual relations than men. (In an age without reliable birth control, having less frequent sexual intercourse was also an effective form of family planning.) To promote this ideal, such groups as the Boston Female Moral Reform Society attacked the sin of licentiousness, dedicating themselves to rescuing women, usually lower class, who had "fallen" into prostitution. More controversially, these groups also aimed to publicize—and ostracize—the men who visited these prostitutes. All of this was done in the name of female moral superiority—and with little awareness of how one class of women was imposing its values on those less privileged.

In essence, these benevolent associations were an attempt to use private charity to deal with many of the social problems that the local, state, and federal governments would later take on. Reformers tackled the problems of destitute widows and orphaned children, conditions for inmates in insane asylums and poorhouses, and public drunkenness. On more strictly religious grounds, voluntary associations supported missionary work abroad and promoted spiritual and personal improvement at home, especially temperance.

These concerns were portrayed as especially well matched to women's heightened moral sensibilities, although women's rights activist Susan B. Anthony would have none of this, sneering: "Men like to see women pick up the drunken and falling. That *patching business* is 'woman's proper sphere.'" Anthony's dismissal notwithstanding, such benevolence provided access to activities more associated with the public than the private realm. Besides being numerous (as many as 400 female moral reform societies existed in New York and New England by the 1840s), these groups were extremely sophisticated in their organization. Women ran meetings, organized outreach drives, raised and distributed vast sums of money, and publicized their activities, all while managing to keep up with their ongoing domestic responsibilities in the private sphere.

Several religiously-based experiments offered women the chance to explore alternative models of family and sexuality within the Christian faith.

The **Shakers**, who were founded by a woman, Mother Ann Lee, built communities based on reciprocity between the sexes, not patriarchal domination. As part of that commitment, Shakers embraced celibacy, welcoming orphans and converts as a way for their communities to thrive and prosper without relying on internal propagation. **The Oneida Community** in upstate New York took a very different tack. Founded by John Humphrey Noyes in 1848, the utopian undertaking endorsed the collective owning of property and communal child-raising. More controversially, members eschewed monogamy entirely because it interfered with their primary relationship with God. Instead they were free to engage in sexual relations with multiple partners. Of special relevance to women's sexual expression, men in Oneida bore the main responsibility for contraception. Finally, the **Mormons** (or Church of Latter-day Saints, as they preferred to be called), founded by the prophet Joseph Smith in upstate New York in 1830, practiced polygamy, where Mormon men took multiple wives, a practice accepted by men and women alike as a way to ensure that all women were safely provided for within families. All these antebellum religious experiments offered alternatives to the traditional nuclear family—and its sexual underpinnings—at the heart of the **Cult of Domesticity**.

 # THE INTERTWINED ORIGINS OF ABOLITION AND WOMEN'S RIGHTS

Until the 1830s almost all of women's benevolent and charitable work was in some way church-related. (In contrast, men were free to join a range of civic, political, and religious associations.) At the core of women's benevolence was allegiance to the ideal of **moral suasion**, that is, trying to convince individuals to change their erring ways through personal persuasion. But there were limits to how much society could be transformed in this manner, and by the 1840s and 1850s some women had concluded that "moral suasion is moral balderdash." Beware, however, of seeing an inevitable progression from moral reform and benevolence to more radical undertakings. Only a hearty and bold minority made that leap.

Two of the most important movements that captured their energies were abolitionism and women's rights. Slavery was both a political and a moral question for the early republic, and it was only resolved (and then incompletely) by the Civil War of the 1860s. Starting in the 1830s, as slavery became more entrenched and profitable in the South, Northern abolitionists began to challenge the institution as morally wrong in a democratic society. Taking the lead were free African Americans, a classification that included those who had been manumitted by gradual emancipation in the North, those who

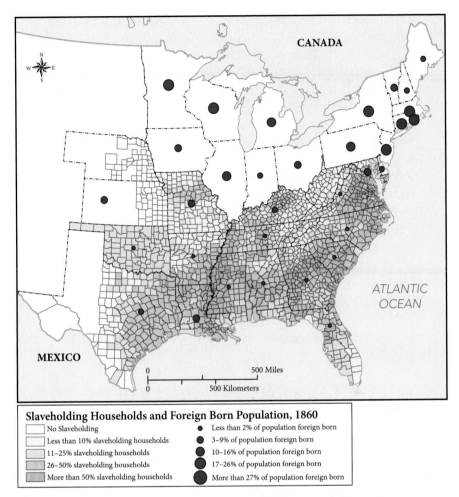

**Slaveholding Households and Foreign Born Population, 1860**

|  | Slaveholding |  | Foreign Born Population |
|---|---|---|---|
| ☐ | No Slaveholding | ● | Less than 2% of population foreign born |
| ☐ | Less than 10% slaveholding households | ● | 3–9% of population foreign born |
| ☐ | 11–25% slaveholding households | ● | 10–16% of population foreign born |
| ☐ | 26–50% slaveholding households | ● | 17–26% of population foreign born |
| ☐ | More than 50% slaveholding households | ● | More than 27% of population foreign born |

**MAP 3.2**

had escaped from slavery in the South, or those who had always been free. By 1820 the free Black community counted close to 250,000 members.

African American women were central to activism on both abolitionism and women's rights. In 1832 Maria W. Stewart became the first American woman, Black or white, to speak in public about politics and women's rights before a mixed-sex (or in the terminology of the time "promiscuous"), mixed-race gathering. Stewart boldly challenged her audience, which included both Black and white members: "Who shall go forward, and take off the reproach that is cast upon the people of color? Shall it be a woman?" By speaking out so forthrightly in public, Stewart literally embodied "the woman question" and affirmed that women should play an essential role in the struggle for freedom of both African Americans and women.

## DOCUMENTING AMERICAN WOMEN

# Maria W. Stewart Speaks on the "Woman Question" in Boston, 1832

Maria W. Stewart was the first American woman, Black or white, to speak in public about politics and women's rights. In her lecture, Stewart issued a double challenge: for African Americans to aim higher and overcome the barriers placed in their paths, and for white Bostonians to confront their complicity in the oppression of Black people. Threaded throughout was an affirmation of the essential role that African American women should play in the larger freedom struggle.

. . . Methinks I heard a spiritual interrogation—"Who shall go forward, and take off the reproach that is cast upon the people of color? Shall it be a woman?" And my heart made this reply—"If it is thy will, be it even so, Lord Jesus!"

I have heard much respecting the horrors of slavery; but may Heaven forbid that the generality of my color throughout these United States should experience any more of its horrors than to be a servant of servants, or hewers of wood and drawers of water! Tell us no more of southern slavery; for with few exceptions, although I may be very erroneous in my opinion, yet I consider our condition but little better than that. Yet, after all, methinks there are no chains so galling as the chains of ignorance—no fetters so binding as those that bind the soul, and exclude it from the vast field of useful and scientific

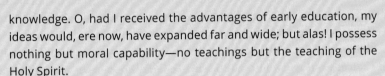

knowledge. O, had I received the advantages of early education, my ideas would, ere now, have expanded far and wide; but alas! I possess nothing but moral capability—no teachings but the teaching of the Holy Spirit.

I have asked several individuals of my sex, who transact business for themselves, if providing our girls were to give them the most satisfactory references, they would not be willing to grant them an equal opportunity with others? Their reply has been—for their own part, they had no objection; but as it was not the custom, were they to take them into their employ, they would be in danger of losing the public patronage.

And such is the powerful force of prejudice. Let our girls possess what amiable qualities of soul they may; let their characters be fair and spotless as innocence itself; let their natural taste and ingenuity be what they may; it is impossible for scarce an individual of them to rise above the condition of servants. Ah! Why is this cruel and unfeeling distinction? Is it merely because God has made our complexion to vary? If it be, O shame to soft, relenting humanity! "Tell it not in Gath! Publish it not in the streets of Askelon!" Yet, after all, methinks were the American free people of color to turn their attention more assiduously to moral worth and intellectual improvement, this would be the result: prejudice would gradually diminish, and the whites would be compelled to say, unloose those fetters!

*SOURCE: Maria W. Miller Stewart, "Lecture, Delivered at the Franklin Hall,"* in **Productions of Mrs. Maria W. Stewart, Presented to the First African Baptist Church and Society, of the City of Boston** *(Boston: Friends of Freedom and Virtue, 1835), 51–56, found on https://www.blackpast.org*

White abolitionists such as William Lloyd Garrison also took up the cause. In 1831 Garrison founded the New England Anti-Slavery Society and welcomed women who shared his views, such as Quaker activist Lucretia Mott and former enslaved woman Sojourner Truth. Two early converts were Angelina and Sarah Grimké, sisters and Southerners who turned against their heritage by embracing **abolition**. (Angelina would later marry fellow abolitionist Theodore Weld). Their presence caused consternation in the movement, however, when following the example of Maria Stewart, Sarah began to speak in public to audiences of both men and women, an act that continued to be too controversial even for a bunch of committed radicals. But she would not be silenced, and soon other women added their public voices to the cause. This participation opened their eyes not just to the plight of enslaved African Americans but eventually to women's plight as well. As white abolitionist and women's rights activist Abby Kelley Foster put it eloquently, "We have good cause to be grateful to the slave. In striving to strike his irons off, we found most surely, that we were manacled ourselves."

White women such as Lucy Stone and Elizabeth Cady Stanton also came to women's rights through abolitionism. Stone was one of the first women to attend college (Oberlin Class of 1847) and after graduation became an itinerant speaker for abolitionism and women's rights. She would later marry abolitionist Henry Blackwell in a ceremony in which she refused to promise to obey her husband or take his name, hence the designation of women who followed her example as "Lucy Stoners."

Elizabeth Cady grew up as the daughter of a judge in upstate New York, where his library of books on jurisprudence indelibly introduced her to discrimination against women in the law. In 1840 she married reformer Henry Stanton and the couple spent their honeymoon in London at a world antislavery

*I Sell the Shadow to Support the Substance.*

SOJOURNER TRUTH.

3.3: Sojourner Truth sold these cartes de visites (postcards) to raise money when she lectured–hence the caption "I Sell the Shadow to Support the Substance." (Early photographs were often referred to as shadows.) Small in size (2½ by 4 inches, about the size of an iPhone) but powerful in their impact, this one dates to 1864.

conference. When women delegates were forced to sit in a balcony separately from the men, this slight was too much for Stanton and Lucretia Mott. On the spot they vowed to hold a convention dedicated to women's rights. It took eight years before it came off, and when it did, it was in a tiny village in upstate New York, where the Stantons had settled with their growing family.

The **Seneca Falls convention** of 1848 was not, as is often asserted, the first gathering ever held on the question of women's rights, but it has assumed a preeminent place in the history of feminism and women's rights. On two days in July, approximately 300 people, including forty men, convened in the local Methodist church in response to a call to discuss "the social, civil and religious condition of Woman" that had been drafted by Stanton, Mott, and Martha Coffin Wright at Stanton's kitchen table. (That table is now in the Smithsonian Institution.) Often these women are portrayed as simple housewives, but they were already savvy and experienced reformers, and they were determined not to back down, even when Henry Stanton threatened to leave

3.4: The women's rights movement was an easy target for satire, as seen in this engraving captioned "Woman's Emancipation" published in *Harper's New Monthly Magazine* in August 1851. All the women are sporting the controversial fashion statement of bloomers or wearing other male-inspired attire.

town. Elizabeth Cady Stanton was their wordsmith, and she turned to the Declaration of Independence for inspiration, boldly restating its central concept in this unforgettable way: "All men and women are created equal."

The **Declaration of Sentiments** (see Appendix) adopted at Seneca Falls presented eighteen instances of "repeated injuries and usurpation on the part of man toward woman," including the denial of the basic right of citizenship, the lack of married women's property rights, the exclusion of women from profitable employment, and the lack of access to education. All of these issues had been circulating separately for the past few decades, but the document pulled them together to make a compelling case for women as necessary subjects of a reform movement of their own. Eleven resolutions followed, all of which passed easily, with the exception of the call "to secure to themselves their sacred right to elective franchise," which just squeaked by. Why was women's suffrage so fraught? Because women voting alongside men in the 1840s would have been the ultimate challenge to the notion of politics and public life as solely men's sphere. Not until 1920, a full seventy-two years after Seneca Falls, would the Nineteenth Amendment stating that the right to vote "shall not be denied" on account of sex be added to the U.S. Constitution.

Absent from Seneca Falls was Susan B. Anthony, who was living in nearby Rochester and about to embark on a career as a temperance lecturer after a decade of teaching school. Soon dissatisfied with the secondary roles that women were expected to play in the temperance movement, she gravitated toward women's rights. In 1851 she met Elizabeth Cady Stanton, and the two formed one of the greatest political partnerships in women's history.

By then the notion of a separate women's sphere was clearly under assault. As a resolution at another early women's rights convention stated, "The proper sphere for all human beings is the largest and highest to which they are able to attain." Margaret Fuller, unquestionably the most prominent woman intellectual in antebellum America, was thinking along similar lines in her influential *Woman in the Nineteenth Century*, published in 1845: "We would have every arbitrary barrier thrown down. We would have every path laid open to Woman as freely as to Man." She went on: "If you ask me what offices they may fill, I reply—any. . . . Let them be sea-captains, if you will." Thus did the political and intellectual ferment originally unleashed by the American Revolution continue to deepen and grow.

This ferment was actually a worldwide phenomenon, as a wave of uprisings and insurrections swept Europe in the revolutions of 1848. Margaret Fuller reported on these developments from Italy for Horace Greeley's *New-York Tribune*, making her America's first female war correspondent. Women on both sides of the Atlantic seized the moment to demand changes in women's status at the same time they agitated against slavery and other social ills, constituting what was arguably the first international women's movement.

In the Western Hemisphere, 1848 marked the end of the Mexican-American War and the signing of the Treaty of Guadalupe Hidalgo, by which Mexico ceded its vast northern territories stretching from Texas to California to the United States. It was not just at Seneca Falls, therefore, that new ideas about citizenship and democracy, as well as empire and nationalism, were beginning to reshape American society, indeed the whole world.

 ## WOMEN'S CIVIL WARS

In 1846 an African American couple in Missouri, Dred and Harriet Robinson Scott, filed legal petitions suing for their freedom. By the time the Supreme Court decided *Dred Scott v. Sanford* in 1857, ruling that Congress has no authority to eliminate slavery in the territories and that slaves were not citizens of the United States, Harriet Robinson Scott's role in the proceedings had been completely eclipsed. And yet this case was not just about one individual: it was very much a Scott family story of trying to keep their marriage intact and protect their two daughters' futures over the eleven years the litigation worked its way through the courts. Despite the devastating language of the Supreme Court decision (it called African Americans "beings of an inferior order . . . and so far inferior, that they had no rights which the white man was bound to respect"), it was not the end of the story for the Scotts—they were manumitted by a private arrangement that year, gaining their freedom after all. That outcome, however, does not negate *Dred Scott*'s ignominious place in the history of American constitutional law.

The Supreme Court was not the only American institution grappling with the divisive issue of slavery in the 1850s. The Congress, the political parties, and public opinion all weighed in, forging temporary compromises designed to hold the Union together only to face new challenges threatening to tear it apart. The final break came in 1861 when Southern states seceded from the Union. What had been an increasingly intractable political, legal, and moral question now became, literally, a civil war. "We shall never any of us be the same as we have been," Lucy Buck observed two years into the conflict. Buck was a white Southerner, but she spoke for the multitudes of American women, few of whom escaped the four-year struggle untouched. And yet that impact differed by region and race, with Southern women, Black and white, bearing the heaviest burdens as their states became the battleground for the bloodiest war in American history.

Northern white women embraced the challenge of war patriotically. Many channeled their contributions through the U.S. Sanitary Commission, which despite its name was not a formal arm of the federal government but

3.5: This photograph of the camp of the Thirty-First Pennsylvania Infantry near Washington, DC, in 1862 confirms that women and children were part of the Civil War military experience. The baby's face is blurred because she likely couldn't sit still long enough while the photograph was being taken.

rather a huge voluntary association that took on the task of supplying the needs of the Northern fighting force. Mainly propelled by women's volunteer efforts, the commission operated on an unprecedented national scale, including in the West. Women organized fundraising efforts called sanitary fairs, collected supplies and funds, and sewed and knitted for the benefit of Union soldiers and their kin. White women then transferred these newly acquired organizational skills into many of the institutional and reform movements they participated in for the rest of the nineteenth century. For example, Clara Barton drew on her wartime experiences to found the American Red Cross in 1881.

Although photographs of Civil War battlegrounds suggest an exclusively male terrain, women were not simply relegated to organizing charity fairs and knitting socks. Perhaps as many as three thousand women signed on as nurses under the supervision of Dorothea Dix, who followed in the footsteps of Crimean War pioneer Florence Nightingale. One of these eager nurses was Louisa May Alcott, whose beloved novel *Little Women* would be published in 1868. "I want new experiences, and am sure to get 'em if I go," she exclaimed, although she lasted less than a month before she contracted typhoid fever and had to return home. In addition to nurses, Northern women also served as spies and soldiers, but only clandestinely. Far more prevalent were the camp followers who tagged along on the edges of the Union army, following husbands, brothers, and sons as they fought, just as they had during the Revolutionary War.

African American women, many of them formerly enslaved, also participated actively in the Northern war effort. Susie King Taylor, who escaped from slavery in Georgia at the age of fourteen and sought protection from Union forces deployed on Georgia's barrier islands, first drew the attention of military leaders for her ability to read and write; soon she was tasked with organizing a school for African Americans who had liberated themselves by joining Union encampments. She later became an army nurse and wrote a memoir about her wartime experiences, *Reminiscences of My Life in Camp with the 33d United States Colored Troops, Late 1st S. C. Volunteers.*

Harriet Tubman escaped from slavery in the border state of Maryland in 1849 and then made multiple trips back to guide family and friends to freedom through what was known as the **Underground Railroad**. In all she made nineteen such rescue missions. When war broke out, Tubman offered her services to the Union Army, serving as a scout, a nurse, and a spy. One of her most noted achievements was guiding the 1863 raid at Combahee Ferry, South Carolina, which liberated more than 750 African Americans. Tubman's raid in turn provided the inspiration for the 1977 Combahee River Collective's "A Black Feminist Statement," a foundational text of Black feminist thought.

Whereas just under half of the eligible Northern men served in the Union army, closer to four-fifths of eligible Southern men joined the Confederate ranks, leaving white women to constitute "a second front," literally running farms and plantations and supervising the people they enslaved as well as taking on new roles as nurses, clerks, and teachers while their men went off to war. Of course slaveholding women had been performing many of those roles before the conflict, but instead of seeing these responsibilities as an opportunity for expanded civic and familial roles (as many Northern women did), Southern white women often experienced these additional

3.6: Along with Sojourner Truth, Harriet Tubman was one of the most widely known African American women of the nineteenth century, noted especially for her role as a conductor on the Underground Railroad helping enslaved people escape to freedom. This recently discovered photo shows Tubman soon after her Civil War exploits.

DOCUMENTING AMERICAN WOMEN

# Susie King Taylor's Reminiscences of Her Service as an Army Nurse

Susie King Taylor, born a slave on a Georgia plantation in 1848, "self-liberated" herself in 1862 by escaping to St. Simons Island, then occupied by Union forces. Quickly recognized for her literacy, she established a school on the island at the request of authorities. After her marriage to a Black non-commissioned officer, she traveled with her husband's regiment and served as a nurse. Her reminiscences of her wartime service, published in 1902, end with this meditation on the role that African Americans like herself and her husband played in the conflict.

My dear friends! do we understand the meaning of war? Do we know or think of that war of '61? No, we do not, only those brave soldiers, and those who had occasion to be in it, can realize what it was. I can and shall never forget that terrible war until my eyes close in death. The scenes are just as fresh in my mind to-day as in '61. I see now each scene,—the roll-call, the drum tap, "lights out," the call at night when there was danger from the enemy, the double force of pickets, the cold and rain. How anxious I would be, not knowing what would happen before morning! Many times I would dress, not sure but all would be captured. Other times I would stand at my tent door and try to see what was going on, because night was the time the rebels would try to get into our lines and capture some of the boys. It was mostly at night that our men went out for their scouts, and often had a hand to hand fight with the rebels, and although our men came out sometimes with a few killed or wounded, none of them ever were captured.

We do not, as the black race, properly appreciate the old veterans, white or black, as we ought to. I know what they went through, especially those black men, for the Confederates had no mercy on them; neither did they show any toward the white Union soldiers. I have seen the terrors of that war. I was the wife of one of those men who did not get a penny for eighteen months for their services, only their rations and clothing.

I cannot praise General David Hunter too highly, for he was the first man to arm the black man, in the beginning of 1862. He had a hard struggle to hold all the southern division, with so few men, so he applied to Congress; but the answer to him was, "Do not bother us," which was very discouraging. As the general needed more men to protect the islands and do garrison duty, he organized two companies.

I look around now and see the comforts that our younger generation enjoy, and think of the blood that was shed to make these comforts possible for them, and see how little some of them appreciate the old soldiers. My heart burns within me, at this want of appreciation. There are only a few of them left now, so let us all, as the ranks close, take a deeper interest in them. Let the younger generation take an interest also, and remember that it was through the efforts of these veterans that they and we older ones enjoy our liberty to-day.

*SOURCE: Susie King Taylor,* Reminiscences of My Life in Camp with the 33d United States Colored Troops, Late 1st S. C. Volunteers *(Boston, 1902), pp. 50–52.*

**DOCUMENTING AMERICAN WOMEN**

# A White Southern Woman Reflects on Daily Life during the Civil War

Ella Gertrude Clanton Thomas is best known for the extensive journal she kept from 1848 to 1889. Born into a wealthy slaveholding Georgia planter family, she married in 1852, bore ten children over the next twenty-three years (seven survived), and helped supervise a large plantation including numerous enslaved workers. A strong supporter of the Confederacy, these excerpts describe the disruptions to daily life during wartime and her thoughts about slavery in the face of a looming Confederate defeat.

September, 1862

Two months and more have passed since I wrote last and in that time how much has happened both of an individual and national character. To begin with Mr Thomas has resigned his position in the army and is at home again. I am writing confidentially to you my Journal and I will tell you exactly how I feel with regard to this matter. While he was contented, and satisfied with camp life and soldier's fare I never should have been the woman to have urged him to come home, however much I might have missed his society, but when col [Gen.] Tom Cobb by the promotion of several others over him did him great injustice and he wrote me that "a due sense of self respect demanded his resignation" I wrote him "to come" —Previous to doing so he was ill in Richmond at Miss Lyons' and it was with difficulty that he succeeded in having his resignation accepted. He remained several days in North Carolina with Jule and reached home on the -day of August. For more than a week he had fever but has gradually been improving although still suffering a little from dyspepsia but never at any period of my life, not even in the sunny hours of courtship or those immediately after our marriage, have I ever enjoyed such quiet happiness, such perfect enjoyment of his society. I said I would not have recalled him from the service. I say now that I would most heartily oppose his joining again unless the enemy were at our doors. I shall never regret the one year spent in service but I feel that he has escaped with his life —Oh when I think of the thousands and thousands of desolate homes and hearts, of the many bright intellects and manly forms hushed in death I turn to my Husband and thank God that he is home again.

Saturday, September 17, 1864

. . .

I have sometimes doubted on the subject of slavery. I have seen so many of its evils chief among which is the terribly demoralizing influence upon our men and boys but of late I have become convinced the Negro as a race is better off with us as he has been than if he were made free, but I am by no means so sure that we would not gain by his having his freedom given him. I grant that I am not so philanthropic as to be willing voluntarily to give all we own for the sake of the principle, but I do think that if we had the same invested in something else as a means of support I would willingly, nay gladly, have the responsibility of them taken off my shoulders.

. . .

March, 1865

I know I will regret hereafter that I have made no record of time and events which are fraught with so much interest, record of events which are hourly making history—but I cannot. I shrink from the task. At times I feel as if I was drifting on, on, ever onward to be at last dashed against some rock and I shut my eyes and almost wish it was over, the shock

encountered and I prepared to know what destiny awaits me. I am tired, oh so tired of this war. I want to breathe free. I feel the restraint of the blockade and as port after port becomes blockade, I feel shut up, pent up and am irresistibly reminded of the old story of the iron shroud contracting more and more each hour, each moment. I live too fast. A strange contradiction, yet true. A life of emotion, quick rapid succession of startling events will wear upon the constitution and weaken the physical nature. I may perhaps be glad hereafter that I have lived through this war but now the height of my ambition is to be quiet, to have no distracting cares—the time to read—leisure to think and write—and study.

*SOURCE: Virginia Ingraham Burr,* Secret Eye: The Journal of Ella Gertrude Clanton Thomas, 1848–1889 *(Chapel Hill, NC: UNC Press, 1990). Online at https://search.alexanderstreet.com/preview/work/bibliographic_entity%7Cbibliographic_details%7C4359063*

# *Timeline*

| | | |
|---|---|---|
| **1816** | **1831** | **1848** |
| Founding of Dorchester (Massachusetts) Maternal Association | William Lloyd Garrison creates the New England Anti-Slavery Society | Founding of the Oneida Community |
| **1830** | | **1848** |
| Joseph Smith publishes the Book of Mormon | **1832** | Seneca Falls Convention |
| | Maria W. Stewart becomes the first woman to speak in public about politics and women's rights before a mixed-sex, mixed-race gathering | **1850** |
| **C. 1830–1840** | | Passage of the Fugitive Slave Act |
| Women flock to Lowell mills | | |

demands as a burden. Managing enslaved workers and keeping them on the job while war with its tantalizing possibilities of freedom and liberation was raging all around them was especially tricky.

Some Southern women wanted nothing more than to be rid of their slaves entirely. "You may give your Negroes away," wrote a Texas wife to her husband in 1864. "I cannot live with them another year alone." But the vast majority of white women remained deeply invested in the Southern way of life and the continuation of the institution of slavery. Far from innocent bystanders or mere witnesses to the Confederate war effort, Southern white women took on active roles as smugglers, spies, and members of rebel guerilla networks. Such actions confounded military authorities, who initially thought of white Southern women as somehow outside the theater of war on account of their sex. When confronted with spies like Clara Judd, who was arrested in Tennessee in late 1862 and sent to military prison in Illinois, they revised their opinions quickly. In hindsight the American Civil War blurred the lines between civilian and combatant in ways that foreshadowed many twentieth century conflicts.

Those lines were similarly murky for enslaved African Americans, a population that included approximately 1.9 million women. Enslaved women too could function as a second front, emerging as leaders and rebels of small and large-scale rebellions on Confederate plantations. And they too joined with African American men in "self-liberation," which involved escaping from their places of enslavement to join Union encampments behind enemy lines. Soon the numbers of formerly enslaved people were so high that these military sites basically became refugee camps. Military officials

**1852**

*Uncle Tom's Cabin* is published

**1857**

Supreme Court decides *Dred Scott v. Sanford*

**1860–1861**

Southern states secede from the Union; beginning of Civil War

**1863**

Harriet Tubman guides raid at Combahee Ferry, South Carolina, which liberates more than 750 African Americans

**1868**

Louisa May Alcott publishes *Little Women*

**1881**

American Red Cross is founded by Clara Barton

declared former slaves "contraband" and offered men the chance to earn their freedom by waged labor or military service, thus setting the stage for the valuable roles that Black troops played in the Civil War. But what was to become of contraband women and children in these camps? Joining up to fight was not an option, so the military held out the prospect of marriage and the creation of traditional nuclear families to African American women as their ticket to freedom, an extremely gendered route to emancipation and citizenship but probably their best hope for legal and financial protection in these unsettled times. The Civil War may have ended the institution of slavery, but in many ways it reconfirmed the role of marriage as an organizing principle of state and society.

The Civil War took a terrible toll: more than a million men were killed or wounded. Each of those casualties left mothers, sisters, wives, and daughters; the lives of widows and the young women who would never have a chance to marry because so many men in their age cohort died in the fighting were especially upended. In the end, the Union was saved and slavery abolished, but at a terrible human cost. The resolution of the conflict also offered a truly remarkable promise: a life of freedom for those emancipated from slavery. How that would play out, and what role gender would play in the story, occupied American society for the rest of the nineteenth century, indeed right up to the present day.

## KEY TERMS

abolition

benevolent
  societies

Cult of Domesticity

Cult of True
  Womanhood

Declaration of
  Sentiments

Fugitive Slave Act
  of 1850

Hartford Female
  Seminary

industrialization

moral suasion

Mormons

Oneida Community

Second Great
  Awakening

Seneca Falls convention

separate spheres

Shakers

Underground Railroad

voluntary associations

## Suggested Readings

Anderson, Bonnie. *Joyous Greetings: The First International Women's Movement, 1830–1860* (2000).

Boydston, Jeanne. *Home and Work: Housework, Wages, and the Ideology of Labor in the Early Republic* (1990).

Ginzberg, Lori. *Women and the Work of Benevolence: Morality, Politics, and Class in the Nineteenth-Century United States* (1990).

Jones-Rogers, Stephanie. *They Were Her Property: White Women as Slave Owners in the American South* (2019).

McCurry, Stephanie. *Women's War: Fighting and Surviving the American Civil War* (2019).

Tetrault, Lisa. *The Myth of Seneca Falls: Memory and the Women's Suffrage Movement, 1848–1898* (2014).

Learn more with this chapter's digital tools at http://www.oup.com/he/warele.

# four

# Reconstruction and Beyond, 1865–1890

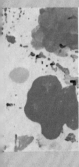

This three-quarter-length portrait of poet and activist Frances Ellen Watkins Harper was taken in 1895 when she was seventy years old. Three years earlier she had published her widely acclaimed novel *Iola Leroy*.

"We are all bound up together in one great bundle of humanity." So spoke the African American poet Frances Ellen Watkins Harper at the Eleventh National Woman's Rights Convention held in New York in 1866. Unfortunately her powerful rhetorical formulation was no match for the increasingly fraught political landscape in the aftermath of the Civil War. The original women's rights movement and the abolitionist cause had worked in tandem in the 1850s, but when the war ended, the old coalition linking race and gender split irrevocably over the proposed constitutional amendments intended to guarantee the political rights of recently freed African Americans. The dispute was over who had priority: African American men, or women, white as well as African American, who also wanted to be included in the post–Civil War expansion of political liberties. The nod went to African American men, but at the cost of a unified women's rights movement.

When Harper addressed the convention, however, the movement was still committed to the idea of supporting universal suffrage, or in Elizabeth Cady Stanton's words, "burying the black man and the woman in citizen." And Harper had newfound reason to be considering her status as a woman as well as an African American. Born in 1825 to free parents in the slave state of Maryland, she was orphaned at the age of three and raised by an aunt. She attended a school for free Black people in Baltimore run by her uncle, the Reverend William Watkins, but her formal education ended at thirteen. After that she supported herself with a variety of jobs, including seamstress, nursemaid, and teacher. In the 1840s and 1850s she made a name for herself as a poet and antislavery lecturer. Her first book of poetry, *Poems of Miscellaneous Subjects*, was published in 1854 and sold 10,000 copies over the next five years. In 1860 she married Fenton Harper, a widower with three children, and bore the family's fourth child. Her world changed dramatically in 1864 when he died suddenly and she found herself at the mercy of the legal system, not because of her race but because she lacked legal rights as a married woman.

Frances Ellen Watkins Harper shared the story of her bereavement and its aftermath with the audience at the women's rights convention in 1866. She began by saying that she considered herself "something of a novice upon this platform," because previously most of her life had been spent battling against the wrongs associated with her race rather than dwelling on what she had in common with women. But when her husband died in debt, a court administrator stripped her and her four children of their property and belongings. How different it would have been, she realized, if she had died instead of her husband. It was at this point that she asserted her intersectional vision: "We are all bound up together in one great bundle of humanity," adding, powerfully, "and society cannot trample on the weakest and feeblest of its members without receiving the curse in its own soul."

Frances Ellen Watkins Harper refused to be defeated by her circumstances. She rebuilt her life in the decades after the Civil War and published a novel, *Iola Leroy; or, Shadows Uplifted* (1892), which is considered one of the first books on the subject of **Reconstruction** by an African American writer. In the years from 1865 to 1890 American society also struggled to rebuild itself after the fissures of the Civil War, beginning to address the unresolved questions about the political and economic status of newly freed African Americans. Meanwhile in the West, the expansion of white settler colonialism resumed, setting up new conflicts between Native American populations and emigrants from the East and Midwest over how land and property rights were to be apportioned. As always, women were at the center of these larger forces, trying to build their lives in the midst of sweeping social and political change.

 # RECONSTRUCTING A FRACTURED NATION

For white Southerners, the Confederate surrender at Appomattox in April 1865 signaled a massive change in the social, economic, and political underpinnings of their society. The end of slavery meant not just the end of an economic system of production, but also the evaporation of the major source of personal wealth for white slaveowners, who found their "assets" (the people they enslaved) no longer of value. As Ella Thomas confided to her diary in 1865 in a massive understatement, "The fact is our Negroes are to be free and a change, a very [great] change will be affected in our mode of living." These direct economic losses, which affected white women as well as men, were traumatic and widespread, sometimes literally sending a family from affluence to beggary overnight. Non-elite, non-slaveholding white Southerners were also affected, but more by the general collapse of the economy and the widespread physical destruction that had occurred on Southern terrain during the fighting, devastation that the North and West were largely spared. With so much of their old way of life in disarray, white Southerners clung to whatever privileges they could, setting the stage for the intensification of white supremacy and the glorification of white Southern womanhood in the decades to come.

Newly freed African Americans in the South faced challenging conditions as well when the war ended, with their top priority being the reestablishment of family ties. Newspapers and circulars were full of announcements seeking out family members who had been scattered by wartime disruptions or sundered earlier by the domestic slave trade, which continued even during hostilities. Joining husbands and wives together in legal matrimony (something that had been denied under slavery) represented a powerful personal and political statement. Another top priority was education, especially literacy. The white Northern schoolteachers, many of them New England "schoolmarms," who opened schools in areas like the Sea Islands in Georgia, represented an early (if not sustained) attempt at interracial cooperation in the new South.

The transition from slavery to freedom was economic as well as familial, as newly emancipated African Americans learned the difficulties of coping in an economy based on waged labor. (Former white slaveowners underwent a similar learning curve, but with more assets and power at their disposal.) Unfortunately, the resources available to the **Freedman's Bureau**, the federal agency set up to aid newly freed men and women (who were essentially war refugees), never came close to the immense demand for those services. Despite hopes of individual land ownership at war's end, captured by the aspiration for "forty acres and a mule," most African American families found themselves landless and working for white landowners as agricultural workers. Black women were an important component of these family units, but their domestic labor was often not counted as such.

4.1: Anna J. Cooper was part of Washington, DC's vibrant African American community. A graduate of Oberlin College, where one of her classmates was Mary Church Terrell, she taught Latin at the celebrated (but segregated) M Street High School in the nation's capital. Cooper later received a PhD from the Sorbonne.

**Sharecropping** for a white owner was better than slavery, but not all that much, so many who were freed relocated to Southern cities such as Atlanta, Charleston, and New Orleans to seek better opportunities. In many ways Black men had more options than Black women, since under slavery they had sometimes learned a skilled trade like blacksmithing or carpentry. Black women seeking wages had only one option: domestic service. For example, in Atlanta in 1880, 98 percent of employed Black women worked as domestic servants. The work was hard, but in contrast to the bondage of slavery, these domestic workers enjoyed certain advantages beyond just wages. When faced with a demanding white employer or her lecherous husband (both circumstances all too common in this line of work), the domestic servant could give notice and seek employment in another household. Even with the meager wages they earned, Black women's economic contributions were essential to family survival.

These postwar transitions occurred in a deteriorating racial climate. White Southerners may have been defeated militarily, but their racial attitudes hardened. The 1866 founding of the **Ku Klux Klan** in Pulaski, Tennessee, was a direct response to Black Americans asserting their new freedoms, especially in public life. Though the late 1860s saw some political breakthroughs when Black men won elected office as Republicans in the overwhelmingly Democratic South, many of these gains evaporated when federal troops withdrew at the end of Reconstruction in 1877 and white Southerners returned to power.

In this changing—and challenging—landscape, African American women exhibited a style of political activism that put notions of family and community at the forefront of their vision. Working through churches, voluntary organizations, schools, and other self-help vehicles, African American women aimed at improving conditions not just for individuals but also for the community at large. The goal of racial uplift was integrally connected to expanded roles for African American women, including a demand for dignity and a call for self-governance. As educator Anna Julia Cooper argued in her 1892 book *A Voice from the South*, "Only the BLACK WOMAN can say, 'When and where I enter in the quiet, undisputed dignity of my womanhood, without violence and without suing or special patronage, then and there the whole NEGRO RACE ENTERS WITH ME.'"

African American churches, often the core of their local communities, proved an especially congenial site for women to exercise influence and power. In fact, women were granted authority and autonomy in religious institutions far in advance of securing political rights in the larger society. In response to a spirited campaign to allow women to vote in churches, female A.M.E. (American Methodist Episcopal) Zion church members won the right to hold office and vote on church matters in 1876. Women also took on larger roles in the Baptist Church and in missionary societies, using these platforms to advance their larger agenda of racial uplift.

This approach became even more necessary as **Jim Crow** restrictions were codified in the 1880s and 1890s, enforcing legal segregation of the races throughout the South and robbing Black men of the political rights, including voting, that had been guaranteed by the Fourteenth and Fifteenth amendments. Undaunted, Black communities persevered. An increase in residential segregation, for example, created the need but also the opportunity to build autonomous Black institutions, especially churches and schools, which African American women made part of their agenda of "lifting as we climb." In North Carolina after Black men lost the vote, Black women like Charlotte Hawkins Brown became the diplomats to the white community, lobbying for services and benefits and working to modify white attitudes by their dignified example.

In 1896 the Supreme Court upheld the practice of **separate but equal** in *Plessy v. Ferguson* but the educational, employment, and charitable services

DOCUMENTING AMERICAN WOMEN

# Anna J. Cooper's *A Voice from the South*

Anna J. Cooper was a Black feminist intellectual who never doubted the central role that African American women played in the struggles for civil rights and women's rights. Like many African American women of her generation, she was an active supporter of the Black women's club movement. Her 1892 book, *A Voice from the South, by a Black Woman of the South*, calls on Black women to take wider social responsibilities in their communities in order to uplift themselves and the entire Black population.

Fifty years ago woman's activity according to orthodox definitions was on a pretty clearly cut "sphere," including primarily the kitchen and the nursery, and rescued from the barrenness of prison bars by the womanly mania for adorning every discoverable bit of china or canvass with forlorn looking cranes balanced idiotically on one foot. The woman of to-day finds herself in the presence of responsibilities which ramify through the profoundest and most varied interests of her country and race. Not one of the issues of this plodding, toiling, sinning, repenting, falling, aspiring humanity can afford to shut her out, or can deny the reality of her influence. No plan for renovating society, no scheme for purifying politics, no reform in church or in state, no moral, social, or economic questions, no movement upward or downward in the human plane is lost on her. A man once said when told his house was afire: "Go tell my wife; I never meddle with household affairs." But no woman can possibly put herself or her sex outside any of the interests that affect humanity. All departments in the new era are to be hers, in the sense that her interests are in all and through all; and it is incumbent on her to keep intelligently and sympathetically *en rapport* with all the great movements of her time, that she may know on which side to throw the weight of her influence. She stands now at the gateway of

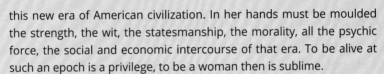

this new era of American civilization. In her hands must be moulded the strength, the wit, the statesmanship, the morality, all the psychic force, the social and economic intercourse of that era. To be alive at such an epoch is a privilege, to be a woman then is sublime.

In this last decade of our century, changes of such moment are in progress, such new and alluring vistas are opening out before us, such original and radical suggestions for the adjustment of labor and capital, of government and the governed, of the family, the church and the state, that to be a possible factor though an infinitesimal one in such a movement is pregnant with hope and weighty with responsibility. To be a woman is such an age carries with it a privilege and an opportunity never implied before. But to be a woman of the Negro race in America, and to be able to grasp the deep significance of the possibilities of the crisis, is to have a heritage, it seems to me, unique in the ages. . . .

. . .

Everything to this race is new and strange and inspiring. There is a quickening of its pulses and a glowing of its self-consciousness. Aha, I can rival that! I can aspire to that! I can honor my name and vindicate my race! Something like this, it strikes me, is the enthusiasm which stirs the genius of young Africa in America; and the memory of past oppression and the fact of present attempted repression only serve to gather momentum for its irrepressible powers. Then again, a race in such a stage of growth is peculiarly sensitive to impressions. Not the photographer's sensitized plate is more delicately impressionable to outer influences than is this high strung people here on the threshold of a career. What a responsibility then to have the sole management of the primal lights and shadows! Such is the colored woman's office. She must stamp weal or woe on the coming history of this people. May she see her opportunity and vindicate her high prerogative.

SOURCE: Anna J. Cooper, *A Voice from the South, By a Black Woman of the South* (Xenia, OH: Aldine Printing House, 1892), 142–45.

available to Blacks were never equal to those available to whites. In combination with the self-help efforts so prevalent in Black communities, African American women's actions helped to make Black life bearable as race relations plunged to their nadir by century's end.

 # THE MULTICULTURAL WEST

The United States is a land of immigrants, the textbooks tell us, a fact invariably illustrated by a photograph of New York's Ellis Island or the Statue of Liberty, where in the words of Emma Lazarus's immortal poem, generations of Europeans "yearning to breathe free" found their way to new lives in the New World. The first wave of nineteenth century European immigrants was from Ireland, pushed out of their homeland by the potato famine that ravaged the country in the 1840s. The next surge came in the 1880s, initially driven by an increase of German immigration and then followed by an uptick from South and Central Europe. Conditions of poverty or limited opportunity in European countries such as Poland, Italy, and Russia (and for Jewish families, the added factor of bitter anti-Semitism) certainly pushed the decision to leave, but so did pull factors in America, specifically the prospect of jobs and land.

But New York and the East Coast were not the only points of entry. Angel Island in San Francisco Bay served as a comparable gateway for immigrants arriving from China, Japan, the Philippines, and other parts of eastern Asia to new lives in "Gum Sum" (Gold Mountain), the Chinese equivalent of the Promised Land. In addition, in the aftermath of the Treaty of Guadalupe Hildalgo in 1848, Mexicans became an increasingly significant presence in the West, especially in states such as Colorado, New Mexico, Arizona, and Texas. And homesteaders on the Great Plains, including immigrant groups like the Norwegians and the Swedes, created their own farming frontier.

Between 1860 and 1900, approximately one-quarter to one-third of the residents of the American West had been born in another country, a proportion even higher than in the East. Migration and settlement are thus best understood within a bicoastal, multi-border, multiracial perspective. Just as vital is putting gender at the center of the experience.

The Chinese offer a good starting point. Early Chinese migration to California started around the time of the Gold Rush of 1849 and expanded in the 1860s as Chinese workers became the primary construction source for Western railroads. This migration was predominantly male, a pattern often replicated in other immigrant groups. (One exception was the Irish, where women predominated from the start, lured by strong demand for domestic

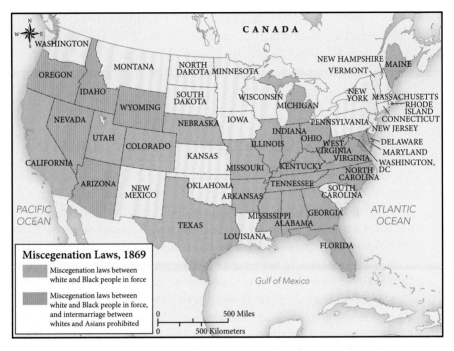

**MAP 4.2**

servants.) With the sex ratio hovering at about thirteen to one, Chinese men created a bachelor society centered around laundries and restaurants, with their sexual needs served by a small number of Chinese prostitutes who worked under near-slavery conditions. In 1860 at least 85 percent of Chinese women in San Francisco were prostitutes, although the proportion had fallen to 28 percent in 1880 because Chinese women had moved into other jobs as domestic servants and garment workers.

From the start the Chinese faced virulent prejudice linked to their perceived status as racial and religious outsiders as well as the economic threat their labor posed to working-class white men. These factors resulted in the passage of discriminatory legislation, the first (although not the last) of its kind designed to limit their entry into the United States. The 1875 Page Law targeting "undesirable" immigrants was only applied to Chinese women suspected of being prostitutes, curtailing their entry. It was followed by the Chinese Restriction Act of 1882 and the **Chinese Exclusion Act** of 1888 banning all immigration, laws which remained in effect until 1943. With so few Chinese women already here, this law made it extremely difficult for Chinese men, an exploited source of cheap labor, to establish families, which seems to have been the point. Because the Chinese learned to exploit loopholes in the law, the Chinese sex ratio in

DOCUMENTING AMERICAN WOMEN

# Mary Tape Challenges the San Francisco Board of Education, 1885

Mary Tape was raised in a Shanghai orphanage and brought to the United States by missionaries at age eleven. She later married a Chinese American interpreter and began a family. When the San Francisco school board balked in 1885 at admitting her eight-year-old daughter Mamie to their neighborhood school out of fears of mixing Chinese and American children, the Tapes successfully took their case to court. In response the school superintendent hastily established a separate school for Chinese students. This letter was written at the height of the dispute.

1769 GREEN STREET,
SAN FRANCISCO, April 8, 1885.

To the Board of Education—DEAR SIRS: I see that you are going to make all sorts of excuses to keep my child out off the Public schools. Dear sirs, Will you please to tell me! Is it a disgrace to be Born a Chinese? Didn't God make us all!!! What right have you to bar my children out of the school because she is a Chinese Decend. They is no other worldly reason that you could keep her out, except that. I suppose, you all goes to churches on Sundays! Do you call that a Christian act to compel my little children to go so far to a school that is made in purpose for them. My children don't dress like the other Chinese. They look just as phunny amongst them as the Chinese dress in Chinese look amongst you Caucasians. Besides, if I had any wish to send

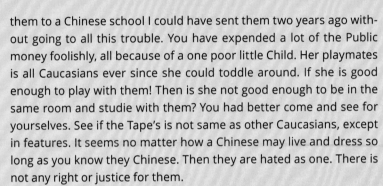

them to a Chinese school I could have sent them two years ago without going to all this trouble. You have expended a lot of the Public money foolishly, all because of a one poor little Child. Her playmates is all Caucasians ever since she could toddle around. If she is good enough to play with them! Then is she not good enough to be in the same room and studie with them? You had better come and see for yourselves. See if the Tape's is not same as other Caucasians, except in features. It seems no matter how a Chinese may live and dress so long as you know they Chinese. Then they are hated as one. There is not any right or justice for them.

You have seen my husband and child. You told him it wasn't Mamie Tape you object to. If it were not Mamie Tape you object to, then why didn't you let her attend the school nearest her home! Instead of first making one pretense Then another pretense of some kind to keep her out? It seems to me Mr. Moulder has a grudge against this Eight-year-old Mamie Tape. I know they is no other child I mean Chinese child! Care to go to your public Chinese school. May you Mr. Moulder, never be persecuted like the way you have persecuted little Mamie Tape. Mamie Tape will never attend any of the Chinese schools of your making! Never!!! I will let the world see sir What justice there is When it is govern by the Race prejudice men! Just because she is of the Chinese decend, not because she don't dress like you because she does. Just because she is decended of Chinese parents I guess is more of a American then a good many of you that is going to prewent her being Educated. MRS. M. TAPE.

SOURCE: Alta, *April 16, 1885, page 1, found in Judy Yung,* Unbound Feet: A Social History of Chinese Women in San Francisco *(Berkeley: University of California Press, 1995), 74–75.*

San Francisco dropped to three and a half to one by 1920, allowing for the emergence of more stable family and community life.

If a Chinese man and a white woman wished to marry, they ran afoul of the miscegenation laws that predominated in the American West, indeed throughout the country. While the best-known examples of these laws were framed to prevent Blacks and whites from marrying (generally Black men and white women), their reach was in fact much broader. Less concerned with preventing interracial sex than upholding the principle of white property inheritance, these laws regulated the institution of marriage by making it difficult for nonwhite men to marry white women. Because the categories of race were more diverse in the multicultural West than the Black/white binary in the North and South, the sweep of miscegenation laws was similarly broader, encompassing the Chinese (sometimes called Mongolians), Filipinos (Malays), Japanese, and occasionally Native Americans. Unfortunately, the virulent racism and commitment to white supremacy behind the laws was nationwide.

4.2: This portrait of the Tape family circa 1885 pictures Joseph and Mary Tape and their three children at the time of their successful legal challenge to the San Francisco Board of Education. *Tape v. Hurley* (1885) established the right of Chinese American students to a public elementary education but generally in separate schools. Only in the 1920s were they allowed to attend integrated high schools.

Another group, members of the Church of Jesus Christ of Latter-day Saints (LDS, popularly known as Mormons), faced distrust and discrimination in the West not because of race (they were white) but religion. Founded by the prophet Joseph Smith in upstate New York in 1830, followers faced persecution from the beginning, which caused them to relocate first to Nauvoo, Illinois, and then after Smith's death in 1844, to follow church leader Brigham Young to the arid desert of Utah, where they set about building a new society (Zion) from scratch.

Already controversial as a new religion, the Mormons faced intense negative scrutiny after the church doctrine of celestial or plural marriage was officially announced in 1852. This pronouncement confirmed the already widespread practice whereby Mormon men were encouraged to take multiple wives, thus guaranteeing every woman a home and family. Opponents could not believe women would willingly enter into such relationships without coercion—something Mormon women heartily disputed. While Mormons saw **polygamy** as a religious duty, most Americans condemned the practice as morally abhorrent and contrary to Judeo-Christian ideals of monogamy and consent. Polygamy soon drew the attention of federal authorities who tried to outlaw it in Utah territory, with little success, since Mormons were a firmly entrenched majority. By the 1880s the Supreme Court had ruled that Mormons did not have a constitutional right to practice this form of marriage. The LDS church formally abandoned the practice in 1890, although whether it would continue informally was another matter.

 # THE WOMEN'S WEST

The Mormons had been drawn to Utah as a place where they believed they could practice their religion undisturbed. They were not the only whites drawn to the great expanses of the Great Plains and beyond. The Civil War had caused a temporary cessation in the westward surge, but once the war ended, the transcontinental migration resumed, as well as the inevitable conflicts with Native Americans who already inhabited the land. Now that federal military forces were no longer occupied with fighting the Confederacy, they were free to be deployed to subdue local Native American populations who challenged the westward migration. Battles such as Little Big Horn in the future state of Montana in 1876 and the massacre at Wounded Knee in South Dakota in 1890 showed how fierce and deadly these military conflicts could be.

With the completion of the **transcontinental railroad** in 1869, California was symbolically linked to the rest of the country and wide swaths of territory in the West opened up to potential settlement. Because of the vastness of the space, however, most homesteaders traveled by covered wagon rather than train. In the 1870s, 1880s, and 1890s these settlers attempted to extend the farming frontier into the Great Plains in areas like the Dakotas, Nebraska, Kansas, and Oklahoma, that previously had been grazing land for Native Americans or cattle ranchers. Unlike the fertile soil in the Midwest or Pacific Northwest, the Great Plains offered far more arid conditions that made farming difficult even under the best of circumstances. Major economic depressions in the 1870s and 1890s added to the precariousness of homesteaders' lives.

The enormously popular "Little House on the Prairie" series written by Laura Ingalls Wilder in the 1930s introduced generations of readers to the

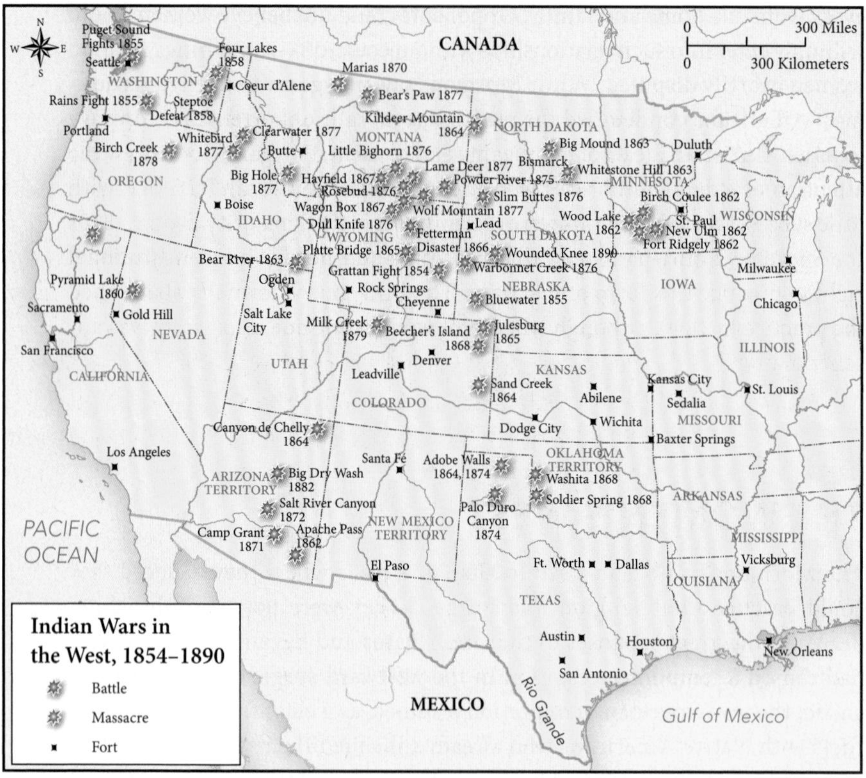

MAP 4.1

challenges and rewards of life on the prairie. Based on Wilder's childhood and early adulthood living in Wisconsin, Minnesota, Kansas, and the Dakota Territory in the 1870s and 1880s, the novels describe how families struggled to make a go of farming, with crop failures and debt often pushing them into bankruptcy and the need to start over again elsewhere. Financial insecurity was a given, as was the demanding physicality and grinding isolation of women's lives. The most vivid images in the books were the ecological disasters that afflicted the settlers: prairie fires that roared across the plains and blackened acres of land, swarms of locusts and grasshoppers that could literally wipe out an entire crop of wheat or potatoes in a matter of hours, white-out blizzards so severe that families huddled in their dugouts and sod houses and hoped that their food wouldn't give out. Willa Cather, a writer who grew up in Nebraska, later captured the love-hate relationship of many settlers when she described the Great Plains as "the happiness and the curse of my life."

Rural dwellers remained the majority of Americans until 1920, and farm wives were an eclectic group, but all experienced moments of extreme loneliness and hard work as they toiled alongside their husbands as part of the family unit. "Quit with a headache. Done too much work" confided an Arizona woman to her diary. In addition to farm chores, rural women kept house, bore and raised children, fed their families and kept them clean, all without the benefits of electricity or running water. Mechanization revolutionized farming starting in the late nineteenth century, but except for a

4.3: This family scene on the South Loup River in Custer County, Nebraska, gives a different slant on the classic Western folk song "Home on the Range." Dugouts built into hillsides or holes provided temporary shelter until more permanent structures could be built.

sewing machine with a foot-treadle to provide power, technology mainly passed rural women by until well into the twentieth century.

Laundry was women's most onerous chore, an all-day affair (usually on Mondays) for which there was no remotely equivalent task for men. Since only one out of ten farms had electricity as late as the 1930s, hundreds of gallons of water had to be pumped by hand and then hauled to the house. The farm wife then heated the water on a woodstove that required constant tending, washed the clothes (often with harsh homemade lye soap), rinsed them, and wrung them out to dry. Then came another all-day task of ironing, which involved six- to seven-pound wedges of metal that had to be individually heated over a fire; a single shirt could take several irons. Southwest Texas farm women called them "sad irons."

To lessen the loneliness of farm life, especially on the Great Plains, where settlement was widely spaced out, farm women and their menfolk turned to collaborative efforts, both political and economic. These included farm cooperatives, which provided services and benefits to members who pooled their resources, as well as organizations like the Grange, a fraternal organization that welcomed women's participation. Rural women also participated in political movements, such as the **Farmers' Alliance** in the 1880s and the **Populist Party** in the 1890s. "What you farmers need to do," Populist orator Mary Elizabeth Lease memorably declared, "is to raise less corn and more *Hell!*"

# The Burden of Rural Women's Lives

In 1901, when this autobiographical piece was published in *The American Kitchen Magazine*, the majority of Americans still lived in rural areas. Rural women had it especially hard. Not only did they have full responsibility for maintaining their households, as did their urban counterparts, but they also made significant contributions to farm labor. And yet farm women, such as this anonymous chronicler who took part in Cornell University's Reading Course for Farmers' Wives, took those challenges in stride.

Two things I have been taught in my long farm life: one is, that work never kills. And the other is, that we must calculate work beforehand in order to save steps and do a great amount of work. I am fifty-eight years old. Have been on a farm all my life until a year ago, when we built a new house on one end of our farm which opens on a public road and is retired from farm labor. My father was a farmer and a minister of the old school, who believed in no salary, but believed in working for a living. I learned to milk when seven years old, and always did my share while at home. I was sent to school, but at fourteen commenced to teach a district school on a third grade license. I soon received a second and then the first grade. I boarded around. I was married at nineteen, and then my farm life began in earnest. We always kept a dairy, from twelve to fourteen head. When we were married we did not own a foot of land. My husband and I bought thirty acres the day after we were married, joining the old homestead of his people with whom we lived. They owned fifty acres, but there was a mortgage of three hundred and fifty dollars on that. We took care of them until they died, paid the mortgage, bought enough more to make us two hundred acres.

We had a sugar orchard and made from three to five hundred pounds of sugar and a great deal of sirup every year. We kept sheep and always worked up the wool, spun, wove, and made full cloth for men's wear and for flannel sheets. We knit our own socks and stockings. I would always rise in the morning at four or half past, winter and summer, and have built my own fires, milked from four to eight cows, prepared the breakfast and had it at six. Until about ten years ago we made butter, and since then have sent it to a factory. I always did my own churning, and many are the books of poems, histories, stories, and newspapers I have read through while churning. I am the mother of eight children, five of whom are living. The others died when small. . . . All this time I had a hired girl only a year and a half. We made our own table linen and toweling, spinning and weaving it, and our flannel dresses. I have been with the sick a great deal, and always went to church and Sunday school, and attended societies which belonged to the church. To-day I can walk a mile or more as quickly as any one. At the present time I have two old people to care for; one of them is eighty-six and the other is eighty-three. There are five in our family, and I am doing all the work myself, and am going to take the teacher to board next year. So you see, work does not kill and there must have been some calculation to save steps. My husband says, "You helped earn and saved more than I did." The boys many times say, "If it had not been for you pushing and helping us to school, we never could have done so well." All this time I have kept up with the general reading of the day.

I never counted my steps but once and that was when I spun a skein of woolen yarn. I went a little over a mile.

SOURCE: *Cornell Reading Course for Farmers' Wives*, The American Kitchen Magazine 14 (October 1900–March 1901), *quoted in* So Sweet to Labor: Rural Women in America, 1865–1895, *Norton Juster, ed. (New York: Viking Press, 1979), 101–102.*

Adventure and independence also beckoned. Case in point: the female **homesteader**. Taking advantage of an 1862 law that offered 160 acres of land to anyone—not just men—who kept up continual residence for five years while improving the land, a surprising number of women, mainly single, took this option: as many as 12 percent in a sample from Lamar, Colorado, and Douglas, Wyoming. And women were more tenacious at sticking it out than men, "proving up" their claims at a rate of 43 percent, versus 37 percent for men. Women's motives varied. Widowed or divorced women might seek a way to provide for their families. Unmarried women could be on the lookout for a good investment—or possibly a husband. But they all shared a sense of self-reliance and willingness to strike out in new directions.

# BROADER EDUCATIONAL OPPORTUNITIES FOR WOMEN

The growth of higher education, one of the most far-reaching changes of the post–Civil War era, was an important precondition for women's new independence. Fears about education making women unfit for roles as wives and mothers had a long history, and in 1873 a Harvard physician named Edward Clarke added a new concern: that using women's "limited energy" for the purpose of studying would harm the "female apparatus." In other words, seeking a college degree would damage women's reproductive capacity. This theory was quickly debunked by female physicians, who pointed out that it was possible to menstruate and think at the same time, but Clarke's fears lingered until the first generations of college graduates conclusively proved him wrong.

Women fought for access to education in different ways in each section of the country. In the West and Midwest the **Morrill Land Grant Act** of 1862 spurred the growth of land-grant colleges and state universities, which were mostly coeducational from the start, a huge boost for women who aspired to learn alongside men. Higher education for women failed to flourish in the post–Civil War South, even for white women, but showed strong growth in the East. While some schools, such as Boston University and Cornell, opened their doors early to women, a more prevalent pattern was the establishment of women's colleges, such as the **Seven Sisters**, starting with Vassar in 1865, followed by Wellesley and Smith (1875), and Bryn Mawr (1884). On the West Coast, a Mt. Holyoke graduate became the first president of all-female Mills College in 1885. Another pattern, again primarily in the East but also in the South, was coordinate colleges, which paired women's instruction in separate institutions alongside the men's. The relationship forged between Harvard and Radcliffe College (founded in 1884) and Columbia and Barnard (1889)

4.4: Bryn Mawr students gather on the steps of a college building under the watchful eyes of male faculty members. Future president Woodrow Wilson was one of Bryn Mawr's inaugural professors when it was founded in 1885, but that experience failed to convert him to the cause of women's suffrage.

typified this pattern, as did the 1886 founding of Sophie Newcomb College as a coordinate to Tulane University in New Orleans.

Black women made access to education a high priority as part of their commitment to racial uplift. While a few schools, such as Oberlin, offered spots to Black women (reformer Mary Church Terrell and educator Anna Julia Cooper both graduated from Oberlin in 1884, the only Black members of their class), the prevailing racial climate meant that most breakthroughs occurred in all-Black settings. Well-regarded colleges such as Fisk in Atlanta and Howard in Washington, DC, were coeducational in large part because single-sex education was deemed too much of a luxury for the African American community. One exception was Spelman, which started as a female seminary in Atlanta in the 1880s and became a women's college in 1925.

Black women also attended vocational institutions such as Alabama's Tuskegee Institute or the Hampton Institute in Virginia for training in domestic and industrial arts. On graduation, many Black women gravitated toward teaching, in large part because the segregated school systems that prevailed in the South (indeed, in the rest of the country) guaranteed that teaching positions, albeit with low pay and poor working conditions, were always available to them.

Education also played an important, if less liberatory, role in the history of Native American women. As written into law by the Dawes Severalty Act of

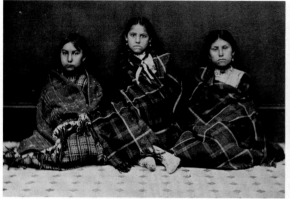

4.5: Government-run boarding schools for Native American children pursued an aggressive program to strip students of tribal customs and dress. These before and after photos were supposed to show success, but the girls' sad faces tell a different story.

1887, the federal government divided reservation lands into individual family allotments and encouraged Native Americans to remake their societies and gender roles along a European model. To facilitate such changes, many Indian children were sent away to federally funded boarding schools, such as the Indian School in Carlisle, Pennsylvania, founded in 1879. At school, female students were expected to learn basic domestic and housewifery skills and conform to Anglo values and customs, including dressing in non-Indian clothing and speaking English. Being torn from tribal customs and familial networks was often a wrenching experience, as students found themselves educated to be part of a white society that had no place for them at the same time they were increasingly out of step with the Native cultures from which they came. This collective trauma is increasingly recognized by scholars in the field as social genocide.

 ## CLAIMING CITIZENSHIP

How can a citizen demand the vote without having that basic political right in the first place? That was the conundrum faced by women's **suffrage** activists as they tried to convince men, especially male elected officials, to share the vote with them—without being able to use the vote as leverage. Suffragists intuitively knew that politics and political influence were about more than casting a ballot, and they devised creative ways to insert themselves directly into the political realm. Even if they could not vote, they could still perform the rituals of citizenship and civic participation that men enjoyed. All they had to do was present themselves as legitimate participants in the political process and act as if they were the full vested citizens they aspired to become.

That task was made both harder and easier by the experience of the United States after the Civil War. Reconstruction is fundamental to understanding the history of women's suffrage. A costly civil war had ended slavery, and a new political order was in the making, but many questions remained to be answered: What would be the relation between the federal government and the states? Who was an American citizen? What responsibilities went along with citizenship? The rights of newly freed African Americans were central to the discussion about how to reconstitute the national state, but the rights of women were far from absent from the deliberations. In this fraught but open-ended political moment, activists believed they might have a fighting chance to win similar rights for women as well. In effect, they tried to insert gender alongside race in the national debate about citizenship.

Two aspects of the Fourteenth and Fifteenth Amendments had huge implications for the women's suffrage movement: the introduction of the modifier "male" when defining voters in the **Fourteenth Amendment** (1868) and the decision not to include "sex" alongside the prohibited categories of "race, color, or previous condition of servitude" in the **Fifteenth Amendment** (1870) guaranteeing voting rights. Prominent reformers like Frederick Douglass and Wendell Phillips believed that this was "the Negro's hour," and that supporting these rights for African American men was the most pressing issue. Suffragists such as Lucy Stone, Henry Blackwell, and Julia Ward Howe agreed. They had hoped for universal suffrage, but

4.6: The *Woman's Journal*, founded in Boston in 1870, played an outsize role in disseminating suffrage news throughout the country, but it was always strapped for cash. One promotion offered a button featuring founder Lucy Stone's portrait attached to a bright yellow ribbon. There was no need explain "I Take Her Paper." The reference would have been self-evident to supporters.

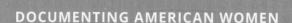

**DOCUMENTING AMERICAN WOMEN**

# Mormon Women's Protest, 1886

Mormon women fiercely defended both their right to vote and their right to practice polygamy in public forums such as a mass protest meeting held on May 6, 1886, in Salt Lake City, which drew nearly two thousand women. One of the speakers was Dr. Romania Pratt, a graduate of the Woman's Medical College in Philadelphia and a plural wife who presented a spirited defense of Mormon marriage practices as both divinely ordained and beneficial to women.

DR. ROMANIA B. PRATT.

One of the most dangerous evils with which we are threatened and against which we most solemnly and earnestly protest, is the ruthless and inhuman invasion of the sanctity of the marriage relation and the destruction of the home circle. It has been said by a prominent Federal official that "the American idea of government is founded on the Christian idea of home, where one father and one mother, each the equal of the other, happy in the consciousness of mutual and eternal affection, rear about the hearth-stone an intelligent and God-fearing family. Patriotism springs from love of country, which is born of love for home; virtue and morality are the flowers which adorn the hearth-stone of the true family."

This word-picture is as true as it is beautiful. Is there anything evil in a plurality of such homes? We wish to deal with stern facts to-day, and we therefore ask if the majority of monogamous families of the United States, or even the world, are very profusely adorned with the flower of virtue and morality. The above quotation, in point of actual fact, we unhesitatingly assert, and with a profound feeling of positive knowledge, to be the very ideal and inspiration of the majority of "Mormon" plural families. Can a true and veritable marriage which receives the divine sanction be immoral or the issue illegitimate?

. . .

Our faith and confidence in the chastity and pure motives of our husbands, fathers, mothers and sons are such that we challenge the production of a better system of marriage and the records of more moral or purer lives. Hand in hand with celestial marriage is the elevation of woman. In church she votes equally with men, and politically, she has the suffrage raising her from the old common law, monogamic serfdom, to political equality with men. Rights of property are given her so that she, as a married woman, can hold property in her own individual right. Women are not thrown off in old age as has been most untruthfully and shamefully asserted. There is nothing in our plural marriage system that countenances any such thing. The very nature of the covenant forbids it. It is binding through all time and lasts throughout eternity. If any woman at an advanced period of her life wishes in a measure to retire from her husband's society with his consent, this is her own individual privilege with which no one has the right to interfere. Instances of wrong-doing may be found in families of plural households, but the exceptions are not the rule; the weight of good results of the majority should be the standard of judgment. It cannot be true, as asserted, that plural marriage is entered into as a rule from sensual motives. It is self-evident that it is not the case with the women, and it is unreasonable to suppose that men would bring upon themselves the responsibilities, cares and expenses of a plural family, when they could avoid all this, yet revel in sin, and, in the language of a distinguished man of the world, "be like the rest of us."

. . .

Therefore, in the name of justice, equity and conscience we protest against special legislation which inhibits the conduct of our lives according to our best judgment for this life and most especially for the future, when our domestic relations do no injury to those who do not agree with our system.

SOURCE: *Mormon Women of Utah,* "Mormon" Women's Protest: An Appeal for Freedom, Justice and Equal Rights *(Salt Lake City, Utah, 1886), 28, 29–30, 31.*

once the amendments were drafted, they supported ratification despite the exclusion of women. Susan B. Anthony and Elizabeth Cady Stanton took a different stance. They adamantly refused to support the amendments, often employing racist language to imply that white women were just as deserving of the vote as African American men, if not more so. Even though African American women prominently participated in this debate, their rights and interests were often left out of the equation.

By 1869 the women's rights movement had split in two over this question, which was both strategic and philosophical. Stone, Blackwell, and Howe founded the Boston-based **American Woman Suffrage Association (AWSA)**, and the Stanton-Anthony wing set up the rival **National Woman Suffrage Association (NWSA)**, which was centered in New York. So deep-seated were the underlying divisions that the two wings would not reunite for two decades, and only when the older generation of original suffragists began to cede power to a rising generation that had not been so traumatized by the Reconstruction-era schism.

As the 1870s dawned, the women's rights movement lacked anything approaching a popular base of support so there was plenty of work to spread around. The AWSA founded the *Woman's Journal* in 1870, later edited by Alice Stone Blackwell (daughter of Lucy and Henry), which brought the powerful ideas and personalities of the movement to subscribers across the nation. Susan B. Anthony managed to register and vote in her hometown of Rochester, New York, in 1872 ("Well I have been & gone & done!! Positively voted the Republican ticket") but was quickly convicted of violating federal voting laws. A court challenge initiated by Missouri suffragist Virginia Minor

## Timeline

**1865**

Confederate surrender at Appomattox

**1866**

Founding of Ku Klux Klan

**1868**

Fourteenth Amendment introduces the word "male" into the Constitution

**1869**

Completion of the transcontinental railroad; The Women's Rights Movement splits into two rival associations; Wyoming territory grants women the right to vote

**1870**

Fifteenth Amendment does not include "sex" alongside the prohibited categories of "race, color, or previous condition of servitude" in voting; the AWSA founds the Woman's Journal

**1876**

Battle of Little Big Horn

claiming that women already had the right to vote because of the general language of citizenship in the Constitution was shot down unanimously by the Supreme Court in *Minor v. Happersett* (1875).

With legal challenges off the table, only two options remained to the suffrage movement. The first was to try to amend state constitutions to include female voters alongside male, a strategy favored by the American Woman Suffrage Association. The second was to work for a federal amendment to the Constitution that would ensure women's right to vote, the approach of the National Woman Suffrage Association. Those two strategies basically defined the next half century of suffrage activism.

The case of Utah shows how complicated suffrage politics could be. Mormon women, who had received the right to vote in territorial Utah in 1870, took their political rights seriously. What role they would play in the national movement was more contested, however. Many prominent Utah suffragists were plural wives, seeing no contradiction between women's rights and their religious beliefs, but conservative suffragists like Lucy Stone and the AWSA would have nothing to do with them because of the controversial issue of polygamy. Elizabeth Cady Stanton and Susan B. Anthony had no such qualms: Mormons' allegiance to suffrage was more than enough to make them good allies. (This capacious approach had gotten NWSA into trouble before, specifically with an eccentric and racist reformer named George Train, who funded their journal *Revolution* and then left them with a huge debt. Their association with the controversial free-love advocate Victoria Woodhull had also backfired.) Caught in the middle were Utah's women, many of whom were strong suffrage supporters. Congress stripped Mormon women of the right

| 1879–1898 | C. 1880–C.1890 | 1890 |
|---|---|---|
| Frances Willard leads the Woman's Christian Temperance Union | Jim Crow restrictions are codified | Massacre at Wounded Knee |
| **1880** | **1887** | **1890** |
| 98 percent of employed Black women in Atlanta work as domestic servants | Congress strips Mormon women of the right to vote because of polygamy | AWSA and NWSA reunite to form the National American Woman Suffrage Association (NAWSA) |
| | **1888** | |
| | Chinese Exclusion Act | **1896** |
| | | *Plessy v. Ferguson* |

to vote in 1887 because of polygamy. Finally in 1896, six years after Mormon leaders had disavowed the practice as part of their quest for statehood, the vote was restored.

The Utah story makes a broader point: the earliest victories came from Western states rather than the more conservative East or South. When Wyoming officially became a state in 1890, it provided the first star for the suffrage flag, followed by Colorado in 1893 and then Utah and Idaho in 1896. At the national level, passions and egos kept the NWSA and the AWSA far apart, but on the ground in localities far from Boston or New York, the differences between the rival groups were less clear. And while the names most associated with the national movement were those of Eastern women, the West supplied a distinguished list of activists for the cause: Abigail Scott Duniway in Oregon, Jeannette Rankin in Montana, Emmeline B. Wells in Utah, Emma Smith DeVoe in Washington, and Caroline Severance and Maud Younger in California, among others.

Women's suffrage also had an interesting comrade in arms in these years: the temperance movement, then at the height of its influence. Under the charismatic leadership of Frances Willard from 1879 until her death in 1898, the **Woman's Christian Temperance Union** (WCTU) grew out of women's grassroots crusades against the power of liquor interests and saloon-keepers and the deleterious effect of drunken men on their families and communities. Willard widened this single-issue focus dramatically by adopting a "Do Everything" strategy that embraced a wide range of social reforms in addition to temperance, such as labor activism, prison reform, international peace, and the establishment of kindergartens. Doing everything included supporting women's suffrage, which the WCTU endorsed in 1884.

In 1890 the two rival factions reunited as the **National American Woman Suffrage Association (NAWSA),** with Elizabeth Cady Stanton serving as its first president. By this point the arguments for suffrage were undergoing a subtle but important shift. Whereas the early demands had rested on questions of equality and fairness—women's right to vote as citizens, as well as a version of the old Revolutionary cry of "no taxation without representation"— by the 1890s the justification increasingly turned to what women would do with the vote, an argument from expediency. While few suffragists ever made grandiose claims that women would end war or clean up the cities, they did hope that women collectively might use their voices to address some of the urgent problems affecting modern life. At the same time, the focus of the movement narrowed from a broad definition of women's rights (including property laws, divorce, economic rights, and dress reform) to a single-minded focus on the vote. Yet final victory was still three decades away.

## KEY TERMS

American Woman Suffrage Association

Chinese Exclusion Act

Farmers' Alliance

Fourteenth Amendment

Fifteenth Amendment

Freedman's Bureau

homesteading

Jim Crow laws

Ku Klux Klan

miscegenation

Morrill Land Grant Act

National American Woman Suffrage Association

National Woman Suffrage Association

polygamy

Populist Party

Reconstruction

separate but equal

Seven Sisters

sharecropping

suffrage

transcontinental railroad

Woman's Christian Temperance Union

## Suggested Readings

Armitage, Susan, and Elizabeth Jameson, eds. *Writing the Range: Race, Class, and Culture in the Women's West* (1997).

Dudden, Faye E. *Fighting Chance: The Struggle over Woman Suffrage and Black Suffrage in Reconstruction America* (2011).

Hunter, Tera. *To 'joy My Freedom: Southern Black Women's Lives and Labors after the Civil War* (1997).

Jones, Martha S. *Vanguard: How Black Women Broke Barriers, Won the Vote, and Insisted on Equality for All* (2020).

Pascoe, Peggy. *What Comes Naturally: Miscegenation, Law and the Making of Race in America* (2009).

Yung, Judy. *Unbound Feet: A Social History of Chinese Women in San Francisco* (1995).

Learn more with this chapter's digital tools at http://www.oup.com/he/ware1e.

# five

# Expanding Horizons,
## 1890–1920

**CHAPTER OUTLINE**

**Working Women**

**Modern Women in the Making**

**Progressive Era Reform**

**The Final Push for Suffrage**

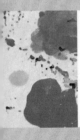

Ida B. Wells called the East St. Louis race riot in July 1917 "the greatest outrage of the century." This Silent Protest organized by the NAACP in New York City included a large contingent of African American women.

**Lynching**, the brutal practice of mobs taking the law into their own hands to kill and maim victims, often by hanging, was the domestic terrorism of its day. While it was a nationwide scourge, it was especially prevalent in the post–Civil War South, where it was used to reinforce white supremacy and keep African Americans "in their place." In 1892, the worst year on record, 155 African Americans were lynched, including seven women; in the decade of the 1890s, 45 Black women were lynched. Southern whites claimed lynching was retribution for the rape of white women by Black men, but the lynching of Black women belies that rationalization. In unpacking the gender and racial underpinnings of these heinous crimes, Ida B. Wells emerged as one of the strongest voices in bringing the issue to the attention of the country, indeed the world.

Ida B. Wells was born into slavery in Holly Springs, Mississippi, in 1862 during the upheavals of the Civil War and spent the rest of her life fighting for full citizenship, both as an African American and a woman. When a yellow fever epidemic killed her parents and a younger sibling in 1878, she dropped out of school and became a teacher to support her family. Seeking more opportunity, she relocated to Memphis, where she became a journalist. Her first brush with challenging discrimination came in 1883, when she was forcibly evicted from the "ladies" car on a Chesapeake and Ohio train and forced to relocate to the "colored" car. Indignant at her treatment, she sued the railroad company, claiming her right to ride in the car for which she had purchased a ticket. The settlement she initially won from the railroad company was later overturned. Confirming the worsening climate for African American rights at the end of the nineteenth century, the Supreme Court upheld the practice of Jim Crow segregation in the 1896 case *Plessy v. Ferguson*.

Wells's anti-lynching epiphany occurred in 1892 in Memphis, where she had become part owner of a newspaper called the *Memphis Free Speech*. When three Black men were lynched by a white mob, Wells exposed the real reason for the racial violence: the economic competition these successful Black shopkeepers posed to white businessmen. As she later wrote in her autobiography, *Crusade for Justice*, "This is what opened my eyes to what lynching really was. An excuse to get rid of Negroes who were acquiring wealth and prosperity and thus keep the race terrorized and 'keep the nigger down.'" She did not stop there. Tackling head-on the claim that Black men were lynched because they raped white women, Wells challenged the assumption that white woman never engaged in consensual sexual relations with Black men. For such provocative statements, the office of her newspaper was trashed, and she was basically run out of town. Several years later she relocated to Chicago, where she married lawyer Ferdinand Barnett and had four children.

Anti-lynching was but one of the many crusades for justice that Ida B. Wells-Barnett (as she was now known) took on. In 1893 she publicly attacked the organizing committee at the World's Columbian Exhibition in Chicago for excluding the contributions of Black women. In 1894 she challenged temperance leader

Frances Willard for her racist statements about Black men's moral character and demanded (without success) that the Woman's Christian Temperance Union make anti-lynching part of its broad reform agenda. In 1913 she organized one of the first Black women's suffrage organizations, the **Alpha Suffrage Club** in Chicago, only to be told by white suffrage leader Alice Paul that she could not march in the suffrage parade timed to coincide with the inauguration of President Woodrow Wilson. Ida Wells-Barnett marched anyway. Slipping into the Illinois delegation as the parade assembled, she dramatically made her point that Black women needed and deserved the vote just as much as white women.

Ida Wells-Barnett's lifelong activism offers a window on many of the pressing issues of American life in the late nineteenth and early twentieth centuries, foremost of which was the struggle for African Americans to find political and economic justice in a deteriorating racial climate. Her career shows the new professional roles opening to women as journalists and business owners, and her temperance and suffrage work demonstrates the importance of women's organizations, as well as the potential tensions between Black and white women in those groups. Finally, as a longtime resident of Chicago, she witnessed firsthand the impact of industrialization, immigration, and urbanization as those historical forces reshaped American life and women's lives as well.

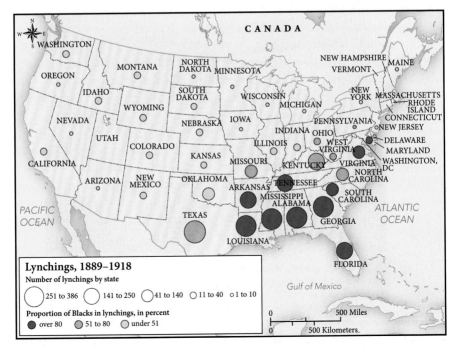

**MAP 5.1**

# WORKING WOMEN

Over the course of the nineteenth century, industrialization reshaped the American economy and caused the United States to emerge as a dominant player on the global stage. Female wage labor was central to this surge as individual women seized new opportunities created by broader economic change. Whereas women made up 14 percent of the workforce in 1870, their percentage had grown to 20 percent by 1910, an increase in absolute numbers from 1.7 million to 7 million. In 1920 8.6 million women were gainfully employed.

The kinds of jobs women held were shaped by the structural needs of the economy as well as deeply ingrained patterns that divided the workplace by gender into men's and women's jobs. Women worked primarily in jobs alongside other women; rarely did they work directly with men or displace men from their jobs. Although the largest single occupational category for women remained domestic service (around one-quarter of the urban female work force in 1900), its predominance was declining as women seized the chance for any work other than the dreaded, dead-end job of servant. Most working women ended up in factories and sweatshops, especially in the sewing and textile trades, as well as working as laundresses, cooks, and beauticians.

5.1: Nineteenth-century offices were initially all-male affairs. When typewriters were introduced after the Civil War, female typists did not have to overcome the prejudice that they were doing "men's work" because it was a new invention that had not yet become gendered. The typewriting department at National Cash Register in Dayton, Ohio, shows how quickly the shift occurred.

Higher status jobs, such as clerical and retail work or teaching, were usually reserved for the daughters of white native-born Americans. The typical nineteenth century office of clerks, stenographers, and accountants had been a male preserve but with the post–Civil War introduction of the typewriter, office work became increasingly feminized. Since the typewriter was a new invention not yet associated with either gender, female typists did not have to overcome prejudices that they were doing "men's" work. Even though the hours were long and the pay sometimes lower than industrial work, the coveted white-collar jobs offered prospects for upward social mobility, especially for recent immigrants.

The typical working woman was young (usually between the ages of fourteen and twenty), single, lived in an urban area, and was the daughter of immigrants. She saw her work as temporary until she married and established a family of her own; very few married women worked for wages at this point. The one exception was in the African American community, where male wages were so low that married women needed to work in order to ensure family survival; a quarter of married Black women worked in 1900, compared to 3 percent of married white women. But they had a far smaller range of options to choose from, mainly domestic service and agricultural work, since they were barred by prejudice from higher paying industrial jobs until well into the twentieth century.

Working conditions were harsh for the women and men whose labor fueled American industrial growth. With few regulations or controls on working conditions except what the market would bear, the average work week for women was sixty hours over six days, with Sundays and part of Saturday afternoon off. In addition to harsh and often dangerous working conditions, seasonal layoffs and periodic unemployment added to the strain. Another hazard was sexual harassment by foremen and supervisors who preyed on vulnerable female workers desperate to keep their jobs. Most working girls lived at home, often turning over their meager wages directly to their mothers.

In their leisure time, urban working girls flocked to the new commercial entertainments such as dance halls, amusement parks, vaudeville theaters, and later movie houses, experiencing the combination of danger and pleasure that such encounters could bring. Dressed in their best clothes and on the lookout for nice chaps to treat them to food or drink, they experimented in new modes of sexuality and commercialized leisure, attracted by the possibility of mixing with men in settings that symbolized the increasingly heterosexual orientation of leisure time. "My mother doesn't know I go out here," said one, "but I want some fun and it only costs ten cents." Needless to say, their immigrant mothers, housebound by domestic responsibilities and language barriers, often disapproved of their high-spirited daughters' attempts to relax after a hard week at work.

# The Story of a Glove Maker

Working in a factory was long, tedious, poorly paid work, as this 1898 description of the experiences of female workers at a glove factory confirms. Agnes Nestor's career as a labor union activist began in Chicago when she led a spontaneous walkout of glove makers over unfair working conditions, especially the issue of machine rent she describes here. For the rest of her life, Nestor devoted herself to the International Glove Workers Union.

The whistle blows at 7 A.M. but the piece workers have until 7.30 to come in to work. The penalty for coming late (after 7.30 A.M.) is the loss of a half day as the girls cannot then report to work until noon. This rule is enforced to induce the girls to come early but it often works a hardship on them when they are unavoidably delayed on account of the cars, etc. Stormy weather is the only excuse.

. . .

When we begin our day's work we never know what our day's pay will be. We have to figure to make up for time we lose. Although it is not our fault it is at our expense. For instance: a dozen gloves may be cut from very heavy leather and very difficult to sew; or perhaps when we go to the desk for work we may have to stand waiting in line ten to twenty minutes; or the belt of our machine may break and we may have to walk around the factory two or three times before we find the belt boy who, perhaps, is hidden under a table fixing a belt, and then we have to wait our turn; or we go to another desk to get our

supplies such as needles, thread, welt, etc. But what we dread most of all is the machine breaking down as we do not know how long it will take to repair it. . . .

. . .

A great many employers give as their reason for preferring the piece-work system and establishing it as much as possible, that they are only paying for the work they receive and have more work turned out in a day. This no doubt is true; but it is too often at the expense of the girl. For she pays not only the loss of time but the loss of health too. I am one of the many who are very much against this system for I have seen too many awful results from it. We have a certain amount of strength and energy and if this is to be used up the first few years at the trade what is to become of the workers after that? This system, moreover, encourages a girl to do more than her physical strength will allow her to do continuously. Piece work is worry as well as work.

When I started in the trade and saw the girls working at that dreadful pace every minute, I wondered how they could keep up the speed. But it is not until you become one of them that you can understand. The younger girls are usually very anxious to operate a machine. I remember the first day that I sewed, making the heavy linings. The foreman came to me late in the day and asked how I liked the work. "Oh," I said, "I could never get tired sewing on this machine." But he had seen too many girls "get tired," so he said "Remember those words a few years from now if you stay," and I have.

SOURCE: *Agnes Nestor, "A Day's Work Making Gloves" (1898) in Nestor, Woman's Labor Leader (Rockford, IL: Bellevue Books Publishing Co., 1954), 37–41.*

A tragic event that occurred in New York City in 1911 serves as a window on the conditions of working women's lives. On a Saturday afternoon in March, fire broke out at the **Triangle Shirtwaist Company** in Greenwich Village; when workers tried to flee, they found the exits had been locked by employers to prevent them from sneaking out from work early. To escape the raging inferno, many jumped or fell from the upper-story windows; their dead bodies soon littered the pavement. In all, 146 workers, mainly women, lost their lives that day.

Just two years before the Triangle fire, garment workers in New York City sweatshops had gone on a strike led by the International Ladies Garment Workers Union (ILGWU)—"the rising of the 20,000"—to protest working conditions. The strike lasted for three months and ended in some concessions, including a fifty-two-hour work week. Tragically, the owners of the Triangle Shirtwaist Company had refused to join the settlement. If they had, those 146 workers would not still have been working late on a Saturday afternoon when the fire broke out.

With the exception of unions such as the ILGWU, relations between the **labor movement** and working women were fraught. Male union leaders often held highly traditional gender expectations and viewed women as temporary workers who really belonged in the home; labor organizers' priority was protecting the wages of male workers so they could support their wives and children (the so-called family wage). Working women had other ideas. Starting

5.2: These delegates to the Knights of Labor convention in 1886, including Elizabeth Rodgers with her two-week-old daughter, Lizzie, demonstrate working women's allegiance to the labor movement. Labor activist Leonora Barry headed the Knights of Labor's Department of Women's Work.

with Leonora Barry in the Knights of Labor in the 1880s and Mary Kenney in the American Federation of Labor in the 1890s, female labor organizers demonstrated that women workers would join unions and be an important part of the labor movement.

Charismatic organizers such as Clara Lemlich, Rose Schneiderman, and Pauline Newman continued that fight in the early twentieth century, working to improve the terrible conditions of waged labor within established unions such as the ILGWU, as well as alongside elite white reformers in organizations such as the National Consumers' League (founded in 1899) and the Women's Trade Union League (1903). It was an uphill fight. By 1920 fewer than 8 percent of women workers belonged to unions, despite making up 20 percent of the workforce.

What about the 80 percent of women who were not engaged in wage labor at the turn of the century? That, of course, does not mean that they did not work, and work hard, just that the work they did for their families was not counted as labor. In rural areas, women played vital economic roles on family farms. Not only did they have the full responsibility for bearing and raising children and maintaining their households, but they also actively participated in farm chores. Even though farm households often worked longer hours than the nation's overworked industrial workers, farm women rarely complained.

In urban areas, the mothers of working girls, often recent immigrants themselves, were tasked with providing for their families under extremely difficult conditions created by poverty and recent arrival. Huddled in tenement housing without access to clean drinking water or indoor plumbing, wives learned to shop, cook, and barter to get what their families needed. With an increasing array of consumer goods available for purchase, there was never enough money to go around. Adapting Old World recipes and customs to New World realities, including different kinds of food, was a daily challenge. So was cleanliness, when most of the heat came from coal and water came from a pump out back. Disease often followed.

##  MODERN WOMEN IN THE MAKING

By the 1890s, a new figure appeared on the American scene, her life tentatively resembling the patterns of women's lives today. This **New Woman** was most readily distinguished by her dress. Instead of heavy corsets, yards of sweeping fabric, and elaborate millinery, she dressed comfortably in long dark skirts with simple white blouses called shirtwaists, a style made for movement and even athletic activity, such as riding a bicycle, the newest craze to sweep the country in that decade. As popularized by artist Charles Dana Gibson, the

# Frances Willard Learns to Ride a Bicycle

History remembers Frances Willard as the indefatigable leader of the Woman's Christian Temperance Union from 1879 to 1898, but she was also an avid sportswoman who taught herself to ride a bicycle at the age of fifty-three and then wrote an entire book about the experience, *A Wheel within a Wheel; How I Learned to Ride the Bicycle* (1895). Willard consciously equated mastering the skill of riding a bike with opening new frontiers for women, but she never lost her sheer sense of joy at the physical freedom being astride "Gladys" (her name for her bicycle) allowed.

If I am asked to explain why I learned the bicycle I should say I did it as an act of grace, if not of actual religion. The cardinal doctrine laid down by my physician was, "Live out of doors and take congenial exercise"; but from the day when, at sixteen years of age, I was enwrapped in the long skirts that impeded every footstep, I have detested walking and felt with a certain noble disdain that the conventions of life had cut me off from what in the freedom of my prairie home had been one of life's sweetest joys. Driving is not real exercise; it does not renovate the river of blood that flows so sluggishly in the veins of those who from any cause have lost the natural adjustment of brain to brawn. Horseback-riding, which does promise vigorous exercise, is expensive. The bicycle meets all the conditions and will ere long come within the reach of all. Therefore, in obedience to the laws of health, I learned to ride. I also wanted to help women to a wider world, for I hold that the more interests women and men can have in common, in thought, word, and deed, the happier will it be for the home. Besides, there was a special value to women in the conquest of the bicycle by a woman in her fifty-third year, and one who had so many comrades in the

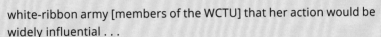

white-ribbon army [members of the WCTU] that her action would be widely influential . . .

It is needless to say that a bicycling costume was a prerequisite. This consisted of a skirt and blouse of tweed, with belt, rolling collar, and loose cravat, the skirt three inches from the ground; a round straw hat; and walking-shoes with gaiters. It was a simple, modest suit, to which no person of common sense could take exception.

As nearly as I can make out, reducing the problem to actual figures, it took me about three months, with an average of fifteen minutes' practice daily, to learn, first, to pedal; second, to turn; third, to dismount; and fourth, to mount independently this most mysterious animal. January 20th will always be a red-letter bicycle day, because although I had already mounted several times with no hand on the rudder, some good friend had always stood by to lend moral support; but summoning all my force, and, most forcible of all, what Sir Benjamin Ward Richardson declares to be the two essential elements—decision and precision—I mounted and started off alone. From that hour the spell was broken; Gladys was no more a mystery: I had learned all her kinks, had put a bridle in her teeth, and touched her smartly with the whip of victory. Consider, ye who are of a considerable chronology: in about thirteen hundred minutes, or, to put it more mildly, in twenty-two hours, or, to put it most mildly of all, in less than a single day as the almanac reckons time—but practically in two days of actual practice—amid the delightful surroundings of the great outdoors, and inspired by the bird-songs, the color and fragrance of an English posy-garden, in the company of devoted and pleasant comrades, I had made myself master of the most remarkable, ingenious, and inspiring motor ever yet devised upon this planet.

Moral: *Go thou and do likewise!*

SOURCE: Frances Willard, A Wheel within a Wheel; How I Learned to Ride the Bicycle *(1895), in Stephanie Twin,* Out of the Bleachers *(Old Westbury, NY: Feminist Press, 1979), 112–14.*

New Woman was a byproduct of the maturation of the industrial economy and the increasingly urban orientation of the country. As usual, many of these trends were more readily available to white, middle-class women than to recently arrived immigrants from Poland or Mexico or farm wives on the Plains, but there was a definite feeling of change in the air when it came to women's lives. During the period from 1890 to 1920 that historians refer to as the Progressive Era, New Women entered the professions, tackled urban problems, and campaigned for birth control and women's suffrage.

The middle-class home was changing as well, especially in urban areas, as the family completed a long-term shift from being a unit of production to one of consumption. Unlike their counterparts in rural America, urban women were the beneficiaries of technological developments, such as electricity, central heating, indoor plumbing, and kitchen appliances, that eased the burdens associated with housekeeping. Urban women also enjoyed increased availability of consumer goods, including ready-to-wear clothing and processed food.

The declining birthrate was one of the biggest changes in women's lives: over the course of the nineteenth century, the average number of births per woman dropped from seven in 1800 to three and a half in 1900. Women's life spans were also increasing, which meant they no longer spent their entire lives bearing and raising children. The lessened time that middle-class women devoted to housekeeping and childrearing helped pave the way for women's increased activism beyond the home.

While still limited to a tiny minority of American women, the numbers of college women grew steadily after 1870, as did their proportion of total students. By 1900, more than 85,000 women were enrolled in colleges, making up 37 percent of all students; twenty years later, women made up almost 48 percent of students, an astounding rise. In fact, some schools such as Stanford and the University of Chicago became alarmed at what they perceived as the feminization of higher education and took steps to limit women's enrollment. Such a response, which was ineffectual, suggests that many Americans still felt a certain uneasiness about providing college educations for women.

Female students relished the stimulation of intellectual work, strenuous physical activity, and a myriad of extracurricular activities on campus. And yet newly minted college graduates faced a daunting question: "After college, what?" For most, the choice remained marriage, coupled with a wide range of volunteer and civic activities. Yet a minority used their higher education as a stepping-stone to a professional career. Unlike later generations of women who learned to balance marriage and career, back then it was generally viewed as an either/or choice.

One of the greatest benefits of a college education was that it provided a way for women who chose not to marry to establish stable households of their own, rather than remaining an unmarried daughter living at home. Very often these pioneering professional women chose to share their lives with other like-minded women in relationships that provided emotional support and financial security. The term **"Boston marriage"** described the prevalence of these deeply felt female friendships, which won approval from family and society alike as an alternative to what was perceived as lonely spinsterhood. Looking back, historians now feel comfortable labeling many of these relationships as lesbian. More broadly, they can be seen as part of queer history by providing a space where cisgender women felt free to express a wide range of gender-nonconforming behaviors, including but not limited to sexual expression, in both public and private settings. Approximately 10 percent of the cohort of women born between 1860 and 1880 remained single—one of the highest rates ever recorded.

The range of professional options open to educated women at the end of the nineteenth century never matched those available to men, nor did their pay. Teaching and librarianship continued to draw large numbers of trained women, as did newer professions such as nursing, social work, and home economics. Women made up a surprisingly high percentage of doctors at the turn of the century (close to 10 percent in some cities) but much lower proportions in law and business. Women scientists faced an especially daunting task, often consigned to lesser ranks with little hope of advancement either in academe or industry. A professorship at a women's college offered one viable career path.

The **settlement house movement** also drew on the talents of educated women. Jane Addams and Ellen Gates Starr founded Hull House in Chicago in 1889, and soon settlement houses popped up in cities around the country. Settlement houses functioned as a combination of community centers and social service providers, offering recreational and educational services such as day care, poetry readings, literacy classes, and health and hygiene programs to the inhabitants of the poor neighborhoods in which they were located. These services were provided by settlement house residents drawn from the ranks of newly educated

5.3: Poet Annie Adams Fields and novelist and short story writer Sarah Orne Jewett shared their lives in what was called a Boston marriage. Testimony to their affluence, they divided their time between Field's house in Boston's Beacon Hill and Jewett's home in South Berwick, Maine. The two women are pictured here in the overstuffed library of the Beacon Hill residence.

women (and a few men) who lived together communally in an atmosphere that resembled a college dorm. Settlement houses were a win-win situation: they provided crucial services to poverty-stricken neighborhoods whose needs were not being addressed by city and state governments, and they provided a collegial, family-like living situation for their residents. For her stewardship of Hull House, Jane Addams became one of the Progressive Era's most celebrated women. In 1931 she won the Nobel Peace Prize.

 # PROGRESSIVE ERA REFORM

Just four years after the founding of Hull House, the **World's Columbian Exposition** opened in Chicago. A chance to trumpet the industrial, economic, and cultural strength of the United States on the threshold of becoming a world power, the 1893 Chicago World's Fair also showcased the important roles that women were playing in civic life. For example, the Woman's Building featured female contributions to culture, art, and history in a monumental structure designed by architect Sophia Hayden and overseen by a Board of Lady Managers, headed by prominent white Chicago clubwoman Bertha Honoré Palmer. The refusal of the Woman's Building board to include Black women's contributions drew the ire of Ida B. Wells, but that did not keep it from being one of the fair's most popular destinations.

Efforts like the Woman's Building drew on the energies and organizational know-how of the women's club movement, which flourished among women of various racial and ethnic backgrounds. As epitomized by the establishment of the **General Federation of Women's Clubs** in 1890, clubwomen came together in their communities to discuss causes and concerns of interest to them as civic-minded women. While many women's clubs served social functions for an emerging white middle-class elite, they could also be pathways into wider civic engagement. As the Federation's president, Sarah Platt Decker, said forthrightly in 1904, "Dante is dead. He has been dead for centuries, and I think it is time we dropped the study of the Inferno and turned the attention to our own."

Educator Nannie Helen Burroughs supplied an equally forthright manifesto for African American women in 1909: "We specialize in the wholly impossible." Black women also felt the call of civic engagement through the club movement and settlement houses, but due to the prevailing racism at the time, their efforts were generally conducted separately from those of white women. Mary Church Terrell served as the first president of the **National Association of Colored Women,** which was incorporated in 1896 with one hundred member organizations; by 1914, the Association represented 50,000 women in 1,000 clubs.

Often clubs came into existence to work for educational and social welfare goals in local communities, driven by an emphasis on race pride accompanied by strong leadership roles for African American women. The founding of Neighborhood House in Atlanta in 1913 by Lugenia Burns Hope and other local clubwomen reflects this dual focus on racial uplift and female activism. A similar impulse motivated the establishment of the first major Chinese women's club—the Chinese Women's Jeleab [Self-Reliance] Association—in San Francisco in 1913.

African American women also continued to mobilize around issues of lynching, sexual violence, and rape. Ida B. Wells framed the protection of Black women's bodies as a basic right of citizenship and realized long before most that white support, women's and men's, would be necessary for campaigns against lynching and sexual violence to succeed. In 1909 Wells joined W. E. B. DuBois, Mary White Ovington, Mary Church Terrell, and others to found the biracial **National Association for the Advancement of Colored People (NAACP)**, the pioneering civil rights organization.

As these examples of women's activism suggest, women played prominent roles in a wide range of late nineteenth- and early twentieth-century reform initiatives. Much of the impetus for this activism came from women's identities as wives and mothers. How could women provide healthful and safe lives for their families, they argued, if city drinking water was contaminated, garbage filled the streets, and tuberculosis was rampant? More broadly, in

5.4: African American women used women's clubs and churches as launch pads for political activism, including women's suffrage. Here Nannie Helen Burroughs and eight other delegates gather for the Banner State Woman's National Baptist Convention in 1915.

DOCUMENTING AMERICAN WOMEN

# Josephine St. Pierre Ruffin Spearheads the Black Women's Club Movement

Josephine St. Pierre Ruffin was a leading African American clubwoman in Boston. In addition to serving as the publisher of *The Woman's Era*, the first national Black women's newspaper, she founded the New Era Club in 1894. The following year she welcomed the first National Conference of Colored Women to Boston with this speech.

. . .

The reasons why we should confer are so apparent that it would seem hardly necessary to enumerate them, and yet there is none of them but demand our serious consideration. In first place we need to feel the cheer and inspiration of meeting each other; we need to gain the courage and fresh life that comes from the mingling of congenial souls, of those working for the same ends. Next we need to talk over not only those things which are of vital importance to us as women, but also the things that are of special interest to us as colored women, the training of our children, openings for boys and girls, how they can be prepared for occupations and occupations may be found or opened for them, what we especially can do in the moral education of the race with which we are identified, our mental elevation and physical development, the home training it is necessary to give our children in order to prepare them to meet the peculiar conditions in which they shall find themselves, how to make the most of our own, to some extent, limited opportunities, these are some of our own peculiar questions to be discussed. Besides these are the general questions of the day, which we cannot afford to be indifferent to: temperance, morality, the higher education, hygiene and domestic questions. If these things need the serious consideration of women

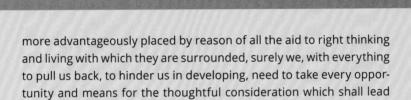

more advantageously placed by reason of all the aid to right thinking and living with which they are surrounded, surely we, with everything to pull us back, to hinder us in developing, need to take every opportunity and means for the thoughtful consideration which shall lead to wise action.

. . .

Too long have we been silent under unjust and unholy charges; we cannot expect to have them removed until we disprove them through ourselves. It is not enough to try and disprove unjust charges through individual effort that never goes any further. Year after year southern women have protested against the admission of colored women into any national organization on the ground of [the] immorality of these women, and because all refutation has only been tried by individual work the charge has never been crushed, as it could and should have been at the first. Now with an army of organized women standing for purity and mental worth, we in ourselves deny the charge and open the eyes of the world to a state of affairs to which they have been blind, often willfully so, and the very fact that the charges, audaciously and flippantly made, as they often are, are of so humiliating and delicate a nature, serves to protect the accuser by driving the helpless accused into mortified silence. It is to break this silence, not by noisy protestations of what we are not, but by a dignified showing of what we are and hope to become that we are impelled to take this step, to make of this gathering an object lesson to the world.

For many and apparent reasons it is especially fitting that the women of the race take the lead in this movement, but for all this we recognize the necessity of the sympathy of our husbands, brothers and fathers. Our women's movement is woman's movement in that it is led and directed by women for the good of women and men, for the benefit of all humanity, which is more than any one branch or section of it. We want, we ask the active interest of our men, and, too, we are not drawing the color line; we are women, American women,

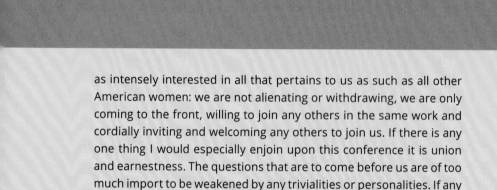

as intensely interested in all that pertains to us as such as all other American women: we are not alienating or withdrawing, we are only coming to the front, willing to join any others in the same work and cordially inviting and welcoming any others to join us. If there is any one thing I would especially enjoin upon this conference it is union and earnestness. The questions that are to come before us are of too much import to be weakened by any trivialities or personalities. If any differences arise, let them be quickly settled, with the feeling that we are all workers to the same end, to elevate and dignify colored American womanhood.

SOURCE: *Josephine St. Pierre Ruffin, "Address at the First National Conference of Black Women's Clubs,"* The Woman's Era, *vol. 2, no. 5 (August 1895), 13–15.*

what progressive reformer Mary Ritter Beard tagged "municipal housekeeping," women reformers pressured city governments to provide city services as a way of protecting the health and well-being of all residents.

There was something larger going on here, and it involved women's changing relationship to the state. In a country known for unfettered capitalism and laissez-faire individualism, the role of the federal government and its state and local equivalents was fairly limited throughout most of the nineteenth century. Women reformers were among the first to realize that the enormous problems that American society faced at the end of the nineteenth century—linked to its rapid industrialization, the explosive growth of its cities, and the arrival of millions of new immigrants—called for coordinated and collaborative responses far beyond the resources of individuals and localities. Who had those resources? The state. And so began a campaign, central to **Progressive Era** reform, to expand the social welfare services of local, state, and federal governments. What had long been women's province through voluntary associations and charitable institutions was increasingly defined as a proper scope for public policy.

This new emphasis, and the rewards it reaped, are best seen in the field of child welfare. A generation of social reformers, many of them settlement house veterans, identified a broad range of issues demanding state intervention, such as the scourge of child labor, the dramatically high rates of infant mortality, and the lack of recreational and play spaces. These problems in turn were related to a host of others: tenement housing, long hours and low pay for women workers, industrial accidents, poor schools, and unsafe food products. Working together with women's clubs and other political and voluntary associations, such as the Women's Trade Union League and the National Consumers' League, determined progressive women won results from recalcitrant elected and appointed officials.

One of the most concrete victories was the creation of the **U.S. Children's Bureau** in 1912, headed by Hull House alumna Julia Lathrop and tasked with investigating and improving the conditions of children's lives. Lillian Wald of the Henry Street Settlement, a pioneering organization in New York City that brought nursing services to the city's poor, thought it was about time. Referring to a federal study of an insect called the boll weevil, which was decimating the Southern cotton crop, Wald observed pointedly, "If the Government can have a department to take such an interest in what is happening to the cotton crop, why can't it have a bureau to look after the nation's child crop?" One important byproduct was that professionally trained women found employment opportunities in government as it expanded its purview to include issues of vital concern to the nation's progressive-minded women. The irony is that women did all this without the vote.

 # THE FINAL PUSH FOR SUFFRAGE

By the 1890s women's suffrage was part and parcel of the larger Progressive Era reform movement. As civic-minded women dramatically increased their involvement in public life and civic affairs, their contributions strengthened the case for giving women the vote. But just as progressive reform never really took hold in the South, the movement for suffrage also foundered in that region, caught up on the complicated question of race. If women won the vote, would Black women be enfranchised, even though Black men were now effectively disenfranchised by a variety of tools such as poll taxes, property requirements, and literacy tests? Alternatively, should suffragists argue that white women's votes would counteract the potential political power of African Americans? As Ida B. Wells-Barnett found when she was told to march at

ANTI-SUFFRAGE CALENDAR-1916

| 1916 JANUARY 1916 | 1916 FEBRUARY 1916 |

Four and twenty Suffragists went to win a male,
Their costumes were the newest, but their arguments were stale.
He shook his weary head at them and made a lowly bow,
"My State has voted NO," he said, "I cannot help you now."

5.5: The anti-suffrage movement, whose ranks included women as well as men, asserted that women didn't want the vote and that voting would threaten women's special privileges and duties. To win converts to their cause, they created publicity gimmicks like this anti-suffrage calendar from 1916.

the back of a 1913 suffrage parade, a pattern of deeply ingrained racism— a definite blind spot—clearly animated suffrage activism, as it did most Progressive Era reform.

As late as 1909, only four states had given women the vote. The original suffrage leaders had died off— Sojourner Truth in 1883, Lucy Stone in 1893, Elizabeth Cady Stanton in 1902, and Susan B. Anthony in 1906. New NAWSA leaders, such as Anna Howard Shaw and Carrie Chapman Catt, proved unable to break the stalemate. Over the next ten years, the momentum dramatically shifted. New tactics, new recruits, and a more supportive political climate paved the way for the final push to victory.

Most prominent was a new focus on spectacle, which literally took the battle to the streets in the form of suffrage parades, open-air meetings, and the hawking of suffrage newspapers on street corners. The movement also branched out into immigrant and working-class communities to mobilize support. Suddenly male voters started taking notice: Washington adopted suffrage in 1910, followed by California in 1911 and Kansas, Oregon, and Arizona in 1912. Note that success still lagged in the conservative East, and certainly the South. Not until 1917 did New York state join the trend, a huge breakthrough.

As a consequence of these suffrage victories, many women were actually voting in local, state, and federal elections well before the passage of the **Nineteenth Amendment** in 1920. Women voters played especially key roles in Western politics and in the 1912 third-party campaign of Theodore Roosevelt on the Progressive Party ticket. Symbolic of women's prominence in Progressive Party leadership, Frances Kellor headed the publicity and research committee, and Jane Addams, who put Roosevelt's name in nomination, was considered a possible cabinet choice.

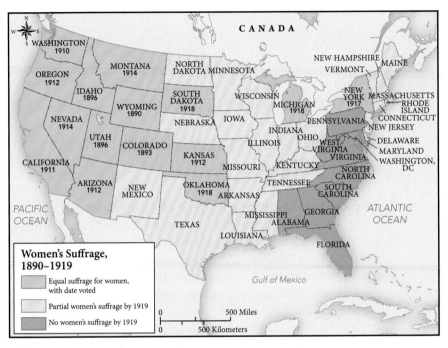

**MAP 5.2**

As suffrage picked up momentum, so did other movements relating to women's issues. One of the most pressing issues was **birth control**, which was illegal throughout most of the United States. Into that fray stepped a young public health nurse named Margaret Sanger, who opened the first birth control clinic in the Brownsville section of New York in 1916—and was promptly arrested. Sanger would remain in the forefront of reproductive rights for the next forty years.

Other activists positioned themselves far to the left of suffrage. Emma Goldman preached anarchism and socialism as part of a broad commitment to revolutionary activism and free love and "rebel girl" Elizabeth Gurley Flynn led general strikes in Paterson, New Jersey, and Lawrence, Massachusetts, for the Industrial Workers of the World (a.k.a. Wobblies). Charlotte Perkins Gilman challenged the theoretical underpinnings of marriage and argued for women's economic independence. Heterodoxy, a club for women "who did things, and did them openly," convened in New York's Greenwich Village in 1912, a harbinger of a strange new thing called **feminism**. (The term was first publicly introduced in the United States at a mass meeting in New York City in 1914.) Staking out their turf, Winnifred Harper Cooley quipped, "All feminists are suffragists, but not all suffragists are feminists," but in fact the suffrage movement deserves a prominent place in the history of modern feminism.

DOCUMENTING AMERICAN WOMEN

# What Margaret Sanger Thought Every Girl Should Know

Sex education has often been a fraught topic, as Margaret Sanger, a nurse and social reformer, found out in the 1910s. Starting in 1912, she published a series of articles on the theme of "What Every Girl Should Know" in the *New York Call*, which were later collected in a 1916 pamphlet. Covering topics such as puberty, menstruation, pregnancy, and menopause, the articles ran afoul of federal and state anti-obscenity laws but that did not stop Margaret Sanger from launching a lifelong crusade for wider access to birth control and contraception.

Students of vice, whether teachers, clergymen, social workers or physicians, have been laboring for years to find the cause and cure for vice, and especially for prostitution. The have failed so far to agree on either the cause or the cure, but it is interesting to know that upon one point they have been compelled to agree, and that is, that ignorance of the sex functions is one of the strongest forces that sends young girls into unclean living.

This, together with the knowledge of the rapidly increasing spread of venereal diseases and the realization of their subtle nature, has awakened us to the need of a saner and healthier attitude on the sex subject, and to the importance of sex education for boys and girls.

. . .

The whole object of teaching the child about reproduction through evolution is to clear its mind of any shame or mystery concerning its birth and to impress it with the beauty and naturalness of procreation, in order to prepare it for the knowledge of puberty and marriage.

There must of necessity be special information for the pubescent boy and girl, for having arrived at the stage in their mental development they no longer take for granted what has been told them by the parents, but

are keen to form their own ideas and gather information independently. It is right, therefore, to give them the facts as science has found them.

There are workers and philanthropists who say there is too much stress put upon the subject of venereal diseases; that the young girl after learning or hearing of the dangers she is likely to encounter in the sexual relation, is afraid to marry and consequently lives a life unloved and alone.

"Your treatment of this subject is dangerous," said a very earnest social worker a few weeks ago. "Such knowledge will prevent our young girls from marrying."

To which I replied that my object in telling young girls the truth is for the definite purpose of preventing them from entering into sexual relations whether in marriage or out of it, without thinking and knowing. Better a thousand times to live alone and unloved than to be tied to a man who has robbed her of health or of the joy of motherhood, or welcoming the pains of motherhood, live in anxiety lest her sickly offspring be taken out of her life, or grow up a chronic invalid.

I have more faith in the force of love. I believe that two people convinced that they love each other and desire to live together will talk as frankly of their own health and natures as they do today of the house furnishings and salaries. Their love for each other will protect them from ill health and disease, and prompt them to procure of their own accord, a certificate of health if each has the right information and knowledge.

There are, however, different phases of nature, the knowledge of which binds and cements the love of two people, other than venereal diseases, for these diseases are only symptoms of a great social disorder.

Every girl should first understand herself; she should know her anatomy, including sex anatomy; she should know the epochs of a normal woman's life, and the unfoldment which each epoch brings; she should know the effect the emotions have on her acts, and finally she should know the fullness and richness of life when crowned by the flower of motherhood.

*SOURCE: Margaret H. Sanger,* **What Every Girl Should Know** *(1916), Project Gutenberg eBook, 7–8, found online at www.gutenberg.org*

By now suffrage, temperance, and feminist activism were all part of vibrant international networks, linking activists across national borders and promoting a rich circulation of ideas and strategies, just as transnational abolitionism and women's rights had done in the 1830s and 1840s. In the 1880s the World's Woman's Christian Temperance Union took the lead, pursuing political equality for women in places such as New Zealand, Australia, and South Africa. In 1888 the International Council of Women was founded to bring together existing women's groups, primarily from North America and Western Europe, with Elizabeth Cady Stanton and Susan B. Anthony its prime instigators. In the 1890s and early 1900s, prodded by the advocacy of German socialist Clara Zetkin, the Second Socialist International made women's suffrage and women's political equality a central demand. In a separate development, the establishment of the International Woman Suffrage Association in Berlin in 1904 "to secure the enfranchisement of the women of all nations" fed the growth of the suffrage movement worldwide and facilitated the emergence of militant suffragism.

This international cross-fertilization is best seen in the impact of the suffrage militancy pioneered in England by the Women's Social and Political Union, led by Emmeline Pankhurst and her daughters Christabel and Sylvia. Their tactics were far more confrontational than petitions and parades: they involved breaking windows, setting bombs, attempted arson, and even (in the case of Emily Davison) running out onto a race course and being trampled to death, all to bring attention to the cause. In return, the militants were arrested and forcibly fed when they went on hunger strikes.

Alice Paul, a young Quaker from New Jersey, fell under the sway of the Pankhursts when she was studying abroad. Returning to the United States in 1911, Paul was determined to shake things up, and she most certainly did. First she organized a huge parade in Washington in 1913 to compete with President Woodrow Wilson's inauguration. (This was the parade Ida B. Wells-Barnett had to sneak into in order to march.) Four years later, when Wilson still refused to support suffrage, Paul and members of the National Woman's Party began picketing the White House, an unprecedented act of civil disobedience. Like their British sisters, they were arrested and thrown in jail; when they, too, went on hunger strikes, they were forcibly fed. The spectacle of elite white women willing to risk death for the cause garnered enormous publicity, and no small amount of sympathy, for the militants. Rose Winslow, who went on a hunger strike after being arrested, put it forcefully: "God knows we don't want other women ever to have to do this over again."

Carrie Chapman Catt, president of the National American Woman Suffrage Association, pointedly distanced her organization from the militants and concentrated, starting in 1916, on what she called her "Winning Plan." The new emphasis downplayed the costly and time-consuming focus

5.6: National Woman's Party protesters representing colleges as diverse as Vassar and the University of Missouri picket the White House in 1918, demanding that President Woodrow Wilson support votes for women. Suffragists were the first political group to deploy the now common tactic of picketing the White House.

on winning referenda state by state in favor of a massive lobbying effort behind a federal amendment. The suffrage amendment passed the House in 1918 and the Senate in 1919, and then was sent to the states for ratification. This was no easy task, but on August 18, 1920, Tennessee became the thirty-sixth state to ratify, which put the amendment over the top.

Many factors help to explain both the length of the struggle and its final success. What began as a truly radical demand for the vote in 1848 had become much less threatening by the early twentieth century, when the boundaries of women's lives stretched much further than the home. Still, political machines, liquor interests, and religious groups such as the Catholic Church were formidable enemies, as was an organized anti-suffrage movement, including many women who inconveniently announced their opposition. In their view, women belonged in the home, not at the polls, and they did not need the vote because they had men to protect their interests. By 1916 the National Organization Opposed to Woman Suffrage headed by Josephine Jewell Dodge had grown into a formidable presence.

To counteract that potent opposition, three generations of suffragists drew on the wealth of experience they had amassed in women's clubs, voluntary associations, charitable organizations, and political parties. Even the schisms that divided the movement—between AWSA and NWSA in the 1870s and 1880s and between NAWSA and the Woman's Party in the 1910s—arguably helped build momentum, each side drawing supporters who might have shunned the other. In the end what made the suffrage movement so powerful—and ultimately guaranteed its success—was that it brought together a diverse range of individuals and organizations in a broad coalition dedicated to a common goal.

Women's home front contributions during World War I finally tipped the balance, even though suffrage leaders were deeply divided over America's entry into the conflict. The National Woman's Party opposed the war and defiantly continued to picket the White House, carrying placards that provocatively countered Wilson's campaign pledge to "make the world safe for democracy" with a call to "make the country safe for democracy." In contrast, Carrie Chapman Catt threw the entire weight of the much larger NAWSA behind the war effort. These patriotic efforts, as well as those by non-suffrage women's groups, led many politicians and ordinary citizens to conclude that women deserved the vote.

World War I was a watershed beyond just women's suffrage. African Americans, dismayed by the worsening racial climate in Southern states, were drawn by opportunities, wartime and other, in Northern and Western cities. Thus began the **Great Migration**, which between 1914 and 1920 saw 500,000 African Americans, half of them women, leave the South for Chicago, Pittsburgh, Los Angeles, New York, Washington, DC, and beyond. After

# *Timeline*

**1883**

Ida B. Wells sues railroad company for forcing her to relocate to a "colored" car

**1888**

The International Council of Women is founded

**1889**

Jane Addams and Ellen Gates Starr found Hull House in Chicago

**1890**

Establishment of the General Federation of Women's Clubs

**1892**

The worst year on record for lynching deaths—155 African Americans are lynched

**1892**

Ida B. Wells becomes part owner of the newspaper *Memphis Free Speech*

**1896**

Supreme Court upholds Jim Crow segregation in *Plessy v. Ferguson*

**1896**

Incorporation of the National Association of Colored Women

**1900**

A quarter of married Black women work, compared to 3 percent of married white women

**1904**

Establishment of the International Woman Suffrage Association

**1909**

National Association for the Advancement of Colored People (NAACP) founded

**1911**

Triangle Shirtwaist factory fire

rising tensions related to jobs and labor strikes, a race riot broke out in East St. Louis in 1917, which left between 100 and 200 African Americans dead and 6,000 homeless. In response the NAACP organized a silent parade down Fifth Avenue in New York that drew 10,000 men and women. Major race riots also occurred in Chicago in 1919 and Tulsa, Oklahoma, in 1921.

In the meantime, on Election Day 1920, some 26 million women were eligible to go to the polls, confirmation of their new status as women citizens and the political equals of men. And yet the fruits of this victory were unequally distributed. While African American women who had migrated to Northern cities such as Chicago and New York could vote, the vast majority of African American women still resided in the South, where they were subjected to the same voter suppression devices that were used to keep African American men from the polls. For African Americans, it was the Voting Rights Act of 1965, not the Fourteenth, Fifteenth, or Nineteenth Amendments, that finally removed the structural barriers to voting.

In a parallel disfranchisement, few Native American women gained the vote. Not until 1924 did Congress pass legislation declaring that all Native Americans born in the United States were citizens, which cleared the way for tribal women to vote. But Native American women still faced ongoing barriers to voting on the state and local levels, especially in the West, as did

| 1912 | 1916 | 1931 |
|------|------|------|
| Creation of the U.S. Children's Bureau | Margaret Sanger opens first birth control clinic in New York | Jane Addams wins Nobel Peace Prize |
| **1913** | | **1935** |
| Wells organizes one of the first Black women's suffrage organizations, the Alpha Suffrage Club in Chicago | **1917**<br>East St. Louis race riot | Puerto Rican women gain the right to vote |
| | **AUGUST 1920** | **1943** |
| **1913** | Tennessee becomes the thirty-sixth state to ratify the Nineteenth Amendment, formally allowing it to be passed | Chinese-American women gain the right to vote |
| Alice Paul organizes parade in Washington to compete with President Woodrow Wilson's inauguration | | **1965** |
| | **1924** | Voting Rights Act prohibits racial discrimination in voting |
| **1914–1920** | Congress passes legislation declaring all Native Americans born in the United States citizens | |
| Great Migration | | |

Mexican Americans. Puerto Rican women did not gain the vote until 1935 and not all Chinese-American women could vote until 1943.

Still the passage of the Nineteenth Amendment remains a major milestone for American women as well as a major step forward for American democracy. Having honed their political skills in the suffrage campaign, women across the political spectrum put that experience to good use after the vote was won. As Crystal Eastman observed, "Men are saying perhaps 'Thank God, this everlasting woman's fight is over!' But women, if I know them, are saying, 'Now at last we can begin.'" When it came to politics and public life, women were saying forcefully, "We have come to stay."

## KEY TERMS

Alpha Suffrage Club

birth control

Boston marriage

feminism

General Federation
 of Women's Clubs

Great Migration

labor movement

lynching

National Association
 for the Advancement
 of Colored People
 (NAACP)

National Association
 of Colored Women

New Woman

Nineteenth Amendment

Progressive Era

settlement house
 movement

Triangle Shirtwaist
 company

U.S. Children's Bureau

World's Columbian
 Exposition

## Suggested Readings

Cooper, Brittney. *Beyond Respectability: The Intellectual Thought of Race Women* (2017).

Feimster, Crystal. *Southern Horrors: Women and the Politics of Rage and Lynching* (2011).

Gilmore, Glenda E. *Gender and Jim Crow: Women and the Politics of White Supremacy in North Carolina, 1896–1920* (1996).

Lange, Allison K. *Picturing Political Power: Images in the Women's Suffrage Movement* (2020).

Manion, Jen. *Female Husbands: A Trans History* (2020).

Orleck, Annelise. *Common Sense and a Little Fire: Women and Working-Class Politics in the United States, 1900–1965* (1995).

Learn more with this chapter's digital tools at http://www.oup.com/he/warele.

# Modern American Women, 1920–1960

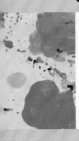

In March 1934 First Lady Eleanor Roosevelt (left) took a fact-finding trip to Puerto Rico, accompanied by female members of the press corps, including her close friend Lorena Hickok. During her husband's twelve years in office, Roosevelt dramatically expanded the role of First Lady.

In a short book called *It's Up to the Women* published in 1933, Eleanor Roosevelt challenged America's female citizens to pull the country through the gravest economic crisis it had ever faced: "The women know that life must go on and that the needs of life must be met and it is their courage and determination which, time and again, have pulled us through worse crises than the present one." When President Franklin D. Roosevelt took office in March, one-quarter of the country was unemployed and the economy had ground to a halt. As FDR took unprecedented steps to address the economic crisis and its underlying causes, Eleanor was at his side, always pushing him to do more. She truly served as the conscience of the New Deal.

Eleanor Roosevelt is perhaps the most influential and admired American woman of the twentieth century, but her early life hardly predicted such an outcome. Born into an elite family in New York in 1884, she felt ugly compared to her beautiful socialite mother and desperately in need of affection from her alcoholic father. Orphaned at age ten, she and her younger brother were shuttled among various relatives. Her life began to open up when she was sent abroad to school in England. At Allenswood, a preparatory school run by a charismatic Frenchwoman named Marie Souvestre, Eleanor cultivated her intellectual aspirations and discovered her leadership abilities. College was not an option for most women of her class background, so she reluctantly "came out" into society as an eighteen-year-old, in effect putting herself on the marriage market. In 1905 she married Franklin Delano Roosevelt, her distant cousin from the Hyde Park branch of the family; her uncle Theodore, then president of the United States, gave the bride away. Eleanor Roosevelt bore six children over the next ten years, five of whom survived infancy, and seemed destined for a life of conventional upper-class womanhood.

It did not turn out that way. In 1910 her husband entered politics in Albany, and she found to her great surprise that she loved the rough and tumble of political life too. Her horizons broadened further as she followed her husband to Washington when he joined the administration of President Woodrow Wilson in 1913. Despite the discovery of her husband's affair with her social secretary during World War I and Franklin's being stricken with polio in 1921, she and FDR forged a strong personal and political partnership. He re-entered political life and she became active in social reform circles and Democratic politics.

When the Roosevelts took up residence at the White House in 1933, Eleanor Roosevelt was already a political force in her own right, a role she played throughout the Depression and war years and after her husband's death in 1945, when she became an advocate for international understanding in the postwar world. One of her last public roles was to chair the President's Commission on the Status of Women in 1961, which helped encourage the revival of feminism in the decades to come. A model of public-spirited womanhood that still resonates today, Eleanor Roosevelt represents the enormous contributions that modern women made to American life in the years after women's suffrage was won.

# NEW DILEMMAS FOR MODERN WOMEN

By the 1920s broad changes in American life marked the emergence of a mass, predominantly urban culture that was significantly different from its nineteenth-century predecessor. Automobiles, movies, radio, telephones, mass-circulation magazines, brand names, and chain stores bound Americans together in an interlocking web of shared national experience, as did a new emphasis on consumption, leisure, and self-realization. Women were at the center of many of these broader developments, although modernity's benefits remained most accessible to the white middle class.

The **flapper** symbolized the new roles for women. With her bobbed hair and slim, boyish figure (achieved by the new fad of dieting), brazenly wearing makeup and smoking cigarettes in public, the flapper symbolized the personal freedom trumpeted by the emerging mass culture, including a freer approach to relationships with the opposite sex. True, the goal was still marriage, but young women had much more freedom to experiment with sex once chaperonage went the way of horse-drawn carriages. Men could be friends and buddies, not just future husbands, reflecting a new heterosociability in modern life.

These new freedoms caused conflict and confusion as well as liberation, especially among parents shocked at the new liberties being taken by what the movies dubbed "our dancing daughters." And this conflict was not just limited to the white middle class. Adolescent Mexican American girls

6.1: Automobiles promised freedom and liberation to women lucky (and affluent) enough to take the wheel. Here three Mexican American women pose in their elegant touring car, likely in Tucson, Arizona, in the 1920s.

embraced the new flapper styles of dress, appearance, and unchaperoned be-havior, much to the horror of their more conservative parents who wanted to keep them under stricter control. And young Japanese American girls of the Nisei (second) generation turned to advice columnists such as "Dear Deidre" (in real life a journalist named Mary Oyama) for help in navigating such new challenges as interracial dating and conflicts between parental expectations about arranged marriages and marrying for love.

Many of these young girls got their modern ideas from the movies, one of the most powerful forms of mass culture and an enormously influential force in shaping women's aspirations from the 1920s on. From watching mov-ies, especially after "talkies" replaced silent films late in the decade, young women learned how to style their hair, covet the latest fashions, even how to act around men, including the proper way to kiss and make out. Hollywood and the growing film industry attracted star-struck teenagers who headed out to California in the hopes of becoming movie stars. Barring that, there were lots of roles behind the cameras as screenwriters, script girls, and wardrobe managers. Hollywood actresses such as Clara Bow, Gloria Swanson, Theda Bara, and Mary Pickford became some of the best known women of their era. Successful too: Pickford was one of the four founders—along with D. W. Griffith, Charlie Chaplin, and Douglas Fairbanks—of the United Artists stu-dio in 1919.

While most of the images on the screen were of white women, there were some exceptions. Lupe Vélez and Dolores del Rio found success, but only by conforming to stereotypes about Latin women: del Rio presented herself as an exotic foreigner, and Vélez pitched herself as a "red hot tamale." Rita Hayworth (born Margarita Carmen Cansino) found an easier path to stardom once she altered her appearance and dyed her hair red. Anna May Wong, the major Asian American actress of her era, challenged the preconceptions of the roles that Chinese American actresses could play. African American actresses such as Hattie McDaniel, Louise Beavers, and Butterfly McQueen faced the most pervasive discrimination, their onscreen roles usually limited to maids and domestics. When criticized for playing into racial stereotypes, McDaniel pointedly replied, "It's better to get $7,000 a week for playing a servant than $7.00 a week for being one."

Affirmations of African American racial pride and cultural identity found more acceptance outside Hollywood. The **Harlem Renaissance**, an ar-tistic movement of young writers and artists in the 1920s who championed racial awareness in the midst of white society, showcased the talents of writ-ers Zora Neale Hurston, Jessie Fauset, and Nella Larsen. And befitting a de-cade that is often referred to as the **Jazz Age**, jazz and blues singers such as Bessie Smith, Ida Cox, and Ma Rainey boldly—and bawdily—sang about women's power and sexuality. Cox's "One Hour Mama" demanded that the

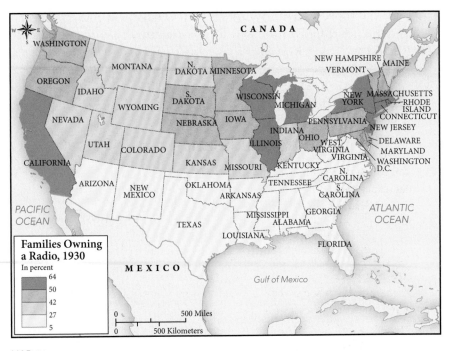

**MAP 6.1**

singer's male lover slow down and pay attention to her intimate needs while Ma Rainey dispensed with men altogether in her 1928 "Prove It on Me Blues": "I went out last night with a crowd of my friends/They must've been women, 'cause I don't like no men." Another prominent member of the queer Black community in Harlem was singer Gladys Bentley, who performed in a white tuxedo and risked arrest whenever she appeared in public in male attire.

Despite the lure of becoming a movie star or a jazz singer, most young women ended up not with glamorous careers but as wives and mothers. But marriage too was changing. Men were still heads of households and primary breadwinners, but there was a higher value placed on the wife's contributions to family life, especially her role in raising children. And there was definitely a higher recognition of women's sexual needs, as long as they were safely confined within marriage. In part because of the popularization of the ideas of Sigmund Freud, the new marital ideal involved satisfying sexual expression for both husbands and wives. The increasing availability and acceptance of birth control, which allowed women to enjoy sexual relations for purposes other than procreation, encouraged this trend. This focus on heterosexual satisfaction came at a price, however: an increasing suspicion of what the medical profession was now calling "sexual deviance" on the part of women who loved other women. Only in safe spaces like gay bars in major urban

# The Harlem Renaissance

African American novelist and folklorist Zora Neale Hurston grew up in the all-Black community of Eatonville, Florida, and became involved in the Harlem Renaissance while studying anthropology at Barnard College in the 1920s. In this 1928 essay she exhibits both race pride and a sense of being beyond race, a mindset shared by other Black writers at the time. Hurston is best known for her 1937 novel *Their Eyes Were Watching God*. A manuscript based on her 1927 interviews with formerly enslaved African American Cudjoe Lewis, *Barracoon: The Story of the Last "Black Cargo"* was published posthumously in 2018.

I am colored but I offer nothing in the way of extenuating circumstances except the fact that I am the only Negro in the United States whose grandfather on the mother's side was not an Indian chief.

I remember the very day that I became colored. Up to my thirteenth year I lived in the little Negro town of Eatonville, Florida. It is exclusively a colored town. The only white people I knew passed through the town going to or coming from Orlando. The native whites rode dusty horses, the Northern tourists chugged down the sandy village road in automobiles. The town knew the Southerners and never stopped cane chewing when they passed. But the Northerners were something else again. They were peered at cautiously from behind curtains by the timid. The more venturesome would come out on the porch to watch them go past and got just as much pleasure out of the tourists as the tourists got out of the village.

During this period, white people differed from colored to me only in that they rode through town and never lived there. They liked to hear me "speak pieces" and sing and wanted to see me dance the parse-me-la, and gave me generously of their small silver for doing these things, which seemed strange to me for I wanted to do them so much that I needed bribing to stop, only they didn't know it. The colored people gave no dimes. They deplored any joyful tendencies

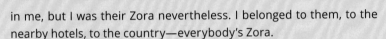

in me, but I was their Zora nevertheless. I belonged to them, to the nearby hotels, to the country—everybody's Zora.

But changes came in the family when I was thirteen, and I was sent to school in Jacksonville. I left Eatonville, the town of the oleanders, a Zora. When I disembarked from the river-boat at Jacksonville, she was no more. It seemed that that I had suffered a sea change. I was not Zora of Orange Country any more, I was now a little colored girl. I found it out in certain ways. In my heart as well as in the mirror I became a fast brown—warranted not to rub nor run.

But I am not tragically colored. There is no great sorrow dammed up in my soul, nor lurking behind my eyes. I do not mind at all. I do not belong to the sobbing school of Negrohood who hold that nature somehow has given them a lowdown dirty deal and whose feelings are all but about it. Even in the helter-skelter skirmish that is my life, I have seen that the world is to the strong regardless of a little pigmentation more [or] less. No, I do not weep at the world—I am too busy sharpening my oyster knife.

At certain times I have no race, I am me. When I set my hat at a certain angle and saunter down Seventh Avenue, Harlem City, feeling as snooty as the lions in front of the Forty-Second Street Library, for instance. So far as my feelings are concerned, Peggy Hopkins Joyce on the Boule Mich with her gorgeous raiment, stately carriage, knees knocking together in a most aristocratic manner, has nothing on me. The cosmic Zora emerges. I belong to no race nor time. I am the eternal feminine with its string of beads.

I have no separate feeling about being an American citizen and colored. I am merely a fragment of the Great Soul that surges within the boundaries. My country, right or wrong.

Sometimes, I feel discriminated against, but it does not make me angry. It merely astonishes me. How can any deny themselves the pleasure of my company? It's beyond me.

*SOURCE: Zora Neale Hurston, "How It Feels to Be Colored Me,"* World Tomorrow, *May 11, 1928.*

centers could queer women openly flaunt their sexual preference. Most lesbians chose to remain closeted.

In an economy increasingly based on consumption, women played vital roles as the primary consumers of the household goods so lavishly advertised in the decade's magazines and newspapers. But all the new appliances did not necessarily free women from domestic chores: a new vacuum cleaner or washing machine could actually create more work if the husband expected a clean shirt every day and the house was now vacuumed daily instead of swept once a week. Women still spent an average of fifty-one hours a week on household chores, little different from their mothers and grandmothers. These new gadgets and appliances were useful only to households that had the disposable income to pay for them and the electricity to run them, conditions that left out much of rural America until well into the 1930s.

As they had been doing since the nineteenth century, women continued to expand their activities beyond the home in volunteer activities and politics. Compared to the organized vitality of the suffrage movement, especially in its last decade, women's activism in the 1920s was more diffuse. As women prepared to go to the polls for the first time after the passage of the Nineteenth Amendment, journalist Emma Bugbee observed: "There are about twenty-six million women voters, but no woman voter. Much less is there a woman vote." But it is wrong to conclude that suffrage did not matter or that women beat a hasty retreat from politics after 1920. As the motto of the National League of Republican Colored Women declared in 1924, "We are in politics to stay and we shall be a stay in politics."

Continuing their Progressive-Era reform priorities, women played a prominent role in the passage of the **Sheppard-Towner Federal Maternity and Infancy Act** of 1921, the nation's first federally-funded public health campaign. Women also moved into the Democratic and Republican parties, often joining separate women's auxiliaries or clubs, although they quickly found that most political decisions were still made by men in smoke-filled rooms. In their new roles as citizens, women joined the **League of Women Voters** or participated in the **Women's Joint Congressional Committee**, a coalition of ten major women's organizations. There were 346 women elected to state legislatures and by the end of the decade, nine women served in Congress.

While former suffragists continued to be associated with social reform, conservative women came together in patriotic or right-wing groups such as the Women Sentinels of the Republic, the Daughters of the American Revolution, and the women's wing of the Ku Klux Klan, which enrolled as many as 500,000 women in the 1920s. Conservative women mobilized in the South to shore up white supremacist policies such as segregation and prohibitions against interracial sex. In tandem with the Republican-dominated political climate of the era, conservative groups in the rest of the country focused

6.2: The Ku Klux Klan, born in the Reconstruction South, experienced a resurgence in the nativist 1920s, targeting Catholics and Jews alongside Blacks. Feeling no compulsion to hide their views, women of the Ku Klux Klan paraded down Pennsylvania Avenue in Washington, DC, in 1928 with the Capitol looming in the background.

on the threat that growing ethnic and racial pluralism posed to the traditional cultural domination of white Protestant Americans.

Other groups of women struggled to gain a toehold in public life. Until the **Indian Citizenship Act** of 1924, Native American women lacked the legal basis to vote. Even after the law's passage, they faced ongoing restrictions to voting on the state and local levels. A few Mexican American women such as Adelina Otero-Warren, who campaigned for Congress as a Republican in 1922, and Soledad Chacon, who ran for New Mexico Secretary of State that same year, sought elected political office (Chacon won, Otero-Warren lost), but in general Mexican American women were either disfranchised by state and local restrictions or excluded from mainstream politics. Instead Mexican American women like Jovita Idar devoted their considerable political talents to local activism, civil rights, and labor organizing in their communities.

African American women's political engagement in the 1920s continued on two fronts. First they pushed for federal anti-lynching legislation, continuing the activism begun by Ida B. Wells in the 1890s. A law to make lynching a federal crime passed the House of Representatives in 1922, but stalled in the Senate because of conservative Southern opposition. (A version of the law did not finally pass until 2018.). A second pressing concern was attempting to register to vote, especially in the South. Despite intimidation and resistance from local white officials, and lack of support from predominantly white groups like the League of Women Voters and the National Woman's Party, which considered voting rights a matter of race not sex, African American women individually and collectively tried to cast ballots in the wake of the Nineteenth Amendment. Even though most did not succeed, their efforts laid the groundwork for the civil rights activism to come.

The most divisive issue for politically active women in the post-suffrage era was the **Equal Rights Amendment**. This may seem surprising: why would women be opposed to equal rights? The controversy came down to the value of the protective labor legislation that had been enacted during the Progressive Era to regulate the hours and working conditions of women workers. The courts interpreted similar legislation for men as an infringement of the freedom of contract, but allowed it for women because of their supposed physical weakness and need for special protection. An equal rights amendment would likely have knocked down those hard-fought gains, which is why social reformers almost universally opposed it. In contrast ERA supporters such as Alice Paul (who wrote and introduced the original amendment in 1923) argued that these laws were demeaning in their stereotyped views of women needing special protection at work and hindered, not helped, women on the job. So divisive was this issue that it basically split the feminist movement into two camps until the 1960s, by which time the extension of workplace protection to both sexes made protective legislation for women unnecessary.

 # MAKING DO IN THE GREAT DEPRESSION

In 1927 the Ford Motor Company produced an automobile every twenty-four seconds, a symbol of the decade's booming economy. Yet the prosperity was never equally distributed: the top 5 percent of the nation's households received one-third of the national income and more than 65 percent of households had incomes under $2,000 a year. The onset of the **Great Depression** in 1929 exposed the economy's underlying structural weaknesses. At its lowest point over the winter of 1932–1933, more than one-quarter of the work force was unemployed and people were literally starving in the cities. Gender—as well as class, race, and geography—profoundly affected the experience of hard times.

In many ways men and women experienced the Depression differently, both in families and on the job. When a man lost his job, he lost his role as breadwinner for his family, but none of the nation's housewives lost their jobs. On the contrary, contributions to their families took on new significance with husbands out of work. By substituting their own labor for goods and services previously purchased, housewives could stretch the family budget to cover periods of unemployment or cuts in pay. Robert and Helen Lynd described this phenomenon in *Middletown in Transition* (1937), their sociological study of Muncie, Indiana: "The men, cut adrift from their usual routine, lost much of their sense of time and dawdled helplessly and dully about the streets; while in the homes the women's world remained largely intact and the round of cooking, housecleaning, and mending became if anything more absorbing." Few were comfortable with this deviation from traditional gender roles. "We had no choice," one woman recalled. "We just did what had to be done one day at a time." These were the women Eleanor Roosevelt addressed in *It's Up to the Women.*

6.3: Dorothea Lange took this photograph of Florence Thompson and her two children at a peapickers camp in Nipomo, California, in 1936 to document migratory farm labor conditions for the Farm Security Administration. This famous image is commonly referred to as "Migrant Mother." Less well-known is that Thompson identified herself as of Cherokee descent.

Women also helped their families by taking jobs: the number of married women working outside the home doubled during the decade and the 1940 census counted 13 million women workers, 25.4 percent of all women aged fourteen and older. It probably seems counterintuitive that women could find jobs when one-quarter of the workforce was unemployed, but the answer is linked to the gendered occupational structure of the economy. Male workers were concentrated in the very sectors hardest hit by the economic collapse: manufacturing, heavy industry, coal mining, and construction. Women's jobs in the clerical and retail fields or domestic and personal service were somewhat less affected by the downturn, although they still faced accusations that they were taking jobs away from men. Addressing that charge, one commentator noted astutely, "Few of the people who oppose married women's employment seem to realize that a coal miner or a steel worker cannot very well fit the jobs of nursemaids, cleaning women, or the factory and clerical jobs now filled by women." Such stereotyping afforded women a small measure of protection in the economic crisis, but at the cost of reinforcing traditional gender norms and confirming women's concentration in lower-status, low-paying jobs.

The Depression affected racial minorities harshly. Mexican Americans in the Southwest and West who had made gains in agricultural and industrial work in the 1920s faced extreme discrimination once hard times hit. One response was forced repatriation to Mexico: from 1931 to 1934 one-third of the Mexican American population (some 500,000 people) returned to Mexico either voluntarily or under threat of deportation, further disrupting families already hurting because of the Depression. To cope, Mexican American women founded **mutual-aid societies** (*mutualistas*) in their communities to counter the racism and economic hardship they experienced in the broader society.

For other groups, such as African Americans, the hard times of the 1930s were not all that different from normal times. As poet Langston Hughes observed, "[T]he depression brought everybody down a peg or two. And Negroes had few pegs to fall." The Great Migration out of the South that had surged in the 1910s and 1920s (bringing 1.3 million migrants to the North, Midwest and West) slowed dramatically in the 1930s, when jobs dried up in urban areas. Even domestic work, the mainstay for Black women, was often undercut by white women now willing to take those jobs to earn a meager wage.

The **New Deal** responded to this broad economic crisis with a mix of relief programs, stimulus spending, and economic reforms. Government relief made a real difference to Mexican American communities in El Paso or San Francisco's Chinatown where federal programs had never reached before. Much later than western European countries, the United States in the 1930s implemented the rudiments of a modern welfare state—that is, the federal government accepted responsibility for the successful performance of the economy and guaranteeing the basic needs of its citizens. Women reformers played a large role in creating and then administering the American welfare state.

Following Eleanor Roosevelt's stellar example, women took on new roles in politics and government in the 1930s. The dramatic expansion of New Deal social welfare programs provided jobs and opportunities for professional women long active in those fields; women's expertise was especially crucial to the Works Progress Administration (WPA) and the Social Security Administration. Women also took on larger roles in the revitalized Democratic party. Bound together in an informal network, women such as Frances Perkins (the first woman to serve in the president's cabinet), Mississippi social worker Ellen Sullivan Woodward and reformer-turned-politician Molly Dewson showed not just the continuity between Progressive Era reform and the New Deal but also demonstrated women's new post-suffrage roles.

Ordinary women fared less well in New Deal programs, which were often organized around the principle of male breadwinners and their dependent wives. Not all women had (or wanted) a man to head their household, so they had to fight relief workers for recognition of their plight. Historian

# The New Deal Comes to Northern New Mexico

When the Great Depression struck, some Mexican Americans returned to Mexico either voluntarily or under threat of deportation, but many remained in the United States, where religion and tradition helped tight-knit communities weather hard times. Starting in 1935, Mexican Americans received an additional resource that had rarely made its way to their communities in the past: federal relief money from programs such as the Works Progress Administration (WPA), Civilian Conservation Corps (CCC), and the National Youth Administration (NYA). Here Elsie Chavez Chilton and Susana Archuleta recall the impact of New Deal programs on their families and communities.

### Elsie Chavez Chilton Recalls Relatives Working with the Civilian Conservation Corps Near Las Cruces, New Mexico, 1930s

At that time there was a lot of bartering. That was pre-depression and I was such a small child I don't remember too much about it. But I know they got along just fine. When the depression hit we were already living in town. We had no money to lose because we had no money in the bank. We did have hard times—especially the families whose fathers didn't have a steady income. I had uncles who had steady incomes. They were ditch riders. One was at Leasburg Dam and one at Mesilla Dam. No matter how small it was, if it was a steady income it meant a lot. Since my father was self-employed that was worse. We managed somehow. Also there was the NYA [National Youth Administration] and the WPA [Works Progress Administration]. . . .

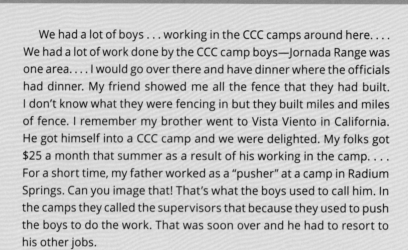

We had a lot of boys . . . working in the CCC camps around here. . . . We had a lot of work done by the CCC camp boys—Jornada Range was one area. . . . I would go over there and have dinner where the officials had dinner. My friend showed me all the fence that they had built. I don't know what they were fencing in but they built miles and miles of fence. I remember my brother went to Vista Viento in California. He got himself into a CCC camp and we were delighted. My folks got $25 a month that summer as a result of his working in the camp. . . . For a short time, my father worked as a "pusher" at a camp in Radium Springs. Can you image that! That's what the boys used to call him. In the camps they called the supervisors that because they used to push the boys to do the work. That was soon over and he had to resort to his other jobs.

Susana Archuleta Looks Back at Jobs with the Civilian Conservation Corps and the National Youth Administration in Northern New Mexico, 1930s

During the Depression, things got bad. My dad passed away when I was about twelve, leaving my mother with eight children and no means of support. . . . My mother took in washings to make a living,

Margot Canaday coined the term "straight state" to describe how federal policies privileged a model of heterosexual marriage at the expense of alternative living arrangements. An offshoot was the increased stigmatization of homosexuality, both for men and women, in areas like welfare policy, immigration, and the military.

Custom also limited women's options in New Deal programs. The WPA put millions of men to work on construction and industrial jobs, but confined

and our job was to pick up the washings on the way home from school. We'd pick up clothes from the schoolteachers, the attorney, and what-have-you. Then. at night, we'd help iron them and fold them. . . .

When I was a teenager, the Depression began to take a turn. Franklin Roosevelt was elected, and the works projects started. The boys and young men who'd been laid off at the mines went to the CCC camps and the girls joined the NYA. . . .

They paid us about twenty-one dollars a month. Out of that we got five and the other sixteen was directly issued to our parents. The same was true of the boys working in the camps. They got about thirty dollars a month. They were allowed to keep five of it. The rest was sent to their families. All of us were hired according to our family income. If a man with a lot of children was unemployed, he was given preference over someone who had less children. . . . Those programs were great. Everybody got a chance to work.

*SOURCES: "As It Was in Chiva Town: Elsie Chavez Chilton," in Rita Kasch Chegin,* Survivors: Women of the Southwest *(Las Cruces, NM: Yucca Tree Press, 1991), 30, 32; "Susana Archuleta," in Nan Elsasser et al.,* Las Mujeres: Conversations from a Hispanic Community *(New York: Feminist Press, 1980), 36–37.*

women's relief work to sewing rooms, schools, and playgrounds. One-quarter of the labor codes established to jump-start the economy allowed women workers to be paid less than men; agricultural and domestic work, where women predominated, were initially excluded from Social Security and the Fair Labor Standards Act coverage. And popular programs like the Civilian Conservation Corps were limited to men only, leading critics to ask, "Where is the she-she-she?" Without the effective mobilization of the women's network at the highest levels of government, ordinary women's needs for relief might have been overlooked, if not forgotten completely, but the results were far from equitable. Still, even these token efforts often meant the difference between making do and doing without.

Another area of dramatic growth for women in the 1930s was in the labor movement. Once the federal government put its force behind labor's right to organize with the **Wagner Labor Relations Act** of 1935, women's union participation surged from 250,000 in 1929 to more than 800,000 by the end of the 1930s. Union membership meant higher wages, better benefits, and job security for women as well as men. And these new union members were not just white ethnic industrial workers: unionized garment workers in Chinatown waged a successful strike against the National Dollar Stores in 1938 and Mexican American women in the cannery industry in California created the powerful United Cannery, Agricultural, Packing and Allied Workers of America (UCAPAWA) in 1937.

 # A WORLD AT WAR

A cloud of ominous international developments hung over the 1930s, especially the rise of Nazi Germany and the aggressive expansion of Japan in the Pacific. Strongly isolationist sentiment limited Franklin Roosevelt's ability to commit the United States to the global war, which began in Europe in 1939, but the economy was already moving toward a war footing before the decisive Japanese attack on Pearl Harbor on December 7, 1941. America was now at war, and American women were too.

Despite all the programs that streamed out of Washington in the 1930s, the New Deal never solved the problem of the Depression: spending for World War II did. The dramatic increase in defense production quickly absorbed all the leftover unemployment from the 1930s and necessitated the recruitment of a new workforce—the nation's women—now that men were off at war. Probably the best-known wartime image is Rosie the Riveter, the iconic Norman Rockwell *Saturday Evening Post* cover of a muscular defense worker in coveralls cradling her riveting gun while she eats her lunch. But Rosie was not just a patriotic housewife who took a job "for the duration": many women already in the labor force used wartime labor shortages to move up into better-paying industrial jobs.

Women also moved geographically, often leaving home for the first time; California, the site of major defense mobilization, gained 1.4 million newcomers. This wartime climate was especially liberating for single women who seized opportunities for increased autonomy and independence in their

**Figure 6.1:** Women Workers in the Manufacturing Sector, 1940–1950 *Source:* United States Department of Labor, https://www.dol.gov/general/topic/statistics

work and personal lives. Things were not quite as easy for African American, Mexican American and Chinese American women, but they too found opportunities because of the wartime emergency. "Americanos Todos" [Americans All] proclaimed the Office of War Information in 1943. In all, the female work force grew 50 percent between 1940 and 1945.

Some 350,000 women played an even more direct role in the war effort by joining the 15 million men who served in the military. The largest number— some 140,000—served with the Women's Army Corps (WAC), followed by 100,000 in the WAVES (Women Appointed for Volunteer Emergency Service) in the Navy. A special group of women pilots comprised the Women's Airforce Service Pilots (WASP). Tasked with ferrying planes between various domestic airbases, these spunky women combined their passion for flying with service to their country, even though it cost thirty-eight of their lives. Their experiences reflected the combination of opportunity and sexism that was the lot of women in the military: they were restricted to the continental United States and denied opportunities for promotion, and their program was phased out as soon as male pilots started returning from service abroad. Like Rosie the Riveter, new roles were acceptable only if they were temporary.

Women of color had to push back even harder to overturn discriminatory practices and seize new opportunities in the military. Despite a serious nursing shortage and strenuous advocacy by Mabel K. Staupers of the National

**IT'S A WOMAN'S WAR TOO!**

*JOIN THE* **WAVES**

*YOUR COUNTRY NEEDS YOU NOW*

JOHN FALTER USNR

*Apply to your nearest*
**NAVY RECRUITING STATION OR OFFICE OF NAVAL OFFICER PROCUREMENT**

6.4: With the slogan "It's a woman's war too!" this 1942 recruiting poster encouraged women to join the WAVES, the women's unit of the U.S. Navy. Other marketing pitches included releasing a man to fight and bringing the troops home sooner.

Association of Colored Graduate Nurses, African American nurses were not permitted to serve in the army and navy until early 1945, just months before the war ended.

Japanese American women had no choice about their wartime roles: along with the men and children in their West Coast communities, they were forcibly detained in the aftermath of Pearl Harbor. "Shikata ga nai" (It can't be helped) was their stoical response but the wartime internment of 110,000 Japanese Americans remains a giant blot on the history of civil liberties in the United States. Conditions in the euphemistically named relocation camps, located in remote sections of California, Nevada, and other Western states, were difficult for women trying to keep up some semblance of family normalcy, but also hard for husbands who lost their roles as patriarchal heads of household in these communal settings. The policy began to ease in 1943 and 1944, in part because of a shortage of agricultural labor and also to allow college-age students to resume their educations, albeit outside the West Coast war zone. When the war ended, Nisei women played key roles in reestablishing the family and community networks that had been sundered by wartime relocation and later took the lead in seeking redress from the U.S. government.

The war had a different impact on the Chinese American community, which benefited from the wartime alliance between China and the United States. As a gesture toward better relations, the 1943 repeal of the Chinese

6.5: Despite sanctioned activities like softball teams and social dances, life was anything but normal in the government-run camps where Japanese Americans on the West Coast were detained during wartime. The Poston internment center located in Yuma County in southwestern Arizona, the location of this Girl Scout troop, was the largest of the camps.

Exclusion Act of 1882 allowed some 40,000 Chinese women to enter the country over the next two decades. War brides married to American soldiers, including many from China, the Philippines, Australia, and Europe, also were allowed to take up legal residence in the United States. The repeal of the 1882 act also finally allowed Chinese-American women to claim full citizenship and exercise their right to vote.

War's end brought the soldiers home but did not lead to a stable international situation. Deteriorating relations with the Soviet Union set in motion the Cold War that gripped the country through the 1960s. Fear of **communism** poisoned domestic politics, leading to loyalty oaths, witch-hunts for subversives in government, and other forms of repression subsumed under the rubric of McCarthyism, named for the Wisconsin senator who was its most forceful champion. Gay men and lesbians in government or the military found themselves specially targeted. "I don't feel like I am being treated like an American citizen," said one suspected lesbian who was called before a military tribunal. "I would like to know why."

# Japanese Relocation

Monica (Itoi) Sone's autobiography, *Nisei Daughter* (1953), tells the story of the wartime detainment of Japanese Americans on the West coast from the perspective of a young woman. The Japanese character *sei* means genera-tion; by adding a prefix as a number, such as *Issei*, *Nisei*, or *Sansei*, it enumerates successive generations. Here second-generation Sone describes her family's evacuation to a tem-porary encampment from their home in Seattle; later "Fam-ily #10710" would be sent to a permanent camp in Idaho.

Mother and Father wandered out to see what the other folks were doing and they found people wandering in the mud, wondering what other folks were doing. Mother returned shortly, her face lit up in an ecstatic smile. "We're in luck. The latrine is right nearby. We won't have to walk blocks."

We laughed, marveling at Mother who could be so poetic and yet so practical. Father came back, bent double like a woodcutter in a fairy tale, with stacks of scrap lumber over his shoulder. His coat and trouser pock-ets bulged with nails. Father dumped his loot in a corner and explained. "There was a pile of wood left by the carpenters and hundreds of nails scattered loose. Everybody was picking them up, and I hustled right in with them. Now maybe we can live in style with tables and chairs."

. . .

We felt fortunate to be assigned to a room at the end of the bar-racks because we had just one neighbor to worry about. The partition wall separating the rooms was only seven feet high with an opening of four feet at the top, so at night, Mrs. Funai next door could tell

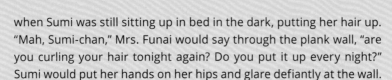

when Sumi was still sitting up in bed in the dark, putting her hair up. "Mah, Sumi-chan," Mrs. Funai would say through the plank wall, "are you curling your hair tonight again? Do you put it up every night?" Sumi would put her hands on her hips and glare defiantly at the wall.

The block monitor, an impressive Nisei who looked like a star tackle with his crouching walk, came around the first night to tell us that we must all be inside our room by nine o'clock every night. At ten o'clock, he rapped at the door again, yelling, "Lights out!" and Mother rushed to turn the light off not a second later.

Throughout the barracks, there [was] a medley of creaking cots, whimpering infants and explosive night coughs. Our attention was riveted on the intense little wood stove which glowed so violently I feared it would melt right down to the floor. We soon learned that this condition lasted for only a short time, after which it suddenly turned into a deep freeze. Henry and Father took turns at the stove to produce the harrowing blast which all but singed our army blankets, but did not penetrate through them. As it grew quieter in the barracks, I could hear the light patter of rain. Soon I felt the "splat! splat!" of raindrops digging holes into my face. The dampness on my pillow spread like a mortal bleeding, and I finally had to get out and haul my cot toward the center of the room. In a short while Henry was up. "I've got multiple leaks, too. Have to complain to the landlord first thing in the morning."

All through the night I heard people getting up, dragging cots around. I stared at our little window, unable to sleep. I was glad Mother had put up a makeshift curtain on the window for I noticed a powerful beam of light sweeping across it every few seconds. The lights came from high towers placed around the camp where guards with Tommy guns kept a twenty-four hour vigil. I remembered the wire fence encircling us, and a knot of anger tightened in my breast.

What was I doing behind a fence like a criminal? If there were accusations to be made, why hadn't I been given a fair trial? Maybe I wasn't considered an American anymore. My citizenship wasn't real after all. Then what was I? I was certainly not a citizen of Japan as my parents were. On second thought, even Father and Mother were more alien residents of the United States than Japanese nationals for they had worked and paid their taxes to their adopted government as any other citizen.

Of one thing I was sure. The wire fence was real. I no longer had the right to walk out of it. It was because I had Japanese ancestors. It was also because some people had little faith in the ideas and ideals of democracy. They said that after all these were but words and could not possibly [e]nsure loyalty. New laws and camps were surer devices. I finally buried my face in my pillow to wipe out burning thoughts and snatch what sleep I could.

*SOURCE: Monica Sone,* Nisei Daughter *(Boston: Little, Brown and Company, 1953).*

And what about the Rosie the Riveter? Women laborers too lost their jobs, to returning veterans. Women understood and accepted that outcome—they were grateful to the men who had served and thought they deserved their jobs back when they came home—but it was harder to stomach when experienced women were passed over for non-veteran men when new hiring started up. Instead of trading their overalls for aprons at home, many defense workers simply went back to the traditional jobs available to women. The percentage of women in the workforce dropped slightly after the war, but by 1950 was back up to 28.6 percent. While historians debate whether World War II was a major turning point for American women, it definitely encouraged the trend of women working outside the home that had been steadily building since the nineteenth century.

# THE 1950S: THE WAY WE WERE?

In the 1950s television challenged movies as the dominant form of American popular culture and created some of the most enduring, if overly simplistic, images of the decade as a time of suburban, family-oriented bliss. Just reciting the names of the shows—*Leave It to Beaver*, *Father Knows Best*, and *I Love Lucy*, among others—conjures up visions of backyard play sets and white picket fences, with Chevy station wagons parked in the driveways. And yet scratch the surface of American life, especially for its women, and the picture is far more complicated.

After two decades of dislocation from depression and war, traditional family values looked quite appealing to the younger generation coming of age in the 1940s. The average age of marriage for women dropped to twenty, and a third of all women in 1951 were married by nineteen. The birth rate, after steadily declining since 1800, and falling below replacement level briefly during the Depression, suddenly shot up and stayed high well into the early 1960s after peaking in 1957. American women on average were now having close to four children on average. Demographers call this phenomenon the **baby boom**, and its ripple effects would play out for the rest of the twentieth century and into the twenty-first.

The baby boom took place in a period of general affluence—Americans experienced a 25 percent rise in real income between 1946 and 1959. This affluence in turn heightened the cultural emphasis on consumption that characterized postwar society. Selling consumer goods

6.6: A portrait of white patriarchy in action from the popular television show *Father Knows Best*, as actress Jane Wyatt looks over the shoulder of Robert Young, who plays her husband. No doubt she will soon be subjected to a dose of "mansplaining" about what he is reading.

and services to growing families fueled the economy and prompted a major expansion of the nation's educational system. The baby boom was also accompanied by the growth of suburbia, one of the most far-reaching trends of postwar America: by 1960, more people lived in suburbs than cities. Suburban life, however, remained far more accessible to whites than members of racial and ethnic minorities, who were often excluded by racial covenants and discriminated against by banks' lending practices.

Women's identification with the home and domesticity was well captured by Betty Friedan in her best-selling *The Feminine Mystique* (1963), which, more than any other source, has shaped our views (not always accurately) of women's lives in the 1950s. In her witty and polemical exposé, Friedan identified "the problem that has no name": "As she made the beds, shopped for groceries, matched slipcover material, ate peanut butter sandwiches with her children, chauffeured Cub Scouts and Brownies, lay beside her husband at night—she was afraid to ask even of herself the silent question—'Is this all?'" The root of that dissatisfaction, Friedan argued, lay in the disconnect between an ideology stressing that "the highest value and the only commitment for women is the fulfillment of their own femininity" and the aspirations of many women to move beyond those increasingly outdated confines.

While some women, mainly white and middle-class, felt trapped in the suburbs, Friedan's stark picture of neurotic and unfulfilled suburban housewives did not necessarily reflect the reality of women's lives. Many highly educated suburban homemakers successfully managed to combine community work with suburban family life. Yet many families could not afford to live the child-centered suburban existence so lavishly profiled in women's magazines like *Good Housekeeping* or *McCall's* or portrayed uncritically on television sitcoms. What relevance did stay-at-home domesticity have for Black or Latina women trapped in poor urban neighborhoods, farm women struggling in rural areas, or working-class families still striving for a toehold in American society? Such a lifestyle would have represented an almost unattainable standard of upward mobility.

Looking at it another way, perhaps the popular culture so relentlessly pushed this domestic ideal precisely because so many women were no longer willing or able to accept its basic tenet that women only belonged in the home. Throughout the 1950s women continued to stream into the workforce, especially married women with children who should have been the prime candidates for the heightened emphasis on domesticity. By 1960 more than one-third of women held jobs outside the home, including 12.4 million working wives. Some women worked for personal reasons (such as needing the stimulation of getting out of the house), but most women worked because they had to. Supporting the new consumer-oriented lifestyles of televisions, automobiles, and family vacations often took two incomes instead of just one, even

# Claudette Colvin, Unsung Heroine of the Civil Rights Movement

On March 2, 1955, a fifteen-year-old Black teenager named Claudette Colvin refused to give up her seat to a white passenger on a Montgomery, Alabama bus. Note the date: nine months before Rosa Parks sparked the Montgomery bus boycott with a similar act of civil disobedience. Like Parks, Colvin was arrested but local civil rights leaders declined to use her as a test case when she became pregnant soon after. She did become one of five plaintiffs in *Browder v. Gayle*, the landmark 1956 Supreme Court decision that ordered Montgomery to end segregation on all modes of public transportation.

I was in eleventh grade.

It started out a normal day. We got out early and thirteen of us students walked to downtown Montgomery and boarded a city bus on Dexter Avenue, exactly across the street from Dr. Martin Luther King's church. As the bus proceeded down Court Square, more white passengers got on the bus. In order for this white lady to have a seat, four students would have to vacate because a white person wasn't allowed to sit across from a colored person. So the bus driver asked for the four seats and three of the students got up. I remained seated.

History had me glued to the seat. Harriet Tubman's hands were pushing down on one shoulder and Sojourner Truth's hands were pushing down on the other shoulder. I was paralyzed between these two women, I couldn't move.

February was, at that time, only Negro History Week, not history month. But the faculty members at my school said we were gonna

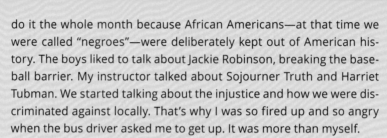

do it the whole month because African Americans—at that time we were called "negroes"—were deliberately kept out of American history. The boys liked to talk about Jackie Robinson, breaking the baseball barrier. My instructor talked about Sojourner Truth and Harriet Tubman. We started talking about the injustice and how we were discriminated against locally. That's why I was so fired up and so angry when the bus driver asked me to get up. It was more than myself.

Some white students [on the bus] were yelling: "You have to get up, you have to get up." And a colored girl, one of the students said, "Well, she don't have to do nothing but stay Black and die."

We were still on our best behavior taking all of the insults from the white passengers. The bus driver knew that I wasn't breaking the law, because these seats were already for colored people. Under Jim Crow law, the bus driver could ask you to give up your seat at any time but the problem was that [the number of seats for black and white people had to be even]. He drove the bus about four stops, and when we stopped, traffic patrol got on the bus and asked me to get up. I told him I paid my fare and said, "It's my constitutional right!" The patrol officer yelled to the bus driver that he didn't have any jurisdiction here.

We thought it was all over with, because the white woman remained standing and I remained seated. I knew she wasn't going to sit opposite me. He drove one block and that's when the policemen from the squad car came in and asked me the same thing, and I was even more defiant.

I don't know how I got off that bus. All the students said they manhandled me off the bus and into the squad car. They handcuffed me,

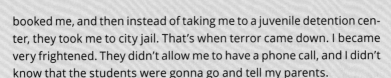

booked me, and then instead of taking me to a juvenile detention center, they took me to city jail. That's when terror came down. I became very frightened. They didn't allow me to have a phone call, and I didn't know that the students were gonna go and tell my parents.

My mother and my pastor come down and bail me out. I had three charges: disorderly conduct, violating segregation law, and assault and battery. They dropped two charges and just kept the one, assault and battery. They said I scratched the policeman because I didn't get up and walk, but I don't recall scratching him.

. . .

That arrest changed my whole life. I was ostracized by people in my community and professional people also. I wanted to be an attorney. My mother would say I never stopped talking. I always had a lot of questions to ask, and I was never satisfied with the answer. A lot of things I wasn't satisfied by.

. . .

All four of us didn't get enough credit. Mary Louise Smith, who was eighteen, was arrested too. I was a little disappointed [at being left out], because the whole movement was about young people, saying we want more from America. We want to stand up and be first class citizens. The discrimination that's going on, whether gender or racial or whatever, religious. We want it to be brought out and defeated.

*SOURCE: Roni Jacobson, "Claudette Colvin Explains Her Role in the Civil Rights Movement,"* Teen Vogue, *October 19, 2017. https://www.teenvogue. com/story/claudette-colvin-explains-her-role-in-the-civil-rights-movement*

in a time of affluence. This trend continued over the following decades, to the point where a stay-at-home mom became the aberration, rather than the norm. But it further disadvantaged female-headed households, which struggled to get by on the low wages women could command in the workplace.

Women also worked for structural reasons related to the maturation of the American economy. Unlike the Depression when women were suspected of taking jobs away from men, postwar women regardless of marital status were welcomed into the workforce, where their preponderance in fields like clerical work, teaching, and health care dovetailed well with the needs of the post-industrial economy. When the choices of these women are included in the history of the decade, the experiences of women look far more diverse and heterogeneous than one would ever expect from reading the popular literature at the time.

Further challenging the perception of the 1950s as an era of conformity and political apathy, women were major agents of change in the postwar period. Groups like the League of Women Voters continued to provide an entry point for women into local civic activities. The political parties welcomed, indeed would have been lost without, the female grassroots volunteer. Women in the labor movement worked to consolidate the gains of the

## *Timeline*

**C. 1918–1935**

The Harlem Renaissance

**1919**

Mary Pickford serves as one of the four founders of the United Artists studio

**1921**

Congress passes the Sheppard-Towner Maternity and Infancy Protection Act

**1923**

Alice Paul drafts the Equal Rights Amendment

**1924**

Native American women gain the legal right to vote

**1929–1939**

The Great Depression

**1929–1939**

Women's union participation surges from 250,000 to more than 800,000

**1931–1934**

Forced repatriation of Mexican Americans to Mexico

**1933**

Eleanor Roosevelt becomes First Lady

**1935**

The Wagner Labor Relations Act

**1937**

Mexican American women in the cannery industry in California establish the United Cannery, Agricultural, Packing and Allied Workers of America (UCAPAWA)

1930s and 1940s, and progressive women came together in groups such as Women Strike for Peace to support disarmament and the banning of nuclear testing. Conservative women rallied against the threat communism posed to American values.

Black women played especially large roles in the emerging **civil rights movement**, which had roots at least as far back as the 1930s and grew during World War II. (Historians call this "the long civil rights movement.") The 1954 Supreme Court decision in *Brown v. Board of Education*, which outlawed segregation in public schools, was an early legal victory. Then the focus shifted to public confrontations: the bus boycott in Montgomery in 1955–1956 after Rosa Parks was arrested for not giving up her seat on a local bus; the tense situation in 1957 when six teenaged girls and three boys integrated Little Rock High School; the sit-ins that targeted segregated public accommodations like lunch counters in 1960 and 1961; and the Freedom Rides that simultaneously challenged segregation on interstate bus travel. Black women were central to all these actions. Ella Baker, one of these trailblazing women, said it best: "The movement of the fifties and sixties was carried largely by women."

The dominant images of the civil rights movement mainly revolve around Black men, often ministers, epitomized by the Reverend Martin Luther King

---

**1938**

Unionized garment workers in Chinatown wage a successful strike against the National Dollar Stores

**1940–1950**

Female work force grows 50 percent

**DECEMBER 7, 1941**

Japanese attack on Pearl Harbor; the United States enters World War II

**1943**

Repeal of the Chinese Exclusion Act of 1882

**1945**

African American nurses are permitted to serve in the army and navy

**1946–1964**

Baby boom

**1954**

*Brown v. Board of Education*

**1955–1956**

Montgomery Bus Boycott

**1957**

Desegregation of Little Rock High School

**1960**

More than one-third of women hold a job outside the home; more Americans live in suburbs than cities

**1961**

Eleanor Roosevelt chairs the President's Commission on the Status of Women

**1963**

Betty Friedan publishes *The Feminine Mystique*

Jr. And yet to focus just on the publicly recognized national leaders miss-
es the energy and support at the grassroots level supplied by Black women.
Grounded in the daily struggle for survival and respect and often facilitated
by Black churches and local chapters of the **National Association for the
Advancement of Colored People (NAACP)**, Black women knew who to
turn to and how to get things done in their communities. Sociologist Belinda
Robnett calls these kind of activists "bridge leaders." Recruiting friends and
relatives through existing kin and friendship networks, women quickly found
themselves on the front lines of boycotts, voter registration drives, demon-
strations, even acts of civil disobedience that landed them in jail. Both young
adults and older, more established community members answered the call.

The roll call of courageous Southern Black women who risked their lives
for the freedom cause is long. Ella Baker, who served as a mentor to the rising generation of student activists, was an impassioned believer in participa-
tory democracy; her motto was "Strong people don't need strong leaders." In
Montgomery Rosa Parks was not just a tired seamstress but a longtime activist
in her local NAACP whose refusal to give up her seat was part of a carefully
crafted strategy to force the issue. And JoAnn Robinson, not Martin Luther
King Jr., was the chief strategist of the Montgomery bus boycott that grew out
of Parks's arrest. Fannie Lou Hamer became a field secretary for the Student
Non-Violent Coordinating Committee (SNCC) after being denied the right
to register to vote in Mississippi. Daisy Bates created a NAACP youth council
in her hometown of Little Rock, Arkansas, and later provided physical and
emotional support to the "Little Rock Nine" who desegregated the high school
in 1957. Representing the younger generation, Ruby Doris Smith was severely
beaten while participating in the Freedom Rides and Diane Nash led sit-ins
in Nashville while a student at Fisk; both later went on to be active in SNCC.

At the core of African American women's civil rights activism was the
imperative to protect the dignity of Black women's bodies from white men's
attacks, especially white men's customary immunity to rape Black women
without legal consequences. Speaking out against sexualized violence and
rape, even when Southern courts were unlikely to prosecute the cases, became
a vehicle to challenge white supremacy, as did protesting police brutality and
the mistreatment of Black girls and women in public spaces such as buses or
parks. Long before the phrase became a catchword for second-wave feminism,
African American women knew that the personal was political.

The emerging civil rights movement had a ripple effect on later social
movements, especially the revival of feminism. Drawing parallels between the
status of African Americans and women (what activist lawyer Pauli Murray
called "Jane Crow"), women individually and collectively challenged the
structures of American life—social, economic, legal—that kept women from
full citizenship and equality. In turn, these challenges to dominant ideas and

institutions provoked a conservative backlash. Many of the political upheavals of the 1960s, 1970s, and beyond thus had strong antecedents in the African American civil rights struggle.

## KEY TERMS

| | | |
|---|---|---|
| baby boom | Jazz Age | Sheppard-Towner |
| civil rights movement | League of Women | Federal Maternity and |
| communism | Voters | Infancy Act |
| Equal Rights | mutual-aid societies | Wagner Labor Relations |
| Amendment | National Association for | Act |
| flapper | the Advancement of | Women's Joint |
| Great Depression | Colored People | Congressional |
| Harlem Renaissance | New Deal | Committee |
| Indian Citizenship Act | Rosie the Riveter | |

## Suggested Readings

Canaday, Margot. *The Straight State: Sexuality and Citizenship in Twentieth-Century America* (2011).

Corder, J. Kevin, and Christina Wolbrecht. *Counting Women's Ballots: Female Voters from Suffrage through the New Deal* (2016).

McGuire, Danielle L. *At the Dark End of the Street: Black Women, Rape, and Resistance—A New History of the Civil Rights Movement from Rosa Parks to the Rise of Black Power* (2010).

Meyerowitz, Joanne, ed. *Not June Cleaver: Women and Gender in Postwar America, 1945–1960* (1994).

Ruiz, Vicki L. *From Out of the Shadows: Mexican Women in Twentieth-Century America* (1998).

Ware, Susan. *Holding Their Own: American Women in the 1930s* (1982).

Learn more with this chapter's digital tools at http://www.oup.com/he/warele.

# seven

# Feminism and Its Discontents, 1960–1992

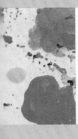
Phyllis Schlafly made no secret of her stance on the Equal Rights Amendment when she took the podium to speak in 1977. She realized that goal in 1982 when the deadline for ratification ran out, but efforts to revive the ERA continue.

"First of all, I want to thank my husband Fred, for letting me come—I always like to say that, because it makes the libs so mad." That was how conservative activist Phyllis Schlafly often opened her talks, knowing that it would drive feminists ("the libs") crazy. And it did. "I'd like to burn you at the stake!" retorted Betty Friedan in the midst of one heated debate in 1973.

Phyllis Schlafly offers a glimpse not just into the raging debates over feminism in the 1970s but also a window on the changing priorities of conservatism within the Republican party, especially the key roles women played in that shift. Born Phyllis Stewart in 1924 in St. Louis into a middle-class family that placed a high priority on education as well as Catholicism, she was raised during the Great Depression. Times were hard, especially after her father lost his job as a salesman, but her mother made sure she had a good education in local Catholic schools. An outstanding student, she won a four-year scholarship to Maryville College, a local Catholic school, but she did not find it academically challenging and arranged a transfer to Washington University, where she worked her way through college, graduating in 1944. The following year she earned a master's degree in political science from Radcliffe College at Harvard University.

Although her family was Republican, her real education as a political conservative began with her first job at the American Enterprise Association (later Institute) in Washington. The next year she returned to St. Louis where she managed a political campaign for a local Republican candidate. In 1949 she married Fred Schlafly, a prominent lawyer who hailed from a wealthy St. Louis Catholic family; she was twenty-four and he was thirty-nine. They bought a house across the Mississippi River in Alton, Illinois, and over the next fourteen years raised six children there.

As a young wife and mother, Phyllis Schlafly threw herself into local civic activities, including volunteering for the Republican Party. In the lead-up to the 1952 election, local party leaders approached her husband about running for Congress, but he declined. Then somebody said, "What about Phyllis?" and she said yes. The twenty-seven-year-old "Alton housewife" (as the press described her) ran a strong campaign, but did not prevail in the heavily Democratic district.

After a decade of local activism, Schlafly became well known in national Republican circles when she co-authored a book about Barry Goldwater, *A Choice, Not an Echo*, that figured prominently in his unsuccessful 1964 presidential campaign. At that point Schlafly and other conservative Republicans were more concerned with promoting a strident anti-communism at the height of the Cold War than with gender and cultural issues. Committed to making sure Republican women were recognized for their roles in party politics, she set her sights on winning the presidency of the National Federation of Republican Women in 1966. Despite strong support from the rank-and-file membership, she was denied that position because the Republican leadership deemed her too far to the right. In 1970 she made a second unsuccessful run for Congress.

Starting in 1972, Schlafly took up the cause of anti-feminism. "It's time to set the record straight," she announced in *The Phyllis Schlafly Report*, which she started in 1967. "The claim that American women are downtrodden and unfairly treated is the fraud of the century. The truth is that American women never had it so good. Why should we lower ourselves to 'equal rights' when we already have the status of special privilege?" A charismatic speaker and superb grassroots organizer, Schlafly successfully wove together homilies about women's traditional feminine roles (even though, as her critics pointed out, she hardly lived such a life herself) with a concrete political agenda. Soon she had become the public face of the conservative backlash against the resurgence of modern feminism.

The broad ranging debates about gender and women's roles unfolded in a contested political landscape after 1960. The civil rights movement expanded to attack the core racism of American society throughout the country, not just in the South. A resurgent youth movement challenged its elders and protested the Vietnam War. The nation endured assassinations, race riots, and a scandal that caused the resignation of President Richard Nixon in 1974. The election of Ronald Reagan in 1980 confirmed the growing ascendancy of a more conservative approach to government and economics, at the same time the social fabric of the country was undergoing fundamental demographic changes after the passage of a wide-ranging revision of the immigration laws in 1965. These broader developments were the backdrop against which Phyllis Schlafly, Betty Friedan, and many others debated the place of feminism in modern American life.

 ## THE REVIVAL OF FEMINISM

In 1960 there were no battered women's shelters, abortion was illegal, want-ads in newspapers were divided into "men's" and "women's" jobs, and the words *sexism* and *Ms.* had not been coined. Not a single university offered a course in women's studies, and women's sports programs were small and underfunded, if they existed at all. Over the next fifteen years, the landscape shifted dramatically. Suddenly women's issues and feminism seemed to be everywhere, challenging the unequal treatment that women received as citizens and members of families and leading to fundamental social change in the nation's laws, institutions, and culture. This revival of feminism (often called "second-wave feminism" (to distinguish it from the first wave of suffrage) had its roots in the 1960s and found its fullest flowering in the first half of the 1970s. Once these issues were on the national agenda, there was no turning back, even when feminist momentum slowed in the 1980s and 1990s.

Social movements do not just spring up when leaders announce a set of demands. Preconditions for the revival of feminism lay in the changing social and demographic bases of women's lives, especially increased labor force participation, greater access to higher education, a declining birth rate, and changing patterns of marriage. Probably the most important factor was the dramatic rise in women working in the postwar years, which undercut traditional gender expectations that domesticity and family were women's primary roles. To be female in America now usually included work and marriage, often childrearing and a career, and possibly bringing up children as a single parent, either by choice or after a divorce. These changing social realities created a major constituency for the revival of feminism in the 1960s and 1970s, especially when they occurred in a broader period of social and political unrest characterized by the civil rights movement, student activism, and opposition to the Vietnam War. They also created a counter-constituency for a backlash against feminism as a threat to traditional gender norms.

At the risk of oversimplifying a complex phenomenon, two different strands of feminism fueled this revival. The first was **women's rights activism**. Many of its followers served in appointive or elective office at various levels of government, and they knew each other through overlapping professional networks. An important spur was the creation of the President's Commission on the Status of Women in 1961 under the leadership of Eleanor Roosevelt. The commission's final report issued in 1963 was a fairly tame call for more equity in the workplace and family, but it did encourage the passage of the **Equal Pay Act** of 1963.

The addition of "sex" to Title VII of the **Civil Rights Act of 1964** was an even more far-reaching legislative achievement because it gave women a crucial legal tool to challenge workplace discrimination. In turn the enthusiastic reaction to Betty Friedan's *The Feminine Mystique* when it was published in 1963 suggested a groundswell of popular dissatisfaction with contemporary women's lives. In 1966 a group of women led by Friedan formed the **National Organization for Women (NOW)**, which styled itself as a civil rights organization for women. Soon NOW was the largest feminist organization in the country.

**Women's liberation** (or "women's lib" as the media dismissively called it) represented the second strand. In contrast to their more mainstream women's rights counterparts, women's liberationists were younger and more radical. They came to feminism through participation in civil rights and the anti–Vietnam War movement, experiences that increased their confidence but also fed frustration when they were primarily treated as coffee makers, note-takers, and sex objects ("Girls say yes to boys who say no"). By 1967 and 1968 women realized they needed a movement of their own. Often in or just out of college, these activists did not want to join NOW's mainstream; they wanted to dismantle patriarchy, replacing it with non-racist, non-sexist institutions. Eschewing hierarchical membership structures, women's liberation was all mass, no organization.

One of the most distinctive features of this brand of feminism was its embrace of the maxim "The personal is political." In consciousness-raising sessions women came together to talk honestly and often painfully about their lives, inevitably experiencing a "click" moment when they realized that other women shared their feelings. As radical feminist Shulamith Firestone said, "Three months of this sort of thing is enough to make a feminist of any woman." Operating independently in various cities such as New York, Boston, Chicago, and San Francisco, women's liberation went public at the **Miss America Pageant** in 1968 where protestors crowned a live sheep and deposited items of female oppression such as girdles and bras in a freedom trash can. Contrary to urban myth, no bras were burned but the name "bra burners" stuck.

After developing separately, the two strands began to coalesce around 1970. By now the media had discovered feminism. Coverage of events like the

7.1: Women's liberation took on beauty pageant culture when protestors targeted the Miss America pageant in Atlantic City on September 7, 1968. In addition to comparing the pageant to a cattle auction, radical feminists attacked Miss America as a "military death mascot" for traditionally entertaining troops in Vietnam.

Women's Strike for Equality organized by departing NOW president Betty Friedan to celebrate the fiftieth anniversary of the passage of the Nineteenth Amendment on August 26, 1970, brought the ideas of this powerful new movement to a much wider audience.

Although still an object of derision and jest, the women's movement (as it was now referred to) managed quite a few accomplishments in a short period of time. In 1972 the Equal Rights Amendment was sent to the states for what looked like speedy enactment. Shirley Chisholm, an African American member of Congress from New York, ran for president, kicking off her campaign at Sojourner Truth's gravesite. Congress passed Title IX of the Education Amendments Act of 1972, providing a huge spur to women's sports, which saw high school participation rates for girls increase from one in twenty-seven in 1971 to one in three by 1979. In January 1973 the Supreme Court upheld women's constitutional right to abortion in the far-reaching *Roe v. Wade* decision. Later that year feminist tennis star Billie Jean King trounced Bobby Riggs in the nationally-televised Battle of the Sexes. Suddenly the topic of women, which had been a dead issue just a decade before, was squarely on the national agenda.

Black and **Chicana feminism** also surged, and not just as a reaction to feeling unwelcome in the predominantly white women's movement, although that certainly was a factor. Among other things, such a scenario downplays

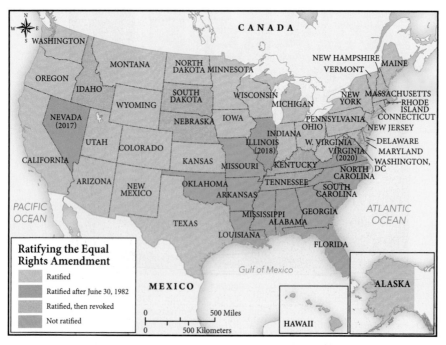

MAP 7.1

women of color's agency in identifying their own oppression and taking steps to address it. More importantly, the timetable is wrong. Black and Chicana feminism cannot be explained as variations or offshoots of the white movement because all three strands were developing simultaneously, shaped by their distinctive experiences in the civil rights movement, the Chicano movement, and the New Left, respectively. To paraphrase scholar Benita Roth, women took their own separate roads to feminism.

Changes in the civil rights movement starting in the mid-1960s, including the militant embrace of Black Power and Black nationalism, set in motion the emergence of Black feminism. As early as 1966, Black women came together as feminists to critique the increasingly masculinist tone of the movement. And they did this in their own groups, such as the Third World Women's Alliance (1968) and the National Black Feminist Organization (1973). Early anthologies such as Toni Cade Bambara's *The Black Woman* (1970), which reprinted Frances Beal's influential article "Double Jeopardy: To Be Black and Female," introduced the Black feminist movement to a wider audience.

More broadly, Black feminism affirmed that attention had to be paid to race and class as well as gender to understand the complexity of Black women's lives. The **Combahee River Collective**, a group of Black feminists in the Boston/Cambridge area who took their name from Harriet Tubman's 1863 guerilla action in the Port Royal region of South Carolina that freed more

7.2: Native American women brought a different agenda to feminism, notably a commitment to tribal sovereignty as a means to ensure the survival of Indian people. Native women also participated in "Red Power" events, such as the seizure of Alcatraz in 1969 and the occupation of Wounded Knee in Pine Ridge, South Dakota, in 1973, pictured here.

DOCUMENTING AMERICAN WOMEN

# Dolores Huerta and the Grape Boycott

Activist Dolores Huerta is often referred to as La Pasion-
ara (the passionate one), a moniker that recognizes her
lifelong commitment to the downtrodden and the power-
less, especially the nation's farm workers. Raised in Stock-
ton, California, Huerta and Cesar Chavez co-founded the
National Farm Workers Association, later the United Farm
Workers, in 1962. Here she describes the genesis of the
nationwide grape boycott that brought the conditions of
farm workers who harvested the crops to the attention of
consumers who bought the products, and the large roles
that women played on the picket lines.

We had been on strike for a few months and the growers were bringing
in strike-breakers from Mexico. They went and got court injunctions
limiting us to five people per field. Can you imagine five pickets on a
big thousand-acre field? So we were kind of stymied in terms of trying to keep the people from breaking the strike. In fact, at that time I
even went to Juárez, Mexico. That's where I met the poet Lalo Delgado,
where he did a leaflet for me, to keep the people from Juárez from
breaking the strike in Delano.

So we were talking about it and there was this Jewish attorney that
was volunteering to help us out, named Stu Weinberg. So, he said,
"Have you thought of doing a boycott? The civil rights movement is
doing a boycott. Have you thought of doing a boycott?" So we said,
"Hey, well, let's try it." So we had these young volunteers that had
come to work with us together with farmworkers, and we had no
money. So these volunteers hitch-hiked out to the East Coast. They
hitch-hiked to St. Louis. They hitch-hiked to New York; they hitch-
hiked to Chicago. Then we picked as our boycott target, because they

say that liquor is easy to boycott, so we picked the Schenley company, who had a wine grape operation, which hired about 400 workers. We picked them as our first target.

The strike broke out in September of 1965. Then the march to Sacramento was decided on, which was done in the Lenten period of 1966. People were marching to Sacramento, the farmworkers were marching to Sacramento, carrying signs that said "Boycott Schenley." So before the march got to Sacramento, the Schenley company decided to recognize the union.

So the strike lasted five years. It was a five-year strike, and we had a lot of the young people who came to join the strike from Berkeley. Then the doors were wide open. I mean, everybody came in and then we were out there on the road raising money for the strike. We invited Luis Valdez to come down and start the *Teatro Campesino*. Which I did, I invited him to come down and he did a *teatro*, which César saw, and César liked it. So then he became a permanent fixture in the strike and that was the beginning of the *Teatro Campesino*.

The whole boycott is a nonviolent tool. It's an economic sanction, so to speak, but it's a way that people can participate. One thing about nonviolence is that it opens the doors for everyone to participate: the children, the women. And women being involved on the picket lines made it easier for the men then to accept nonviolence. They would always say if they didn't have a woman, "We need some women on our picket line. We need some women here." It makes it a lot easier for them. Then they can justify not being macho tough, or macho revenge, you know. Just having the women there made it possible, I think, for the organization to practice its nonviolence.

SOURCE: Vincent Harding, "Interview with Dolores Huerta," found in Mario T. Garcia, ed., A Dolores Huerta Reader (Albuquerque: University of New Mexico Press, 2008), 182–83.

than 750 slaves, penned one of the most influential pieces of Black feminist theory in 1977. Looking at "what oppression is comprised of on a day-to-day basis," they refused to separate the multiple oppressions that shaped Black women's lives, including homophobia, thus staking a claim for Black lesbians in the broader freedom struggle. This theoretical statement anticipated the later concept of intersectionality, which recognizes that there is not one single oppression operating independently, but that all oppressions (especially race, class, and gender) are interrelated.

Chicana feminism also emerged independently from white feminism. The first Chicana feminist organizations began to appear around 1969 and 1970, drawing their energy and recruits from the wider Chicano movement (El Movimiento). Chicana feminists chose to work to increase the visibility and influence of women within the broader Chicano movement, rather than prioritizing cross-racial organizing with groups such as Black feminists. Chicana feminists proudly pointed to a tradition of activism exhibited by foremothers such as Luisa Moreno and Josefina Fierro in Mexican and Mexican American struggles for social change, as well as the prominent roles women played in Mexican-American civil rights groups in the 1940s and 1950s. In addition, labor activists such as Dolores Huerta and Jessie Lopez De La Cruz took key leadership roles in the United Farmworkers Union, which began organizing in the fields of the San Joaquin Valley in 1962. Important organizational milestones included the 1969 formation of Las Hijas de Cuauhtemoc at Long Beach State University, the 1970 founding of the Comisión Feminil Mexicana Nacional, and the first National Chicana Conference held in Houston in 1971.

White, Black, and Chicana feminism are all examples of **identity politics**, a key component of 1970s theory and praxis. The core concept behind identity politics is the existence and creation of a self-identified social group, usually defined in opposition to the dominant society. This shared experience of oppression or exclusion, often articulated through the process of consciousness-raising, leads to a goal of greater self-determination through political action, with the political constituency formed by its shared identity. Such an approach was obviously central to the emergence of second-wave feminism. If women didn't identify themselves as part of a group, where was the "we" in feminism?

Identity politics were extremely important to the emergence of **gay liberation**, commonly dated to the **Stonewall Riot** in New York City in 1969, where male patrons (and a few lesbians and trans women) at a gay bar fought back when busted by the police. The movement brought new pride and a collective sense to those who had been forced to live hidden lives "in the closet" by a society that identified their behavior as deviant. In order to demand better treatment and recognition as a group, gay men and lesbians first had to articulate and accept their shared identity as gay. In other words, they had to come out.

Feminism made particular sense to many (but not all) lesbians, who found the movement a supportive atmosphere to explore their connections with other women. "Feminism is the theory," Ti-Grace Atkinson boldly announced, "lesbianism is the practice." Some heterosexual feminists at first saw the issue of lesbianism as a tangent, or worse yet, a liability in their quest for broader public acceptance; Betty Friedan, for example, complained of a "lavender menace." And yet the realization that lesbians faced many of the same problems in employment, housing, credit, and parenting rights as other women eventually caused the gay/straight split to decrease. Led by such towering figures as Audre Lorde, Adrienne Rich, and Gloria Anzaldúa, a lesbian feminist perspective has been espe-

7.3: Audre Lorde was a self-described "Black, lesbian, mother, warrior, poet." Her most famous essay, "The Master's Tools Will Never Dismantle the Master's House" (1984), is a foundational text of Black feminist thought.

cially important in the fields of literature, poetry, and criticism, as well as foundational to the field of women, gender, and sexuality studies.

 ## NOT SO FAST, SISTERS

Feminists found all this change exhilarating: they really thought they were going to change the world. But powerful social movements run the risk of provoking equally powerful backlashes, which began to happen in the mid-1970s as women, and more than a few men, grew concerned about the rapidity of social change and openly challenged feminist goals. The Equal Rights Amendment and abortion became the main flashpoints.

The language of the Equal Rights Amendment is straightforward: "Equality of rights under the law shall not be denied or abridged by the United States or any State on the basis of sex." When it passed Congress in 1972, activists expected speedy ratification; by 1974, thirty-four states (out of a necessary thirty-eight) had ratified the amendment. The National Organization for Women made passage its highest priority, it was endorsed by a wide range of women's and labor organizations, and public opinion polls showed strong

7.4: Women picket the White House in 1977, rallying opposition to the Equal Rights Amendment, which they feared would cause women to be drafted and lose Social Security benefits. The ERA failed to win ratification by its 1982 deadline, but activists continue to press state legislatures to reopen the debate.

popular support for its adoption. But then the momentum stopped dead in its tracks, except for passage by Indiana in 1977. Activists won a three-year extension on the ratification deadline until 1982, but extensive lobbying in Florida, North Carolina, and Illinois failed to convince legislators to pass the amendment, and it went down to defeat.

A prime reason for the defeat was conservative Republican activist Phyllis Schlafly, whose STOP ERA organization first targeted the issue in 1972. Mobilizing masses of grassroots women, especially from evangelical churches and right-wing groups, the ranks of ERA opponents were swelled by those who feared that women had more to lose than gain by the sweeping (and exaggerated) changes they claimed were possible under the law, such as undermining a husband's responsibility to provide for his family, abolishing child support and alimony, and forcing women into the workforce, to say nothing of unisex toilets. ERA opponents descended on state capitals, dressed in their Sunday best and often bearing home-baked bread and apple pies, symbols of their traditional domestic roles. Their message: we like being treated as women; we don't want to be treated like men. Women have supplied a key constituency, especially at the grassroots level, for conservative mobilization initiatives ever since.

The ERA divide reminds us that the category of women, even politically active women, is too broad to encompass the whole gender. Those conflicting visions were on full display at the 1977 National Women's Conference held in

Houston. Following up on the designation by the United Nations of 1975 as International Women's Year, Congresswomen Bella Abzug and Patsy Mink convinced Congress to authorize $5 million for a conference of American women, with delegates to be selected in each of the fifty states. Feminists dominated the selection process in most states, and close to 20,000 women gathered in Houston as delegates and observers. After four days of intense discussion and politicking, the assembled women unanimously agreed on a national plan of action that included twenty-six resolutions on topics such as the ERA, violence against women, the special problems of minority women, lesbian rights, and reproductive freedom, including the right to abortion.

Across town in Houston, almost 15,000 conservative women, assembled by Schlafly and other right-wing leaders, held their own conference where they loudly asserted their allegiance to more traditional gender roles, especially the fundamental differences between the sexes, which they saw as the basis for family and civic life. Schlafly's message that women had more to lose than gain from feminism continued to resonate in the increasingly conservative political climate of the 1970s and 1980s, ushering in a period of stalemate and retrenchment for the women's movement.

In hindsight, however, the issue of abortion, not the Equal Rights Amendment, proved most divisive. When the Supreme Court handed down

7.5: The facet of the National Women's Conference held in Houston in November 1977 that most captured the popular imagination was a 2,600-mile torch relay that began in Seneca Falls, New York. Here the torch triumphantly arrives in Houston, where it was greeted by Billie Jean King (left), Bella Abzug (middle), and Betty Friedan (far right), among other celebrants. Bettye Lane, the photographer, captured many iconic images of second-wave feminism.

## DOCUMENTING AMERICAN WOMEN

# Conservative Complaints about Title IX

In 1975 Phyllis Schlafly took issue with the Education Amendments Act of 1972, popularly known as Title IX. The original impetus behind the legislation was the widespread discrimination women faced in all aspects of the educational experience, from students to administrators to professors, but gross disparities in access to sports quickly emerged as a primary concern. Here Schlafly criticizes the regulations drafted by the Department of Health, Education, and Welfare to carry out the law in the field of athletics.

The HEW Regulation is based on the "gender-free" approach demanded by the women's lib militants. It is dogma of the women's lib radicals that there really is no difference between men and women (except the sex organs), and they demand that everything touched by Federal and state law, bureaucratic regulation, the educational system, and public funding be absolutely "gender-free" so that males and females have identical treatment.

This dogma demands also that sex be treated as a "suspect" classification, just as race is now treated—so that the burden of proof is on the government (or on the school, or the industry, etc.) to justify any difference of treatment between the sexes at any time.

We reject the "gender-free" approach. We believe that there are many differences between male and female, and that we are entitled to have our laws, regulations, schools, and courts reflect these differences and allow for reasonable differences in treatment that reasonable men and women want.

We reject the argument that sex discrimination should be treated the same as race discrimination. There is vastly more difference between a man and woman than there is between a black and a white, and it is nonsense to adopt a legal and bureaucratic attitude that pretends that those differences do not exist. . . .

. . .

The entire area of intercollegiate athletics should be outside the juris-diction of the HEW Regulation because they are not "education" within the meaning of the Education Amendments of 1972 any more than fra-ternities and sororities are. Physical education classes are properly con-sidered part of the education process, but intercollegiate athletics are not. Furthermore, it is grossly unfair to make the colleges assume the financial burden of taking moneys out of their budget to balance, or even partially balance, moneys spent on income-producing sports which are able to pay their own way by gate receipts. If the American public wants to pay to watch certain athletic contests, that should be their right. But who is HEW to tell us that we must pay taxes to finance other athletic contests that the American public has no interest in watching?

The HEW Regulation is exceedingly arbitrary in assuming Federal control of all athletic programs. It specifies that, if the school or college "operates or sponsors a team in a particular sport for members of one sex but operates or sponsors no such team for members of the other sex, . . . members of the excluded sex must be allowed to try out for the team offered unless the sport involved is a contact sport" (#86.41). This rule would prohibit a school from balancing athletic expenditures by offering one sport for boys and a different sport for girls.

A good example of the result of such an arbitrary rule was what happened in the 1975 girls' bowling tournament in Illinois. An Illinois circuit court made a rule similar to this one in the HEW Regulation. The Dixon (Illinois) High School offered football for boys, but bowling for girls. The boys decided they would take advantage of the court ruling and complete for places on the girls' bowling team. Boys won four out of five places on the team. Then, at the I.H.S.A. girls' state championship bowling tournament held in Peoria, Illinois, in Febru-ary 1975, the Dixon boys easily walked off with the title. Everyone was angry and the tournament was a farce.

Bowling is, of course, a non-contact sport. This example shows how ridiculous it is to put girls against boys in most sports, even non-contact sports. If there is anyone who should be against forcing girls

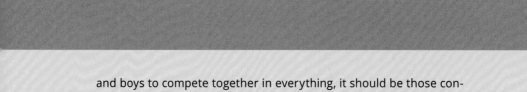

and boys to compete together in everything, it should be those concerned about women's athletics! The girls will be the big losers under
the "gender-free" coed mandate.

*SOURCE: "Statement on the HEW Regulation on Nondiscrimination on the
Basis of Sex by Phyllis Schlafly, National Chairman, National Committee to
Stop ERA,"* **Congressional Record** *(July 10, 1975), 22.147, 22.148.*

*Roe v. Wade* in 1973, it stepped into a minefield of controversy. The 7–2 decision was based on the constitutional right of privacy, which the justices ruled
"broad enough to encompass a woman's decision whether or not to terminate her pregnancy." Feminists, who had been calling for the reform or repeal
of abortion laws since the 1960s, acclaimed the decision as a vital cornerstone of women's ability to control their reproductive choices, but opponents
immediately mobilized to overturn the decision. An increasingly powerful
Right-to-Life movement placed the rights of the fetus (or unborn baby, in
their parlance) ahead of the rights of the woman to decide whether to carry
a pregnancy to term. In 1977 the Congress passed the **Hyde Amendment**,
which prohibited federal funds from paying for abortions for welfare recipi-
ents, even if the procedure was necessary to save the life of the mother; in
1980, the Supreme Court upheld the law.

Finding insufficient support for a constitutional amendment stating that
human life starts at conception, and perhaps mindful of the recent ratification
difficulties of the ERA, anti-abortion activists chose another strategy: system-
atically and deliberately chipping away at the provision of abortion services.
Following the logic of *Roe v. Wade*, which affirmed women's constitutional right
to abortion in the first trimester but opened the door to state regulation after that
point, in coming years abortion opponents pushed state and federal legislation
requiring, among other limits or restrictions, parental or spousal consent, mandated waiting periods, and the outlawing of certain late-term procedures; all of
these restrictions were upheld by the Supreme Court. At the same time violence
and intimidation against abortion providers caused many clinics to close, leaving women in large swaths of the country without easy access to a legal abortion.

The country remains deeply divided between pro-choice and pro-life stances, with support strongest for access to abortion in the first trimester (12 weeks) and in the case of rape, incest, or when the life of the mother is threatened, but declining dramatically after that. At its core this debate is not just about the rights of the fetus but also about women's roles in society, especially the ongoing sexual revolution, which opened to women many of the pleasures and responsibilities of sexual expression that had previously been reserved for men. For heterosexual partners, that new freedom necessitated access to reliable birth control (such as birth control pills, which were first introduced in 1960) as well as protection from unplanned pregnancies. To this abortion opponents replied that maybe they shouldn't be having that sex in the first place, or if they do, they should take the consequences. These ongoing debates show that many of the changes associated with second-wave feminism in the 1960s and 1970s remain controversial decades later.

 ## LEGISLATIVE LANDMARKS

In 1965 Congress enacted two wide-ranging pieces of legislation that had major implications for women, even though that was not their main intent. The first was the **Voting Rights Act** of 1965, one of the most significant pieces of civil rights legislation ever passed. Designed to enforce the voting rights guaranteed by the Fourteenth and Fifteenth Amendments to racial minorities, the law led to a dramatic increase in voter registration, especially by African Americans in the South. It was especially important for African American women, who finally were able to fully exercise the right to vote that had been supposedly guaranteed to them by the Nineteenth Amendment in 1920. As activist Dorothy Height observed in 1970, "Fifty years ago women got suffrage . . . but it took lynching, bombing, the civil rights movement and the Voting Rights Act to get it for Black women and Black people." Amendments to the law in 1975 extended the protections to "language minorities" including Native Americans, Asian Americans, Alaskan Natives and Spanish-speaking citizens, thereby expanding the voting rights of women in those groups as well.

The other significant legislation passed in 1965 was the **Hart-Celler Immigration and Nationality Act**. Since 1924, incoming immigration had been severely curtailed by a quota system that set limits on racial groups based on their percentage of the general population in 1890; southern and eastern Europeans were the main targets, in addition to Asian Americans, who had been excluded since the 1880s. The new law scrapped the old racial quotas, instituting instead general numerical caps for the Eastern and Western Hemispheres. Now many more immigrants came from Asia, the Middle East, and Central and South America, and fewer from Europe.

### DOCUMENTING AMERICAN WOMEN

# A Hmong American Immigrant Story

The journey that brought Shue-Qa Moua to the United States began during the Vietnam War when the Central Intelligence Agency (CIA) recruited thousands of Hmong people in Laos to fight against the communist Pathet Lao in what became known as "the secret war." When the United States withdrew from Southeast Asia in 1975, many of those Hmong soldiers, including her father, fled to Thailand. The next year the family emigrated to the United States. Shue-Qa Moua was born in California and later settled in Minnesota, where she shared this poignant story about a treasured family memento with the Minnesota's Immigrants project of the Minnesota Digital Library.

During the Vietnam War, thousands of Hmong men were recruited to fight alongside the Americans. The fall of Saigon in 1975 would force the Hmong's great leader, General Vang Pao, and more than 100,000 other Hmongs to seek political asylum in Thailand. In that very same year of 1975, my father put my mother, her two brothers, and both my grandmothers on a boat to cross the Mekong River to Thailand while he stayed behind to settle unfinished business as a soldier who fought alongside the Americans.

Before sending them off, he gave my mother a silver bar, or as the Hmong will call it, *choj nyiaj*. During that era, these silver bars could be exchanged for other goods, very similar to currency. Silver bars were traditionally used to pay for one's bride and for medicinal purposes

The law also opened the doors to Vietnamese and Cambodian refugees who were fleeing turmoil and instability after the American withdrawal from Southeast Asia, as well as Cubans fleeing the Castro regime. In addition to the lifting of outmoded racial quotas, the law greatly expanded the ability of

as well. But to my mother, this specific bar that was given to her by my father was a token of his love and the only item that she would have in memory of him if she should never see him again. To this day, the silver bar remains close to my mother, holding great sentimental value.

Some weeks later, my father reunited with my mother in a refugee camp in Thailand. In November 1976, my parents emigrated to the United States and spent some years living in New York, where they had their first child and began to seek the American Dream. During the first decade of living in the United States, my parents moved several times to four different states trying to find steady work to support their growing family. After many years of chasing the American Dream, my father finally found work as a social worker for the county and bought the family their first home in 1988 in California. In 1992, my father passed away unexpectedly. It's been a long time since he's been gone but even so, when my mother tells stories about the life that she and my father lived to the journey they took to cross the Mekong River and to the first years that they spent in America, I can still hear the joy in her voice as she reminisces about the times she and my father spent together. When I look at this silver bar, I not only think about the love that was shared between my parents, but I also use it to remind me of my parents' struggles from one country to another, the cultural values of the Hmong and, most of all, to reflect on myself and to never forget my roots, and to continue the journey that my parents started for me, and then to have my children continue my journey, and their children theirs.

SOURCE: immigrants.mndigital.org/exhibits/show/immigrantstories-exhibit/item/512

relatives to join family members already legally residing in the country without counting against the numerical caps. Many immigrants from Mexico, as well as Central and South America and the Caribbean, took advantage of this second option.

What was so profoundly different about this round of immigration was that women came in equal or greater numbers to men. Only among nineteenth century Irish immigrants did women predominate; in all other groups, the sex ratio always skewed male. As part of this post-1965 chain migration, newly arrived immigrant women, including wives, immediately joined the labor force in numbers comparable to native-born American women, also a dramatic shift from earlier patterns. While some recent immigrants found opportunities in high tech or the professions, especially medicine, new arrivals usually entered the economic structure at the very bottom, taking the least desirable jobs, such as domestic service. And when they exited domestic service, they often were relegated to "dirty work" such as cleaning rooms in hotels and offices or changing bedpans in hospitals and nursing homes. The willingness of recent immigrants to take such jobs happened in tandem with an expansion of options for African American women. As a result, the percentage of Black women who were domestic servants fell from almost 40 percent in 1960 to just 2 percent in 1990.

The changes set in motion by the 1965 law ushered in a period of mass immigration not seen since the early 1900s: the number of immigrants in the country quadrupled from 9.6 million in 1970 to 44.4 million in 2017. The surge coincided with broader developments reshaping both the domestic and global economies. In many areas around the world, rapid urbanization and uneven development had adversely affected both rural and urban dwellers. The increased ease of global travel, plus the option of staying in touch with family back home through cheap phones and the Internet, encouraged outmigration in search of a better life. Simultaneously a shift in the United States

7.6: For many recent immigrants to the United States, the next step was becoming a citizen. Here 5,000 new citizens, including Thu Bich Le, formerly of Vietnam, are sworn in at a mass ceremony held at Boston's beloved Fenway Park on September 14, 2010.

from a manufacturing to a postindustrial, service-oriented economy meant that many relatively well-paid industrial jobs disappeared, often outsourced to other countries, such as China. At the same time the gap between rich and poor widened, especially after the 1980s. As the United States became part of an increasingly globalized economy, so too did women's lives, whether they joined the workforce in the United States or toiled in factories and sweatshops for American corporations abroad.

 # A SHIFT TO THE RIGHT

The presidential election of 1980 marked the first appearance of the **gender gap**, a political phenomenon that has been present in varying degrees in every election since. The gender gap is the difference between the percentage of women and the percentage of men voting for a candidate. In 1980 the gap was 8 percent, with women favoring Jimmy Carter; in 1984 it was 6 percent for Walter Mondale, who made history by choosing the first woman, Geraldine Ferraro, as a vice-presidential candidate on a major party ticket. Despite the gender difference in voting, Ronald Reagan won both elections. Remember that the gender gap works both ways: even if more women tend to vote Democratic, more men are voting Republican. And voting patterns are very much influenced by larger political developments.

The 1980 election represented the culmination of the resurgence of modern conservatism that had been building since the late 1950s. Women, predominantly white, middle-to-upper-middle-class suburban women at the grassroots level, provided a key constituency for this shift. As far back as the anti-suffrage movement, conservative women mobilized around a more traditional view of women's rights and responsibilities. In the 1920s and 1930s conservative women were often identified with patriotic organizations that challenged the growing role of the federal government and adopted an isolationist stance toward world affairs. In the 1950s at the height of the Cold War, conservative women's grassroots activism revolved around anti-communism at home and abroad.

Far from their stereotyped image as "little old ladies in tennis shoes," these politically savvy women often had experienced a "something just doesn't feel right" epiphany that paralleled the "click" moment that drew many women to feminism. Fearful of the threat that communism posed to schools and churches, conservative women scrutinized local institutions carefully for any challenge to the Christian-based, family-oriented society they felt was key to American democratic institutions. Many of these grassroots activists gravitated toward the Republican party, supplying a strong constituency for Dwight Eisenhower's election in 1952 and 1956.

In the late 1950s well-organized conservative women moved beyond local politics to join a broader national conservative movement. Their grassroots energy played a major role in the selection of Barry Goldwater as the Republican candidate in 1964. Even though he lost in a landslide to Lyndon Johnson, there was no denying the growing political clout of the right, which gradually coalesced around Ronald Reagan, a former Hollywood actor who had served as a hard-line conservative governor of California from 1967 to 1975. Grassroots women played a key role in the political realignment that elected Reagan in 1980. And ever since, conservative women have been a vocal force in politics for a pro-family, pro-religion, community-based vision of what American society should look like. Concern about the rapidity of social change and outright disapproval of feminism's goals and priorities remained core principles of the conservative agenda. And conservative activists found welcome partners in popular culture and media.

In a widely read 1991 book titled *Backlash: The Undeclared War Against American Women*, journalist Susan Faludi described the powerful counterattack against the gains American women had won in the 1960s and 1970s, detailing how the media consistently and inaccurately held the women's movement responsible for every ill afflicting modern women—from infertility to eating disorders to rising divorce rates to the "man shortage." For example, Faludi picked apart the statistics put forward by the media showing a drastic decline in the chances for college-educated, unwed women over thirty to marry. In *Newsweek's* inflammatory—and inaccurate—headline in 1986, women over forty were "more likely to be killed by a terrorist" than make it to the altar. She also demolished widely reported stories about supposed trends of widespread emotional burnout among career women or an "infertility epidemic" among professional women who had postponed childbearing. In a climate of backlash, such accusations, even when untrue, seemed plausible.

Faludi proposed a different interpretation. It was a myth that the women's movement and feminism were women's own worst enemy; it was a myth that women were unhappy precisely because they had achieved equality. Instead, many contemporary women's problems were traceable to the fact that they did not have *enough* equality, not that they had too much. As a journalist, Faludi realized the power of the media and popular culture to shape public attitudes and affect public policy. Her agenda was to show that women still had many battles to fight before equality would be achieved, and to reaffirm that many women were consciously resisting the backlash message, both individually and collectively. Nowhere was this more clear than in the rise of **global feminism**.

In the story of how global feminism became a vibrant worldwide phenomenon, the United Nations served as what one scholar called an "unlikely godmother" by sponsoring a series of conferences that brought together women from all over the world. Following the designation of 1975 as International Women's Year, the first UN Women's Conference was held in Mexico City. When it became clear that the myriad issues on the agenda could not possibly be addressed in a year, the initiative was expanded into the International Decade of Women, with additional conferences held in Copenhagen in 1980 and Nairobi in 1985. As Caribbean activist and participant Peggy Antrobus noted, "The Decade opened spaces for women from communities all over the world to meet" and facilitated women "finding their public voice at the international level." Making links between global trends and local realities is at the core of global feminism. So too is a belief in empowering women as agents of social change.

U.S. women played an important, but hardly dominant, role in the rise of global feminism. In the 1980s American feminists, stymied at home, welcomed the chance to take their activism onto the world stage, providing important seed money and talent through organizations such as the Feminist Majority Foundation and the International Planned Parenthood Foundation. Robin Morgan founded the Sisterhood is Global Institute and Charlotte Bunch established the Center for Women's Global Leadership at Rutgers.

Finding common ground about what constituted women's issues was challenging. Especially at the beginning there was a clear rift between women from the Global North (industrialized Europe, North America, Japan, and Northern Asia), who tended to focus on questions of legal rights and women's social and political equality, and women from the Global South (Africa, the Asian subcontinent, and Latin and South America), who looked more broadly at questions of poverty, disease, and the need for economic development as most relevant to women's advancement. "To be equal in poverty with men is no blessing," said one Copenhagen participant succinctly.

In 1995 more than 30,000 citizens of the world journeyed to Beijing for the **Fourth United Nations World Conference on Women**, where they heard First Lady Hillary Rodham Clinton proclaim, "If there is one message that echoes forth from this conference, it is that human rights are women's rights . . . And women's rights are human rights." The conference platform set three preconditions for women's global advancement—equality, development, and peace—and boldly situated women's issues within broader social and economic transformation. In this formulation practically everything was now a women's issue.

The United Nations may have been the unlikely godmother of global feminism, but the Internet and social media have become its lifelines, linking the local to the global and back again in an increasingly interconnected and information-driven world. The possibilities for dispersing critical information and research, sharing contacts and strategies, and mobilizing literally billions of people around the globe are the way of the future, women's and everyone else's.

# Global Feminism

Activist Charlotte Bunch called the United Nations World Conferences on Women "global town meetings." Each conference featured a similar structure of two parallel meetings: official delegates representing their countries met in one, representatives of nongovernmental organizations (NGOs) met in a second. Bunch's speech to the opening NGO plenary in Beijing in 1995 recognized the critical role women would play as a global force in shaping the twenty-first century.

This Conference is occurring at a critical juncture in time throughout the world because it is a time of transition—a time when the ways of governing, the ways of living and of doing business, the ways of interacting amongst people and nations are in flux. In my region, Europe and North America, which has a long history of war and domination that has affected the entire globe, we see this transition in what is called the end of the Cold War. We have now what I call the Hot Peace. Rather than a truly peaceful era, we are seeing a shift in power blocs in which the anticipated peace dividend has turned instead into increased racial, ethnic, religious and gender-based conflicts and violence. In this escalation, the role of women—questions of women's human rights and the violation of women as a symbol of their cultures and peoples—has become central.

. . .

This Beijing conference comes at a critical time in the process of women becoming a global force in the world and has become in many ways a referendum on the role that women will play in the twenty-first century. In that regard, it is also a referendum on the human rights of women. It is about how far we have come in being recognized as full and equal citizens of the world, with equal human rights and with full responsibility for the future direction of the globe. Whether addressing poverty, education, health, violence, etc., all of these are issues of women's access to full humanity, to full human rights, to the conditions necessary to exercise political rights and to take responsibility for enacting visions of where we want to go in the world. This is what it takes for us to become a global political force involved in shaping the twenty-first century.

. . .

. . . I think of these UN world conferences as global town meetings. They are opportunities where we meet and talk to each other across the lines of nationality, across lines that we don't often have other opportunities to cross. But as global town meetings, they are also occasions for us to show the world our visions. Looking at the world through women's eyes is an excellent slogan for this forum because this is the place where we can demonstrate the visions of possibility that come from women. . . . We are participating now, we are watching, we are demanding, and we are here to see if this can become the arena of real participation where global governance and policies can be created with a human face that is both male and female and where all the diversity of both male and female can emerge. And if this does not prove possible, women must say to the United Nations and to all of our governments, that we have a vision for the future and that is where we are going. We hope that they will allow us to participate and to lead. If they don't, we will take leadership anyway and show that the world can be better for all in the twenty-first century.

*SOURCE: Charlotte Bunch, "Through Women's Eyes: Global Forces Facing Women in the 21st Century," speech delivered to the Opening Plenary, NGO Forum '95. Huairou, China, August 31, 1995.*

## *Timeline*

**1963**
Passage of the Equal Pay Act

**1965**
The Hart-Celler Immigration and Nationality Act is signed into law
Voting Rights Act passed

**1966**
Phyllis Schlafly seeks presidency of the National Federation of Republican Women, but is defeated

**1966**
Formation of the National Organization for Women (NOW)

**1967**
Schlafly starts the *Phyllis Schlafly Report*

**1968**
Women's liberation goes public at the Miss America Pageant

**1968**
Formation of the Third World Women's Alliance

**1969**
Stonewall Riot in New York City

**1969–1970**
First Chicana feminist organizations begin to appear

**AUGUST 26, 1970**
The Women's Strike for Equality organized by Betty Friedan

## KEY TERMS

Chicana feminism
Civil Rights Act of 1964
Combahee River Collective
Equal Pay Act
Fourth United Nations World Conference on Women

gay liberation
gender gap
global feminism
Hart-Celler Immigration and Nationality Act
Hyde Amendment
identity politics
Miss America Pageant

National Organization for Women (NOW)
*Roe v. Wade*
second-wave feminism
Stonewall Riot
Voting Rights Act
women's liberation
women's rights activism

## Suggested Readings

McRae, Elizabeth Gillespie. *Mothers of Massive Resistance: White Women and the Politics of White Supremacy* (2018).
Nickerson, Michelle M. *Mothers of Conservatism: Women and the Postwar Right* (2012)

| 1972 | 1973 | 1977 |
|---|---|---|
| Equal Rights Amendment passes Congress and goes to the states for ratification; Title IX of Education Amendments Act increases access to sports | National Black Feminist Organization is founded | Congress passes the Hyde Amendment |
| **1972** | **JANUARY 1973** | **1980** |
| Phyllis Schlafly starts "Stop ERA" campaign | *Roe v. Wade* | Election of Ronald Reagan |
| | **1974** | **1980** |
| | Resignation of Richard Nixon | First appearance of the gender gap |
| | **1975** | |
| | International Women's Year | |

Olcott, Jocelyn. *International Women's Year: The Greatest Consciousness-Raising Event in History* (2017).

Rosen, Ruth. *The World Split Open: How the Modern Women's Movement Changed America* (2000).

Roth, Benita. *Separate Roads to Feminism: Black, Chicana, and White Feminist Movements in America's Second Wave* (2004).

Spruill, Marjorie. *Divided We Stand: The Battle over Women's Rights and Family Values that Polarized America* (2018).

Learn more with this chapter's digital tools at http://www.oup.com/he/ware1e.

# eight

# Our Bodies, Our Politics, 1992–2020

**CHAPTER OUTLINE**

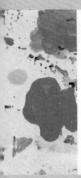

"The Year of the Woman" Just Keeps Happening

Women in the Military

The Changing Terrain of Sex and Gender

Changing American Families

Jobs and Justice

2020: A Moment of Reckoning

Anita Hill takes the oath before testifying in the nationally televised Senate Judiciary Committee hearings on the confirmation of Supreme Court justice Clarence Thomas in September 1991. Her testimony put the issue of sexual harassment squarely on the national agenda.

"Are you a scorned woman?" Anita Hill was asked by a member of the all-male Senate Judiciary Committee. "Do you have a martyr complex?" These were just some of the hostile questions addressed to Hill in October 1991 when she testified at the confirmation hearings of Clarence Thomas for nomination to the U.S. Supreme Court. In her prepared remarks, Hill, an Oklahoma law professor who had been Thomas's subordinate at the Department of Education and the Equal Opportunity Employment Commission (EEOC) in the 1980s, painted a pervasive pattern of inappropriate behavior on the part of her boss, including pressure to date him as well as graphic discussions of pornography and sex during meetings in his office. Even though Hill felt extremely uncomfortable with this unwanted attention, she did not quit her job, which she felt was important to her career advancement. Hill's forceful and measured accusations, broadcast to a national television audience riveted by this unexpected turn in the hearings, were denied by Thomas, who called the event "a high-tech lynching," an especially loaded phrase coming from an African American man.

Anita Hill's personal journey to that Senate conference room began on a farm in Okmulgee County, Oklahoma in 1956. The youngest of thirteen children, her childhood was "one of a lot of hard work and not much money, but it was one of solid family affection as represented by my parents." Her family's Baptist faith was an important part of her upbringing as was an emphasis on education. She graduated from Oklahoma State University in 1977 and then headed east to Yale Law School, where she received her JD degree in 1980.

After a brief stint in private practice in Washington, Hill accepted the offer of Thomas, whom she had met through a mutual friend, to become his assistant at the Department of Education. At first she felt they had a positive working relationship but then he began to pressure her to go out with him, as well as engage in sexually explicit conversations. Nevertheless when Thomas was made chair of the EEOC, she decided to follow him there, attracted by the prospect of interesting professional work. After a short hiatus, the pattern of sexual harassment resumed, and by early 1983 Hill was looking for other employment. She took a teaching position at Oral Roberts University and then joined the University of Oklahoma law faculty in 1986, thinking the experience was behind her. But when a member of the Senate Judiciary Committee reached out to her in 1991 in advance of the confirmation hearings, "I felt that I had to tell the truth. I could not keep silent."

In an attempt to discredit the allegations, supporters of the nomination viciously attacked Anita Hill's personal integrity. Feminists rallied around her, pointing out that her experience of sexual harassment on the job was unfortunately all too common. Opinion polls at the time showed wide divergence in whether people believed Clarence Thomas or Anita Hill, with attitudes failing to break down neatly along race and gender lines. The Senate narrowly confirmed Thomas by a vote of 52–48.

Anita Hill did not choose to initiate a public discussion of sexual harassment, it chose her. In fact the identification of sexual harassment as a specific problem, rather than "just the way things are," was a fairly recent development, a direct outgrowth of second-wave feminism. Legal scholar Catharine MacKinnon helped name the problem in the late 1970s, and then articulated the legal argument that a hostile work environment discriminates against women and thus is a form of sex discrimination. The Supreme Court upheld this view in *Meritor Savings Bank v. Vinson* in 1986.

The skepticism that greeted Hill's accusation on Capitol Hill in 1991 (which had eerie parallels to Christine Blasey Ford's testimony against Supreme Court nominee Brett Kavanaugh in 2018) shows how women who speak out struggle to be taken seriously and believed. And yet the explosion of activism after 2017 set in motion by the **#MeToo** movement and **Black Lives Matter** shows that things can and do change.

In the first two decades of the twenty-first century, the United States saw dramatic surges in women's participation in politics and a new urgency to feminist demands. Those decades also confirmed the continued strength of the conservative movement and a corresponding rise in partisanship, especially in the years after the election of Donald Trump in 2016—all of which unfolded in the midst of an increasingly globalized, interconnected world, which the **COVID-19** pandemic brought starkly home.

# "THE YEAR OF THE WOMAN" JUST KEEPS HAPPENING

Angered at the treatment that Anita Hill received on Capitol Hill and in the national media ("They just don't get it" was a popular refrain), a record number of women successfully ran for public office, earning 1992 the designation of "The Year of the Woman." Patty Murray, Diane Feinstein, Barbara Boxer, and Carole Moseley Braun joined Nancy Kassebaum and Barbara Mikulski in the Senate. Twenty-four new women were elected to the House of Representatives, bringing the total to forty-seven (with Democrats outnumbering Republicans 3–1). Women also increased their representation in state and local elections across the country. Two decades later, many of those women had accumulated the seniority to be major players in politics. First elected in 1986, Nancy Pelosi's ascension to Speaker of the House of Representatives in 2007 made her the highest-ranking female politician in American history.

The 1992 election also introduced voters to a woman who would become one of the most respected but also deeply polarizing figures in recent American life: Hillary Rodham Clinton, the wife of presidential candidate Bill Clinton.

8.1: Future First Lady Hillary Rodham Clinton first got a taste of Washington politics when she served on the staff of the Watergate impeachment hearings in 1974, but she was not introduced to the country until her husband's 1992 presidential campaign, when this official portrait was taken. She has been in the public eye ever since.

Educated at Wellesley College and Yale Law School, whip-smart and committed to her career, she was an awkward fit for the traditional role of First Lady. (Michelle Obama later struggled with this disconnect as well.) Early in the administration, she took a leading role in her husband's failed health care initiative. In his second term she "stood by her man" when the president was threatened with impeachment in 1998 over his sexual involvement with a young intern named Monica Lewinsky. Most feminists likewise stood by Bill Clinton, prioritizing the benefits of having a Democratic president in the White House over speaking out about the clearly inappropriate behavior of its occupant. Hillary Clinton weathered that storm, and when her husband left office, she ran successfully for a New York seat in the U.S. Senate in 2000.

Eight years later the presidential campaign was replete with gender and racial symbolism. In August Republican presidential candidate John McCain chose Sarah Palin as his running mate. Palin, relatively unknown on the national political scene, offered an impressive personal story: the forty-four-year-old mother of five children, she had risen from the town council of tiny Wasilla, Alaska, to the governorship of the state, propelled by a charismatic public persona and conservative fiscal and social values that resonated with Alaskan—and potentially national—voters. But to do that she had to convince the electorate that she had a legitimate claim to political authority, something that has traditionally been more difficult for female candidates than their male counterparts.

On the Democratic side, the 2008 primary campaign pitted an African American man against a white woman, a choice that would have been inconceivable just a few years earlier. Many feminists rallied around Hillary Clinton's candidacy, delighted to finally have such a talented candidate running for national office after years of encouraging women to aim high. But not all feminists signed on to the Clinton campaign. Many were just as drawn to Barack Obama's vision of hope and change for America, and the inspirational prospect of having a young African American family in the White House.

The Republican party learned that gender alone did not determine voting patterns. Their attempt to woo disgruntled female voters disappointed at

Clinton's loss of the nomination by nominating Sarah Palin fizzled. As Gloria Steinem memorably quipped, to "vote in protest for McCain/Palin would be like saying, 'Somebody stole my shoes, so I'll amputate my legs.'" Barack Obama went on to win the general election, and Hillary Clinton served with distinction as his Secretary of State from 2009 to 2013.

The way that gender and voting play out in unpredictable ways in politics was on full display in the 2016 presidential campaign, which pitted Hillary Rodham Clinton against Donald Trump, a New York real estate developer and television personality with no experience in national politics. Clinton assembled a broad coalition of Democratic voters but faced strong hostility from wide swaths of the population who harbored negative views about her candidacy, often linked to her gender. On the Republican side, Trump's vision of "Make America Great Again" spoke to many conservative voters who felt passed over by the direction the country was moving. The thrice-married candidate also appealed successfully to evangelical voters, who looked the other way at his treatment of women, including a boast captured on tape that he could "grab them by the pussy" whenever he wanted.

Clinton led for much of the campaign, but on election night the force of a conservative tide became clear. Even though Clinton won the popular tally by more than 2 million votes, Trump eked out a victory in the Electoral College, mainly bolstered by his wins in previously solidly Democratic states like Michigan, Ohio, and Wisconsin. When the votes were analyzed, once again there were clear—and to many, surprising—gender and racial dimensions: more than half (53 percent) of white women voters cast their ballots for Donald Trump. At the same time 94 percent of Black women who voted and 68 percent of Latina voters chose Clinton. To put it bluntly, white women played a significant role in the election of Donald Trump and women of color will be key to the future of the Democratic Party.

Smarting from the Trump electoral victory, feminists redoubled their efforts to elect Democratic women to political office, with dramatic results in the 2018 election. The results for the 116th U.S. Congress were especially striking: 106 women in the House of Representatives and 25 women in the Senate, one-quarter of the upper chamber. Continuing a trend that had been building since the 1990s, Democrats put forward and elected far more women candidates than Republicans.

Just as striking as the numbers was the diversity of these elected officials, including the first two Native American women (Deb Haaland of New Mexico and Sharice Davids of Kansas, who identifies as **LGBTQ**) and the first two Muslim women (Ilhan Omar of Minnesota, a refugee from Somalia, and Rashida Tlaib of Michigan). Most press attention gravitated towards "the Squad"—Alexandria Ocasio-Cortez of New York (quickly dubbed AOC), the youngest woman ever elected to Congress; Ayanna Pressley of Massachusetts; and Omar and Tlaib—who made it clear they intended to be heard, despite their freshman status. Said Representative Katie Porter, another newly

8.2: As a result of the 2018 election, the U.S. Congress boasted a record number of women in the House and Senate, including two Muslim American women, two Native American women, and twenty-nine-year-old Alexandria Ocasio-Cortez. Here the 84 women in the House of Representatives, led by Majority Leader Nancy Pelosi, assemble for a group portrait on the steps of the Capitol.

elected member of Congress from California, "Yeah, we have to fix this shit." Unfortunately Porter didn't last long, forced to resign after allegations of an affair with a female aide circulated by Porter's estranged husband (Porter identified as bisexual). As always, women in elected office were forced to navigate complicated terrain, political and otherwise.

There is no question that the political climate has changed for the better for women over the last fifty years. And yet women in politics, both as candidates and as office holders, continued to be subjected to stereotypes and discrimination that limited their progress. That 131 women served in Congress in 2019 was a definite improvement over the 19 serving in 1960, but still far from gender equity. As a political scientist sagely pointed out after the 2018 election, "We are not going to see, in one cycle, an end to underrepresentation of women in American politics that we've seen for 250 years. The concern is, we need this energy and engagement for the long haul. This is a marathon, not a sprint."

 # WOMEN IN THE MILITARY

Back in the 1970s the idea of drafting women was so unimaginable that it helped derail the Equal Rights Amendment. Now women serve and die in the armed forces alongside men. The story of women in the military is recent history in the making, closely aligned with the priorities of American foreign policy before and after the terrorist attacks on the World Trade Center on September 11, 2001. One of the most salient trends is the prevalence of what are often called "forever wars," endless conflicts with no clear paths to victory that are undertaken under the rubric of the War on Terrorism. The deployment of U.S. troops to Iraq and Afghanistan fits this pattern.

It is hard to imagine an institution more "male" than the military and yet women have volunteered and served throughout the twentieth century, including both world wars and in Vietnam. As the Vietnam War wound down, the military instituted a draft lottery and in 1973 conscription ended. President Jimmy Carter proposed reinstituting draft registration in 1980, and there was discussion of registering women alongside men, but the idea of universal conscription was rejected by the Supreme Court in *Royster v. Goldberg* in 1981. At that point the United States committed to an all-volunteer army, and women were suddenly much more part of the

8.3: Women play increasingly large roles in the United States military, where they find opportunities but also face challenges from a macho military culture. In 1990 Sergeant Carol LaRoche from Birmingham, Alabama, proudly deployed with the U.S. 24th Infantry Division of the U.S. Army to Saudi Arabia during Operation Desert Shield.

picture. Post-Vietnam, armed services morale was low and a military career not very desirable. One way to fill the quotas was to recruit and train more women.

In retrospect, the first Gulf War in 1990–1991 was an important turning point in popular acceptance of women's new roles in the military. More than 40,000 women deployed in Operation Desert Storm and Desert Shield and twelve women lost their lives. By the time of Operation Iraqi Freedom in 2003, women comprised approximately 14 percent of the armed forces. The American public was riveted by the story of Private Jessica Lynch, who was captured and later released to great fanfare, but the fate of her best friend, Lori Piestewa, got much less attention. Piestewa, who was driving the Humvee in which Lynch was riding, was fatally wounded in the attack, the first woman to die in that conflict.

Piestewa, who was the daughter of a Hopi father and a Hispanic mother, represents the diverse racial and ethnic makeup of the modern army where between a third and half of enlisted women are Hispanic or a racial minority. Female recruits are more diverse than male recruits and the general civilian population as a whole, although their overall numbers are lower than men's. In 2017 women comprised 16 percent of the active duty force (up from 9 percent in 1980 and 1 percent in 1970), and 18 percent of commissioned officers.

### DOCUMENTING AMERICAN WOMEN

## Sexual Assaults in the Military

Despite—or perhaps because of—playing an increasingly large role in the military, women in all branches of the armed services face deeply engrained patterns of misogyny that affect their ability to do their jobs, most notably a military culture that condones and often leaves unpunished sexual harassment and assault. In 2013 a Senate subcommittee heard testimony on this topic from women service members, including Anu Bhagwati, a former Marine Corps captain who became executive director of SWAN (the Service Women's Action Committee).

Military sexual violence is a very personal issue for me. During my five years as a Marine officer, I experienced daily discrimination and sexual harassment. I was exposed to a culture rife with sexism, rape jokes, pornography, and widespread commercial sexual exploitation of women and girls both in the United States and overseas.

My experiences came to a head while I was stationed at the School of Infantry at Camp Lejeune, NC, from 2002 to 2004, where I witnessed reports of rape, sexual assault, and sexual harassment swept under the rug by a handful of field grade officers. Perpetrators were promoted or transferred to other units without punishment, while victims were accused of lying or exaggerating their claims in order to ruin men's reputations.

As a company commander at the School of Infantry, I ultimately chose to sacrifice my own career to file an equal opportunity investigation

As had traditionally been true for men, many women saw joining the armed forces as a chance to earn good pay and gain technical training and opportunities for advancement. Unfortunately the military put up roadblocks practically every step of the way. The rule that really tripped women up was the one excluding them from "combat-related" job categories, which in 1980 kept

against an offending officer. I was given a gag order by my commanding officer, got a military protective order against the officer in question, lived in fear of retaliation and violence from both the offender and my own chain of command, and then watched in horror as the offender was not only promoted but also given command of my company.

Many of the women who were impacted by these incidents, including me, are no longer in the military. However, all of the officers who were complicit in covering up these incidence (sic) have since retired or are still serving on Active Duty.

I was devastated because I loved and still love the Marine Corps.

I wish my experience was unique, but in the last few years of working on these issues, and in the hundreds of cases we handle each year on SWAN's helpline, I have discovered that rape, sexual assault, and sexual harassment are pervasive throughout the military. Sexual violence occurs today in every branch of service in both operational and non-operational environments, in both combat arms, as well as support units, and affects both men and women.

. . .

I will close by saying that today we are looking at an institution that desperately needs to be shown the next steps forward. Senators, do not let today's servicemembers become another generation of invisible survivors.

*SOURCE: "Testimony on Sexual Assaults in the Military," Hearing before the Subcommittee on Personnel of the Committee on Armed Services, United States Senate, 113th Congress, First Session, March 13, 2013 (Washington, DC: Government Printing Office, 2014), 10, 11.*

them out of a whopping 73 percent of all positions. Even though more categories gradually opened over time, the combat exclusion meant that it was very difficult to get the experience and training necessary for promotion. The lines between combat and non-combat became especially porous during the Iraqi and Afghanistan operations, where there were no front lines, just the constant threat of engagement. Not until 2012 was the combat exemption finally lifted.

The deeply ingrained misogyny of traditional military culture made women ripe for sexual harassment and assault. A shockingly high proportion reported being sexually assaulted while in the service: at least one in three, and probably much higher. And these sexual assaults did not come from enemy combatants as a congressional panel was told in 2004: "Women serving in the U.S. military today are more likely to be raped by a fellow soldier than killed by enemy fire in Iraq."

Military women who were lesbians or gender non-conforming faced special challenges. In the 1990s the Clinton administration instituted a "**Don't Ask, Don't Tell**" policy, which forced gay soldiers to keep quiet about their sexual orientation as the price of continued service. In 2007 a Pentagon study showed that a much higher proportion of those discharged for being openly gay were women: 46 percent in the army, even though women made up only 14 percent of the personnel, and 49 percent in the air force, compared to their 20 percent representation. That policy was lifted in 2011, but LGBTQ service members continue to face lingering homophobia and a host of challenges not faced by straight soldiers. **Transgender** soldiers face an especially difficult struggle for acceptance, particularly if they transition while on active duty.

The story of women in the military is therefore both celebratory and cautionary. Old fears that they would falter in combat, prove too frail to carry heavy equipment, or be unable to perform duties while menstruating or pregnant have been shown to be false. And yet there is a palpable resentment among many hard-core military leaders that women are getting a softer deal, which fuels a culture of sexual assault and sexual violence that is rampant in military life. There is still much more to be done before women are fully integrated into the modern army. But don't lose sight of how far they have come in infiltrating one of the last bastions of male privilege left in contemporary American life. To put it another way, if a woman can make it in the military, she probably can make it anywhere.

 ## THE CHANGING TERRAIN OF SEX AND GENDER

In the popular mind, the sexual revolution of the 1960s is associated with a new openness about sex in popular culture (think miniskirts and the birth control pill), but the current expansion of popular thinking about the fluidity of gender may turn out to be even more far-reaching. Think how quickly phrases like LGBTQ+, cisgender, gender-nonconforming, genderqueer, and nonbinary have become part of our vocabulary, along with a movement to declare our pronouns (she/her/hers) and an increasing tendency to adopt singular terms like "they" that move beyond gender entirely. Just in the past few years, it seems, sexual identities and expression have expanded far beyond normative heterosexuality as increasing numbers of people refuse to identify themselves by traditional gender norms. When sex as well as gender is up for grabs, the possibilities for sexual expression and personal identity emerge as far more fluid and variable than a simple male/female binary. And that trend is likely to continue to blossom and unfold in the years ahead.

One of the most useful new terms is the "Q" in LGBTQ: queer. Less a specific sexual identity and more of an attitude or point of view, it covers a range of sexual preferences, orientations, and habits that do not conform to dominant sexual or gender norms. The term "queer" has a long history as an extremely derogatory term for gay men, along with "fag" or "faggot." But it has been positively and affirmatively embraced by queer activists for precisely that shock value, conveying an identity that is proudly at odds with whatever is defined as normal. **Queer theory** has been enormously influential in academe, especially in cultural, literary, and historical studies (as in "queering the suffrage movement"), providing alternative—or queer—readings of texts as part of a broader challenge to fixed meanings for the categories of sex, gender, and sexuality.

Feminist scholars learned early on to be suspicious of socially-constructed categories and assumptions based on the differences between men and women but until recently, there was less inclination to question the biological differences between the sexes that underlay those gender definitions. Popular belief in those immutable biological differences, along with the corollary that notions of masculinity and femininity follow logically from them, is accepted as a key organizing concept by many people, what scholars call an "incorrigible proposition." And yet a subset of humans, perhaps as high as 10 percent, share secondary sex characteristics of both sexes, making it hard to label them simply as male and female. This has proved especially tricky in the world of sports competition, which remains rigidly segregated by older notions of sex.

How to deal with feeling that you are trapped in the body of the wrong sex is the challenge faced by trans people. At the tricky interface between biology and socially constructed notions of gender and sexuality, transgender individuals have won increasing support for their decisions and actions, including from the legal system. In June 2020 the Supreme Court ruled that an employer who fires an individual merely for being gay or transgender violates Title VII, the 1964 law that prohibits employers from discriminating based

# The First Time Jennifer Finney Boylan Said, "I'm Trans"

In 2001 Colby College English professor James Boylan began to transition from male to female, asking to be known as Jennifer Finney Boylan by her colleagues and family. In 2003 she published a bestselling autobiography entitled *She's Not There: A Life in Two Genders*. Now a professor at Barnard College and a regular contributor to the *New York Times*, in this column Boylan reflects on the moment when she shared her identification of herself as transgender with her wife and children and what has changed (or not) in the intervening twenty years.

On January 6, 2000, I did it. *I'm transgender*, I said.

So much has changed since then. In some ways, this country has become safer, as more and more of us step forward to proclaim our realness.

In other ways, we're more threatened than ever.

When I came out, no one had yet been schooled on the finer points of hating me; most bigots in this country didn't know a trans woman from the Trans-Siberian Railway.

Because my existence was so far off their radar, few people had bothered to come up with laws to make my life worse. No one lost much sleep over trans folks serving their country. Caitlyn Jenner and Chaz Bono and Janet Mock were not publicly out; Laverne Cox was thirteen years from her epic role in "Orange Is the New Black."

There had been plenty of public fighters for trans people before me—including the iconic Sylvia Rivera, as well [as] my friend Kate Bornstein. But still, there were times when trans advocacy was a lonely place to be.

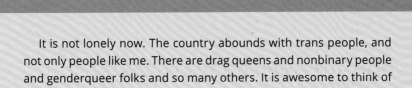

It is not lonely now. The country abounds with trans people, and not only people like me. There are drag queens and nonbinary people and genderqueer folks and so many others. It is awesome to think of how far we have come.

But it's also scary. Because now that we're on the radar, conservatives (and others) have developed a new language with which to demonize us.

. . .

My theory is that people objecting to the sanctity of the powder room, or tearfully defending women's athletics, or terrified by the prospect of us serving our country, are not actually concerned with those issues at all. What they really object to, when you come right down to it, is the fact that trans people exist in the first place.

Our existence, to use a technical term, weirds them out.

I guess I can understand that. When I was a child, it weirded me out too.

But what they never suggest is what trans people should do instead of being ourselves. We still don't know what, if anything, makes people trans, but it's clear that conversion therapy does not work. You can be upset that trans people exist, I suppose, but no amount of upset about us can erase the absolute fact that we are here, same as you, and that we have been here for centuries.

Transgender people were not put here to make Mike Pence—or Germaine Greer—unhappy. Transgender people, like everything else, were created by God—or nature, if you prefer, glorious evidence of creation's inventiveness. We were not made to hurt your feelings. We were made to see if you meant it when you said, "Love each other as I have loved you." Did you?

*SOURCE: Jennifer Finney Boylan, "The First Time I Said, 'I'm Trans,'"* New York Times, *January 22, 2020.*

on sex. Aimee Stephens, a trans woman who was a plaintiff in the case, was fired after she notified her employer she would be transitioning. Left outside the decision were the rights of nonbinary or genderqueer people who didn't fit in the categories "male" and "female," but this decision nevertheless was a major breakthrough for gay and trans rights.

 # CHANGING AMERICAN FAMILIES

Despite occasional nostalgia for the model of male breadwinner and female housewife, that pattern applies only to a tiny minority of families in the twenty-first century. Barely half of all adults in the United States are currently married, and 30 percent have never been married at all. In 1960 the average age of first marriage was twenty-two for men and twenty for women, but it has been rising steadily ever since: twenty-six for men and twenty-three for women in 1990, and thirty for men and twenty-eight for women in 2018. Also rising, quite dramatically for several decades before leveling off, has been the divorce rate: one in two marriages now end in divorce. But many divorced people re-marry, often multiple times, resulting in a range of blended families. After the pathbreaking Supreme Court decisions in *United States v. Windsor* (2013) and **Obergefell v. Hodges** (2015), the right to marry was extended to same-sex couples. Others, gay, straight, and trans, live in committed relationships without benefit of marriage. All these indicators point to an institution in flux.

Confirming a long-term trend only briefly interrupted by the baby boom of the 1950s, the American birth rate continues to fall. In 2018 the total fertility rate was 1.73 per woman, well below the 2.1 replacement rate. The number of women in their early twenties having children has fallen to a record low, whereas the proportion of women in their late thirties and early forties having children is rising, thanks in part of breakthroughs in reproductive technology like in vitro fertilization. For parents who cannot conceive, adoption remains an option, including international adoptions, which numbered almost 250,000 between 1999 and 2012, mainly from China, Russia, and South Korea. These international adoptions helped make American families even more diverse.

The biggest change over the past fifty years is the growing number of single mothers. In 2016 some 42 percent of children were born to unmarried mothers, up from 5 percent in 1960, 18 percent in 1980, and 33 percent in 2000. In 2016 69 percent of African American births were to unmarried women, as were 66 percent of American Indian and Alaskan Native births and 53 percent of Hispanic births. Asian and Pacific Islander women recorded the smallest proportion (17 percent). This upswing in unmarried births is far broader than unlucky teenagers lacking access to reliable birth control. The United States is reaching a point where marriage and having children are no longer inextricably bound, although the consequences differ dramatically depending on class and often race.

At the upper end of the economic strata, women are embracing new patterns of family life. The best example is the number of never-married professional women who decide to become single mothers by choice. Who needs a husband in order to have a baby and a family? Usually this decision occurs when the woman is somewhat older and thus more established in her career, so that she can afford this step. Lesbian couples pioneered this approach, with increasing social acceptance, even before same-sex marriage was legalized.

But the experience of single motherhood is vastly different at the other end of the economic spectrum. The most direct consequence of the growth of female-headed households, a category that includes single, widowed, divorced or deserted women who are the sole support of their family, is a dramatic rise in childhood poverty, which is directly linked to the low wages that many women, especially women of color, command in the modern low-wage service economy. Households headed by single mothers are five times as likely to be below the poverty line as two-parent families. The United States ranks a shocking first in terms of child poverty in the developed world.

A single mother has to do everything by herself, but in a two-parent household, there is at least another adult to share the burdens. And yet those families still struggle to cram everything that needs to be done into the waking hours of the day. Most families now contain two wage earners, with women contributing about 42 percent of overall family income, up from 30 percent several decades ago. Even when both parents work, women still shoulder a larger share of domestic responsibilities for household management, child care, and elder care: twenty-eight hours a week to men's sixteen. Perhaps one of the most positive shifts in recent years is that balancing work and family is increasingly seen not just as a women's issue but also relevant to men. But at the end of the day, despite men's shouldering a larger share of domestic work and child care, it is still primarily the working woman who adds a second shift at home when her income-producing job is done.

 # JOBS AND JUSTICE

Despite the opening of industrial and professional jobs to women, almost three-quarters of the female labor force remains in predominantly female occupations, such as teaching, nursing, clerical and sales work, health

# Why Is "Having It All" Just a Women's Issue?

The media never tires of debating "Can women have it all?", often complete with stories of individual women's struggles to balance high-powered jobs with the responsibilities of childrearing and family life. Note how the terms of the debate are already skewed: this question is presented as a matter of choice for elite women, but few talk about the challenge for working women who have no choice but to combine the two. And men are often left out of the discussion completely. In this op-ed piece for CNN from 2012, sociologist and author Stephanie Coontz tries to reframe the question.

The July/August cover story of the *Atlantic*, "Why Women Still Can't Have It All" by Anne-Marie Slaughter, has ignited a firestorm.

One side accepts the author's argument: that feminism has set women up to fail by pretending they can have a high-powered career and still be an involved mother. The other side accuses Slaughter, who left her job as the first female director of policy planning at the State Department, of setting women back by telling them to "rediscover the pursuit of happiness," starting at home.

Slaughter's article contains a powerful critique of the insanely rigid workplace culture that produces higher levels of career-family conflict among Americans—among men and women—than among any of our Western European counterparts, without measurably increasing our productivity or gross national product. And she makes sensible suggestions about how to reorganize workplaces and individual career paths to lessen that conflict.

Unfortunately, the way the discussion is framed perpetuates two myths: that feminism is to blame for raising unrealistic expectations about "having it all" and that work-family dilemmas are primarily an issue for women.

Let's start by recognizing that the women's movement never told anybody that they could "have it all." That concept was the brainchild of advertising executives, not feminist activists. Feminism insists on women's right to make choices—about whether to marry, whether to have children, whether to combine work and family or to focus on one over the other. It also urges men and women to share the joys and burdens of family life and calls on society to place a higher priority on supporting caregiving work.

Second, we should distinguish between high-powered careers that really are incompatible with active involvement in family life and those that force people to choose between work and family only because of misguided employment requirements and inadequate work-family policies.

. . .

Slaughter ultimately suggests some excellent reforms that would allow both men and women to meet their work and family commitments more successfully, although she inexplicably describes them as "solutions to the problems of professional women." Later she acknowledges that work-family issues plague all American workers, regardless of their sex, income level, occupational niche or even parental status since many childless workers have responsibilities to aging parents or ill partners. In fact, according to the New York–based Families and Work institute, men now report even higher levels of work-family conflict than women do.

It was great victory for gender equality when people finally stopped routinely saying, "She's awfully good at her job—for a woman." The next big step forward will be when people stop saying, "It's awfully tough to balance work and family—for a woman." It's tough for men and women. We need to push for work-family practices and policies that allow individuals to customize their work lives according to their changing individual preferences and family obligations, not just their traditional gender roles.

*SOURCE: Stephanie Coontz, "Why Is 'Having It All' Just a Women's Issue?,"*
*June 25, 2012. https://www.cnn.com/2012/06/25/opinion/coontz-women-*
*have-it-all/index.html*

care, and personal service. Along with women's work go women's wages. By 2018 the median wage for women who held full-time, year-round jobs had risen to 81 percent of men's median wages, a significant increase from 59 percent in 1970. White women posted the greatest increases, although the Institute for Women's Policy Research reported that the typical female college graduate would still lose a staggering $440,000 over twenty-years because of the pay gap. The wages of African American women and Latinas lagged behind: 65 percent and 61 percent respectively of white men's median earnings in 2018. In contrast Asian women's earnings were 93.5 percent of white men's, although only 75 percent of Asian men's. While progress had been made, there still is a long way to go before women reach wage equity.

Those aggregate figures applied to full-time employment, which was becoming less widespread in a service-oriented economy where dead-end "McJobs" were becoming the norm. Full time employees are expensive for corporations and other employers because they are covered by federal and state laws protecting wages and hours as well as working conditions. Contract employees have no such protection. As independent contractors, they are considered temporary workers, a loophole employers are

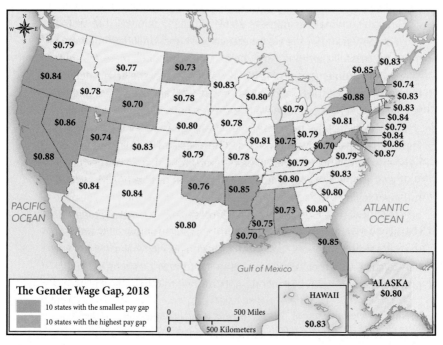

The Gender Wage Gap, 2018

- 10 states with the smallest pay gap
- 10 states with the highest pay gap

MAP 8.1

eager to exploit. These workers have no job security, little control over their schedules, and limited chances for advancement—and often don't earn enough to live on, relying on food stamps and other aid programs to get by. This applies to those who work for gigantic employers like Walmart, McDonald's, and Amazon, as well as members of the so-called **gig economy**, like Uber and Lyft drivers, home-care providers, and the adjunct professors who do the bulk of teaching at the nation's colleges and universities. "We are all fast-food workers now," says Bleu Rainer, a former McDonald's employee turned labor activist.

Sometimes these workers are referred to as "the precariat" because of their precarious situation, but the phrase really should be the "female precariat," since the low-wage service economy is disproportionately made up of female workers, especially women of color, in areas like domestic service, health and beauty, hotels and hospitality, and food service. The Bureau of Labor Statistics predicts that jobs like home health aides and personal care workers will see the largest increase in the coming decade, even with wages hovering at about $12 an hour, well below what it takes to support a family. The economic and social disruptions caused by the COVID-19 pandemic underscored how essential—and often invisible—such work was to the functioning of the modern economy.

The poverty wages earned by wide swaths of American workers stand in stark contrast to the increasing concentration of wealth found at the very top of the economic ladder, where (pick your shocking statistic) six members of the Walton family that founded Walmart control as much wealth as 40 percent of American households or the 62 richest people in the world control more wealth than 3.8 billion people. Activists took note, with the protestors who organized **Occupy Wall Street** in 2011 familiarizing the country with the notion of the "1 percent" versus the "99 percent." Flash mobs organized through social media descended on corporate headquarters or flagship stores and protestors became increasingly savvy about getting their message out, tweaking corporate slogans with taunts like "Poverty Wages: Not Loving It" and "Just Don't Do It."

As part of this reckoning with the growing income inequality, **Fight for $15** launched a nationwide campaign to raise the minimum wage (set by law at $7.25 since 2009) to $15 an hour. The movement began in New York City in 2012 when 200 fast-food workers walked off the job; since then Fight for $15 has posted significant victories in states and localities across the country. Other attempts to mobilize low-waged workers included the National Domestic Workers Alliance, an advocacy group founded by Ai-Jen Poo in 2007 that drafted a **Domestic Workers' Bill of Rights** calling for overtime pay and time off, protection from sexual harassment, and inclusion in state and federal labor laws. Linking their domestic work directly to women's work outside the home, they coined this slogan: "I do my job so you can do yours. Domestic Work Deserves Respect."

Neither of those groups are traditional unions, but the labor movement also found that its areas of strongest growth were in the sectors where women predominated, with public-sector unions of government and municipal workers like the Service Employees International Union (SIEU) leading the way. Women may in fact hold the key to the future of organized labor, which now represents only 10 percent of the general population, down from a peak of 35 percent in the mid-1950s.

Organizing efforts in the United States were part of a global uprising against poverty wages that had been building for several decades. Many of the world's service and retail workers, small farmers, and contract workers are women, and they are organizing not just around wages and working conditions but also to demand gender justice on the job, including protection from sexual harassment. Conditions have been especially dire in the world of "fast fashion"—the factories in Cambodia, Bangladesh, India, Vietnam, and China where predominantly female workers (between 60 and 75 million in 2016) toil to make cheap clothes for the rest of the world. Often workers don't even know

8.4: Marchers converged on Washington, DC, on January 21, 2017, as part of a worldwide protest against the inauguration of President Donald Trump. With distinctive pink hats and colorful banners, the marches were reminiscent of when suffragists took to the streets one hundred years earlier to demand the vote.

who their owners are. Only by tracing the labels have activists been able to hold giant multinational corporations like Nike, Old Navy, H&M, and Adidas accountable for the low wages and unfair labor standards under which their goods are produced.

The activism around poverty wages and inequality is part of a broader progressive coalition seeking racial justice and gender equity for all Americans. Three of the most significant recent manifestations have been Black Lives Matter, the **Women's March** of 2017, and the burgeoning #MeToo movement.

The hashtag #BlackLivesMatter was created in 2013 by organizers Alicia Garza, Patrisse Cullors, and Opal Tometi after George Zimmerman was acquitted in Florida of the murder of Trayvon Martin, an unarmed African American teenager. In 2014 its focus expanded to police brutality and the systematic harassment of Black communities by local authorities, such as the murder of Mike Brown in Ferguson, Missouri, by white officers; the death of Eric Garner in New York, who repeatedly cried out, "I can't breathe," as he struggled against restraints while in custody; and the shooting of twelve-year-old Tamir Rice in Cleveland by a white police officer for carrying a toy replica of a gun. As evidence of police brutality mounted, Black Lives Matter expanded to a global network of forty chapters, although the movement remains decentralized and anti-hierarchical in its structure. Another group called #SayHerName draws attention to the killing of Black women by police.

#BlackLivesMatter exploded in 2020 after an agonizing 8-minute-43-second video captured a white police officer in Minneapolis pressing his knee against the neck of George Floyd while under arrest, despite Floyd's repeated cries that he could not breathe. This incident, which ended in Floyd's death, provoked massive protests throughout the country, despite the COVID-19 pandemic restrictions on large-scale gatherings, and provided what felt like a seismic shift in the willingness of white America to finally confront the role that systemic racism played in all aspects of contemporary life, indeed throughout American history.

The Women's March held on January 21, 2017, to protest the inauguration of President Donald Trump the day before were the largest single-day protest in United States history, mobilizing between 3 and 5 million marchers in this country. Overall 673 marches took place worldwide, representing all seven continents. Often wearing distinctive pink "pussy hats" to create a stunning visual panorama, the diverse and peaceful crowds put the new administration on notice that Trump's history of shabby treatment of women, as well as his racism and anti-immigrant baiting, would not stand unchallenged. Protestors made their points by displaying posters such as "It's Day One and I've #had enough," "Girls Just Want to Have Fun-damental Rights,"

# Black Women's Lives Matter

The killing of George Floyd by Minneapolis police in May 2020 sparked national protests that also brought attention to female victims of police brutality, especially the case of Breonna Taylor, a twenty-six-year-old unarmed African American woman who was fatally shot in her Louisville apartment in March 2020 by white officers conducting a drug investigation. The belated outcry over Breonna Taylor's death popularized the hashtag #SayHerName, first coined by the African American Policy Forum in 2015 in response to Sandra Bland's death in jail after her arrest for a routine traffic stop. This statement from the Forum lays out the importance of a gender-inclusive movement to end state violence.

## Why We Must Say Her Name: The Urgent Need for a Gender-Inclusive Movement to End State Violence

There are several reasons why the resurgent racial justice movement must prioritize the development of a gender-inclusive lens.

First, including Black women and girls in the narrative broadens the scope of the debate, enhancing our overall understanding of the structural relationship between Black communities and law enforcement agencies. In order to comprehend the root causes and full scope of state violence against Black communities, we must consider and illuminate all the ways in which Black people in the U.S. are routinely targeted for state violence. Acknowledging and analyzing the connections between anti-Black violence against Black men, women, transgender and gender-nonconforming people reveals systemic realities that go unnoticed when the focus is limited exclusively to cases involving Black non-transgender men.

Secondly, both the incidents and consequences of state violence against Black women are often informed by their roles as primary caretakers in their communities. As a result, violence against them has ripple effects throughout families and neighborhoods. Black women are positioned at the center of the domestic sphere and of community life, yet their marginal position with respect to economic and social power relations creates the isolating and vulnerable context in which their struggle against police violence, mass incarceration and low wages occurs. In order to ensure safe and healthy Black communities, we must address police violence against Black women with equal outrage and commitment.

Third, centering the lives of all segments of our community will permit us to move away from the idea that to address police violence we must "fix" individual Black men and bad police officers. Moving beyond these narrow concepts is critical if we are to embrace a framework that focuses on the complex structural dimensions that are actually at play. Through inclusion it becomes clear that the problem is not a matter of whether a young man's hands were held up over his head, whether he had a mentor, or whether the police officers in question were wearing cameras or had been exposed to implicit bias trainings. It becomes clear that the epidemic of police violence across the country is about how police relations reinforce the structural marginality of all members of Black communities in ways that are similar and unique to one another.

Fourth, including Black women and girls in this discourse sends the powerful message that indeed all Black lives do matter. If our collective outrage is meant to serve as a warning to the state that its agents cannot kill without consequence, our silence around the cases of Black women and girls sends the message that certain deaths do not merit repercussions.

*SOURCE: Kimberle Williams Crenshaw and Andrea J. Ritchie,* Say Her Name: Resisting Police Brutality Against Black Women, *Center for Intersectionality and Social Policy Studies, 8–9. https://44bbdc6e-01a4-4a9a-88bc-731c6524888e.filesusr.com/ugd/62e126_9223ee35c2694ac3bd3f 2171504ca3f7.pdf*

"Tweet Women with Respect" and (from an older feminist) "I Can't Believe We Are Still Protesting This Shit." This surge of female energy in reaction to Trump's election played a major role in the electoral successes of women candidates in the 2018 election and also was a factor in the outcomes of many races in 2020.

The #MeToo movement against sexual harassment and sexual assault also surged in the early years of the Trump administration. The hashtag was first used in this context by sexual harassment survivor and activist Tarana Burke in 2006, but it had clear antecedents in Anita Hill's 1991 testimony against Clarence Thomas. The spurt of activism and attention in 2017 was set in motion by the willingness of a cadre of women, often Hollywood actresses or others in the entertainment business, to speak out publicly against prominent men who had used their positions of power and influence to extract sexual favors from women vulnerable to exploitation because of concern for their careers. Hollywood film mogul Harvey Weinstein was the prime focus of the investigations, which *New York Times* reporters Megan Twohey and Jodi Kantor along with Ronan Farrow of the *New Yorker* broke in October 2017. The willingness of victims to speak openly about what they had endured unleashed a floodgate of similar stories. Alas, it seems that almost every woman has her own #MeToo story. All these issues would play a significant role in the 2020 election.

8.5: On August 26, 2020, the centennial of the ratification of the Nineteenth Amendment, a fourteen-foot bronze statue by sculptor Meredith Bergmann depicting Sojourner Truth, Susan B. Anthony, and Elizabeth Cady Stanton was dedicated in New York City's Central Park. The three suffragists seem to be having quite an animated conversation.

# 2020: A MOMENT OF RECKONING

On August 26, 2020, the country marked the centennial of the adoption of the Nineteenth Amendment giving women the vote, the culmination of a series of events and commemorations of this milestone in American women's history. One prominent theme was increased recognition of the roles African American women and other women of color played in the women's suffrage movement, a history that had often been overlooked or ignored. Without denying the racism of much of white suffrage leadership, this new emphasis on diversity offered a history that not only documented the past but also spoke to our own times.

In an eerie coincidence, the final stages of the suffrage struggle occurred during the global flu pandemic of 1918–1919, which killed 675,000 Americans and 50 million people worldwide. The centennial was celebrated in the midst of another global pandemic caused by the coronavirus COVID-19, which first appeared in China in late 2019 and spread throughout the world the following year. Suddenly epidemiologists were rock stars, offering public health guidelines in an increasingly polarized political

8.6: When Vice-President-Elect Kamala Harris took the podium on November 7, 2020, at the Democratic victory celebration, she proudly said, "While I may be the first woman in this office, I will not be the last." For the occasion Harris wore a white pantsuit paired with a white pussy-bow blouse, a clear political shout-out to the suffrage movement and women's long struggle to break through the glass ceiling in politics.

situation where the Trump administration consistently downplayed the severity of the virus and its potential impact on the already shaky health care system. Lockdowns and limits on normal activity like travel bans and working from home helped to "flatten the curve" to avoid overwhelming the system, but each time restrictions were relaxed or lifted, the virus surged back. The promise of the quick development of a vaccine offered hope, but until widespread vaccination occurred it was anything but business as usual for the foreseeable future.

The pandemic had a clear gender dimension: its impact fell more heavily on women, not necessarily in terms of getting sick or dying at a greater rate but in their never-ending roles as the primary care givers for their families and communities. When schools and day care facilities shut down and many workers began to work remotely from home, it was the working women

## *Timeline*

**1986**

In *Meritor Savings Bank v. Vinson* the Supreme Court upholds the view that a hostile work environment is a form of sex discrimination

**1990–1991**

First Gulf War

**1991**

Anita Hill testifies at the confirmation hearing of Clarence Thomas for nomination to the U.S. Supreme Court

**1992**

The Year of the Woman

**1998**

Bill Clinton is threatened with impeachment over sexual involvement with Monica Lewinsky

**2000**

Hillary Clinton runs successfully for the U.S. Senate from New York

**SEPTEMBER 11, 2001**

Terrorist attacks on World Trade Center

**2003**

Operation Iraqi Freedom

**2007**

Nancy Pelosi ascends to Speaker of the House of Representatives

**JANUARY 2009**

Barack Obama becomes president

**2009**

Hillary Clinton appointed Secretary of State

**2011**

"Don't Ask, Don't Tell" policy is lifted

**2012**

Military rule excluding women from "combat-related" job categories is lifted

**2013**

Beginning of Black Lives Matter movement

**2013, 2015**

The Supreme Court rules that right to marry is extended to same-sex couples in *United States v. Windsor* and *Obergefell v. Hodges*

in those households who shouldered the majority of responsibility for juggling their families' needs, especially the supervision of their children's online schooling. They were literally working double duty.

The pandemic also brought to the forefront the plight of health care workers and service providers, often low-waged women, who were the backbone of the provision of care in this economy. For them the pandemic meant a terrible juggling act between putting themselves on the front lines to fight COVID-19 and worrying about endangering their families and loved ones if they unwittingly carried the virus home. Whether the post-pandemic world will learn from these lessons and devote more resources to the widespread provision of day care, better appreciation of the role of teachers, and improved wages and working conditions for health care workers—all areas where women predominate—remains to be seen.

**2016**

42 percent of children are born to unmarried mothers

**2017**

Emergence of the #MeToo movement

**JANUARY 20, 2017**

Donald Trump becomes 45th president of the United States

**JANUARY 21, 2017**

Women's March worldwide in protest of the inauguration of Donald Trump and mistreatment of women and minorities

**OCTOBER 2017**

Harvey Weinstein story breaks

**2018**

Christine Blasey Ford testifies against Supreme Court nominee Brett Kavanaugh

**2018**

106 women are elected to the House of Representatives and 25 women to the Senate for the 116th U.S. Congress

**2018**

Median wage for women who hold full-time, year-round jobs rises to 81 percent of men's median wages

**2020**

The death of George Floyd sparks massive Black Lives Matter protests across the country

**JANUARY 9, 2020**

WHO announces mysterious coronavirus in Wuhan, China

**JUNE 2020**

The Supreme Court rules that an employer who fires an individual merely for being gay or transgender violates Title VII

**DECEMBER 2020**

The Electoral College confirms Joe Biden as president-elect and Kamala Harris as vice-president-elect

Like the forever wars of Afghanistan and Iraq, the campaign cycle can often seem endless. In fact, the lead-up to the 2020 election basically started the moment Donald Trump was inaugurated in January 2017. Democratic gains in the 2018 election seemed to bode well for that party's prospects, but then the pandemic struck in March 2020 just as the political parties were gearing up for the fall election. There was never any question that Donald Trump would be the Republican nominee, but the Democratic field was wide open. In the end Joe Biden prevailed, giving the country the prospect of choosing between two white men in their seventies. The selection of California Senator Kamala Harris as the vice-presidential candidate, the first woman of color ever chosen, pointed to a different vision of the future.

Despite fears of voter suppression or interference from a foreign country, the 2020 election featured the highest voter turnout—66 percent—since 1900, with women's votes recognized as significant factors in both the Democratic and Republican coalitions. Even though more voters cast their ballots for Trump in 2020 than in 2016, Joe Biden won both the popular vote and the Electoral College. But with partisan polarization unchanged and a pandemic still raging as he took office, Biden confronted a challenging political landscape.

Any time of crisis brings comparisons to past moments in American history when the country faced major challenges: the American Revolution, the Civil War, the Great Depression, World War II, or 9/11. In each of those moments, American women were significant actors in responding to crisis as well as key players in what came afterward. In 1776 Abigail Adams reminded her husband John to "remember the ladies" and in 1933 Eleanor Roosevelt told her readers that "it's up to the women." Timely sentiments indeed, in 2020 and beyond.

## KEY TERMS

| | | |
|---|---|---|
| Black Lives Matter | Fight for $15 | Occupy Wall Street |
| COVID-19 | gig economy | queer theory |
| Domestic Workers' Bill | LGBTQ | transgender |
| of Rights | #MeToo | Women's March |
| "Don't Ask, Don't Tell" | *Obergefell v. Hodges* | |

## Suggested Readings

Abrams, Stacey. *Our Time Is Now: Power, Purpose, and the Fight for a Fair America* (2020).

Coontz, Stephanie. *The Way We Really Are: Coming to Terms with America's Changing Families* (1998).

Cooper, Brittney. *Eloquent Rage: A Black Feminist Discovers Her Superpower* (2019).

Gidlow, Liette, ed. *Obama, Clinton, Palin: Making History in Election 2008* (2011).

Nadasen, Premilla. *Household Workers Unite: The Untold Story of African American Women Who Built a Movement* (2015).

Orleck, Annelise. *"We Are All Fast-Food Workers Now": The Global Uprising against Poverty Wages* (2018).

Learn more with this chapter's digital tools at http://www.oup.com/he/warele.

# APPENDIX

## *DECLARATION OF SENTIMENTS AND RESOLUTIONS*, SENECA FALLS CONVENTION, 1848

When, in the course of human events, it becomes necessary for one portion of the family of man to assume among the people of the earth a position different from that which they have hitherto occupied, but one to which the laws of nature and of nature's God entitle them, a decent respect to the opinions of mankind requires that they should declare the causes that impel them to such a course.

We hold these truths to be self-evident: that all men and women are created equal; that they are endowed by their Creator with certain inalienable rights; that among these are life, liberty, and the pursuit of happiness; that to secure these rights governments are instituted, deriving their just powers from the consent of the governed. Whenever any form of government becomes destructive of these ends, it is the right of those who suffer from it to refuse allegiance to it, and to insist upon the institution of a new government, laying its foundation on such principles, and organizing its powers in such form, as to them shall seem most likely to effect their safety and happiness. Prudence, indeed, will dictate that governments long established should not be changed for light and transient causes; and accordingly, all experience hath shown that mankind are more disposed to suffer, while evils are sufferable, than to right themselves by abolishing the forms to which they are accustomed. But when a long train of abuses and usurpations, pursuing invariably the same object, evinces a design to reduce them under absolute despotism, it is their duty to throw off such government, and to provide new guards for their future security. Such has been the patient sufferance of the women under this government, and such is now the necessity which constrains them to demand the equal station to which they are entitled.

The history of mankind is a history of repeated injuries and usurpations on the part of man toward woman, having in direct object the establishment of an absolute tyranny over her. To prove this, let facts be submitted to a candid world.

He has never permitted her to exercise her inalienable right to the elective franchise.

He has compelled her to submit to laws, in the formation of which she had no voice.

He has withheld from her rights which are given to the most ignorant and degraded men—both natives and foreigners.

Having deprived her of this first right of a citizen, the elective franchise, thereby leaving her without representation in the halls of legislation, he has oppressed her on all sides.

He has made her, if married, in the eye of the law, civilly dead.

He has taken from her all right in property, even to the wages she earns.

He has made her, morally, an irresponsible being, as she can commit many crimes with impunity, provided they be done in the presence of her husband. In the covenant of marriage, she is compelled to promise obedience to her husband, he becoming, to all intents and purposes, her master—the law giving him power to deprive her of her liberty, and to administer chastisement.

He has so framed the laws of divorce, as to what shall be the proper causes of divorce; in case of separation, to whom the guardianship of the children shall be given; as to be wholly regardless of the happiness of women—the law, in all cases, going upon the false supposition of the supremacy of man, and giving all power into his hands.

After depriving her of all rights as a married woman, if single, and the owner of property, he has taxed her to support a government which recognizes her only when her property can be made profitable to it.

He has monopolized nearly all the profitable employments, and from those she is permitted to follow, she receives but a scanty remuneration.

He closes against her all the avenues to wealth and distinction, which he considers most honorable to himself. As a teacher of theology, medicine or law, she is not known.

He has denied her the facilities for obtaining a thorough education, all colleges being closed against her.

He allows her in Church, as well as State, but a subordinate position, claiming Apostolic authority for her exclusion from the ministry, and with some exceptions, from any public participation in the affairs of the Church.

He has created a false public sentiment, by giving to the world a different code of morals for men and women, by which moral delinquencies which exclude women from society, are not only tolerated, but deemed of little account in man.

He has usurped the prerogative of Jehovah himself, claiming it as his right to assign for her a sphere of action, when that belongs to her conscience and to her God.

He has endeavored, in every way that he could, to destroy her confidence in her own powers, to lessen her self-respect, and to make her willing to lead a dependent and abject life.

Now, in view of this entire disfranchisement of one-half the people of this country, their social and religious degradation—in view of the unjust laws above mentioned, and because women do feel themselves aggrieved, oppressed, and fraudulently deprived of their most sacred rights, we insist that they have immediate admission to all the rights and privileges which belong to them as citizens of the United States.

In entering upon the great work before us, we anticipate no small amount of misconception, misrepresentation, and ridicule; but we shall use every instrumentality within our power to effect our object. We shall employ agents, circulate tracts, petition the State and National legislatures, and endeavor to enlist the pulpit and the press in our behalf. We hope this Convention will be followed by a series of Conventions, embracing every part of the country.

   \* \* \*

The following resolutions ... were adopted:

*Whereas*, the great precept of nature is conceded to be, "that man shall pursue his own true and substantial happiness." Blackstone, in his Commentaries, remarks, that this law of Nature being coeval with mankind, and dictated by God himself, is of course superior in obligation to any other. It is binding over all the globe, in all countries, and at all times; no human laws are of any validity if contrary to this, and such of them as are valid, derive all their force, and all their validity, and all their authority, mediately and immediately, from this original; therefore,

*Resolved*, That such laws as conflict, in any way, with the true and substantial happiness of woman, are contrary to the great precept of nature and of no validity, for this is "superior in obligation to any other."

*Resolved*, That all laws which prevent woman from occupying such a station in society as her conscience shall dictate, or which place her in a position inferior to that of man, are contrary to the great precept of nature, and therefore of no force or authority.

*Resolved*, That woman is man's equal—was intended to be so by the Creator, and the highest good of the race demands that she should be recognized as such.

*Resolved*, That the women of this country ought to be enlightened in regard to the laws under which they live, that they may no longer publish their degradation by declaring themselves satisfied with their present position, nor their ignorance, by asserting that they have all the rights they want.

*Resolved*, That inasmuch as man, while claiming for himself intellectual superiority, does accord to woman moral superiority, it is pre-eminently his duty to encourage her to speak and teach, as she has an opportunity, in all religious assemblies.

*Resolved*, That the same amount of virtue, delicacy, and refinement of behavior that is required of woman in the social state, should also be required of man, and the same transgressions should be visited with equal severity on both man and woman.

*Resolved,* That the objection of indelicacy and impropriety, which is so often brought against woman when she addresses a public audience, comes with a very ill-grace from those who encourage, by their attendance, her appearance on the stage, in the concert, or in feats of the circus.

*Resolved,* That woman has too long rested satisfied in the circumscribed limits which corrupt customs and a perverted application of the Scriptures have marked out for her, and that it is time she should move in the enlarged sphere which her great Creator has assigned her.

*Resolved,* That it is the duty of the women of this country to secure to themselves their sacred right to the elective franchise.

*Resolved,* That the equality of human rights results necessarily from the fact of the identity of the race in capabilities and responsibilities.

*Resolved, therefore,* That, being invested by the Creator with the same capabilities, and the same consciousness of responsibility for their exercise, it is demonstrably the right and duty of woman, equally with man, to promote every righteous cause by every righteous means; and especially in regard to the great subjects of morals and religion, it is self-evidently her right to participate with her brother in teaching them, both in private and in public, by writing and by speaking, by any instrumentalities proper to be used, and in any assemblies proper to be held; and this being a self-evident truth growing out of the divinely implanted principles of human nature, any custom or authority adverse to it, whether modern or wearing the hoary sanction of antiquity, is to be regarded as a self-evident falsehood, and at war with mankind.

*Resolved,* That the speedy success of our cause depends upon the zealous and untiring efforts of both men and women, for the overthrow of the monopoly of the pulpit, and for the securing to woman an equal participation with men in the various trades, professions, and commerce.

SOURCE: From Elizabeth Cady Stanton, *A History of Woman Suffrage,* vol. 1 (Rochester, NY: Fowler and Wells, 1889), pages 70–72.

# GLOSSARY

**#MeToo:** A movement against sexual harassment of women that surged on social media during the early years of the Trump administration.

**abolition** A pre–Civil War social movement devoted to the emancipation of enslaved African Americans and their inclusion in American society as citizens with equal rights.

**Alpha Suffrage Club** One of the first suffrage organizations for Black women, organized by journalist and activist Ida B. Wells-Barnett.

**American Woman Suffrage Association (AWSA)** Boston-based suffrage organization established in 1890 and led by Lucy Stone, Henry Blackwell, and Julia Ward Howe. It supported passage of the Fourteenth and Fifteenth Amendments despite their not granting the right to vote to women.

**baby boom** The temporary but noteworthy increase in birth rate in the United States, Great Britain, and Europe in the years immediately following World War II.

**benevolent societies** Voluntary associations founded by women for the purpose of charity, they were an outgrowth of the Second Great Awakening.

**birth control** The ability to prevent pregnancy. Feminists fought for access to legal birth control from the late 19th century on. Margaret Sanger was a pioneer in providing birth control and sex education to women starting in the 1910s.

**Black Lives Matter** Movement that began in 2013 that promotes nonviolent civil disobedience in response to police brutality.

**Boston marriage** A relationship between two women who set up a household together in lieu of a more traditional marriage. These relationships were most prevalent in the late nineteenth and early twentieth centuries.

**Californio** Term used by Anglos in California to draw racial and ethnic lines between elite, landowning California families with supposedly Spanish heritage from non-elite families with supposedly Mexican heritage.

**Cherokee** Culture native to the Southeast that adapted to European cultural expectations in an attempt to maintain their independence and land ownership. They were evicted from their land in the 1830s and the majority were forced to migrate to Oklahoma on the Trail of Tears.

**Chicana feminism** The rise of an equal rights and social justice movement among Chicana women, largely in response to their experiences in the Chicano movement, but also a reaction to feeling unwelcome in the white feminist movement.

**Chinese Exclusion Act (1882)** Congressional act that barred the immigration of Chinese laborers. This law all but ended Chinese immigration and remained in effect until 1943.

**Civil Rights Act of 1964** Congressional act that prohibited discrimination in employment or the use of public spaces on the basis of race, sex, religion, or national origin.

**civil rights movement** A campaign by African Americans and their allies to end racial discrimination, segregation, and disenfranchisement.

**Combahee River Collective** A group of Black feminists in the Boston area. Their work anticipated the idea of intersectionality, that in order to understand the lives of Black women, attention had to be paid to race and class as well as gender.

**communism** A political and economic ideology, the aim of which is the common ownership of the means of production.

**consumer revolution** A slow and steady increase over the course of the eighteenth century in the demand for, and purchase of, consumer goods.

**COVID-19** An acutely contagious disease caused by a coronavirus first identified in Wuhan, China, in December 2019. The spread of the disease caused a worldwide pandemic.

**Cult of Domesticity** The mindset among the middle and upper classes that a woman's role was in the home. It prioritized the traditional Protestant nuclear family and the importance of motherhood. Black, working class, and immigrant women were excluded from this social construct.

**Cult of True Womanhood** An emphasis on the importance of a woman's piety, purity, submission, and domesticity spread primarily by prescriptive literature—women's magazines, books, and religious tracts. White women were its main targets.

**cultural mediators** Native American women who acted as mediators, especially in trading relationships, between European settlers and Native American tribes.

**Declaration of Sentiments** Declaration of women's rights, including the right to citizenship, property rights, and the right to vote, adopted at the Seneca Falls convention in 1848.

**disappearing Indian** A myth perpetuated by settler colonialism that Native cultures were disappearing as tribes became assimilated or forced onto reservations.

**Domestic Workers' Bill of Rights** Originally proposed by the National Domestic Workers Alliance, guarantees basic rights such as overtime pay, paid vacation days, and protection from sexual and racial harassment to domestic workers.

**"Don't ask, don't tell"** A policy in effect from 1994 to 2011 that barred openly gay, lesbian, or bisexual persons from military service while prohibiting military personnel from discriminating against soldiers who kept silent about their sexual preferences.

**Equal Pay Act** Federal law passed in 1963 that amended the Fair Labor Standards Act and aimed at abolishing wage disparity based on sex.

**Equal Rights Amendment (ERA)** Proposed amendment to the U.S. Constitution first introduced in 1923 that banned the denial or abridgment of rights on the basis of gender.

**Farmers' Alliance** An umbrella movement of agricultural organizations, founded in Texas in 1876, that encouraged men and women to cooperate in running their households and their farms. The Alliance provided the foundation for what would become the Populist Party.

*feme covert* A legal term for a married woman who was "covered" or protected by her husband. Before the law, women lost the ability to act independently when they married.

**feminism** An ideology insisting on the fundamental equality of women and men. In the 1960s and 1970s feminists differed over how to achieve that equality: while liberal feminists mostly demanded equal rights for women in the workplace and in politics, radical feminists more thoroughly condemned the capitalist system and male oppression and demanded equality in both private and public life. Black and women of color feminists foregrounded the intersectionality of oppressions shaping women's lives.

**Fifteenth Amendment** An 1870 constitutional amendment forbidding discrimination in voting on the basis of race, color, or previous condition of servitude.

**Fight for $15** Advocates that the federal minimum wage be raised to $15 an hour. The movement began in New York City in 2012.

**First Great Awakening** A series of Christian revivals that swept Great Britain and the colonies in the 1730s and 1740s. It reshaped Protestant Christianity with a focus on individual piety and emotional worship.

**flapper** The youthful new woman in popular culture of the 1920s who, rebelling against her mother's generation, celebrated her freedom by wearing short skirts, bobbing her hair, and smoking and drinking openly.

**Fourteenth Amendment** An 1868 constitutional amendment defining national citizenship, mandating equal justice before the law, and guaranteeing essential civil rights, primarily for formerly enslaved African American men.

**Fourth United Nations World Conference on Women** The final world conference organized by the United Nations held in Beijing in 1995. Earlier UN conferences had taken place in Mexico City in 1975, Copenhagen in 1980, and Nairobi in 1985.

**Freedman's Bureau** The Bureau of Refugees, Freedmen, and Abandoned Lands, a government agency formed in 1865 and administered by the army, that afforded aid and protection to formerly enslaved people, among others.

**Fugitive Slave Act (1850)** Congressional act that nationalized the process of capturing people who had escaped enslavement and returning them to those who had enslaved them by requiring federal judges to appoint "commissioners" to hear cases of accused fugitives and by requiring the active complicity of state officers.

**gay liberation** Social movement that demanded better treatment and recognition for gay and lesbian citizens, including getting rid of laws that criminalized homosexuality.

**gender gap** The difference between the number of men and the number of women voting for a candidate.

**General Federation of Women's Clubs** National federation of women's clubs that were an acceptable way for middle class women to expand their civic engagement while also providing a social outlet.

**gig economy** A segment of the 21st century economy made up of non-employee laborers, including rideshare drivers, delivery workers, and adjunct faculty. This group is disproportionately made up of female workers.

**global feminism** A movement pushing for women's rights on a global scale, with local activists worldwide providing much of its energy. The movement began in earnest during the UN's Year of the Woman in 1975.

**Glorious Revolution (1688)** Uprising of the English Parliament against King James II that transformed the English system of government from an absolute monarchy to a constitutional monarchy and the rule of Parliament.

**Gold Rush** An influx of migrants, primarily single men, into California after the discovery of gold there in 1849.

**Great Depression** International economic depression and the United States' worst economic downturn to date. Beginning at the end of 1929 and lasting for ten years, the catastrophe spread to every corner of the country, wrecking lives and leaving people homeless, hungry, and desperate for work.

**Great Migration** The large-scale movement of African Americans during and after World War I from the South to the North, Midwest, and West, where jobs were more plentiful.

**Harlem Renaissance** An African American cultural and arts movement of the 1920s centered in the Harlem neighborhood of New York City.

**Hart-Celler Immigration and Nationality Act** Federal legislation passed in 1965 that ended the racial quota system of immigration. Instead it instituted general caps on immigration from the Eastern and Western hemispheres and expanded the ability of family members of citizens or legal residents to immigrate.

**Hartford Female Seminary** A pioneering education institution for women founded by Catharine Beecher.

**homesteading** The process of accepting land in western territories from the federal government that came with the requirement to live on it and improve it by farming or building.

**Hyde Amendment** Federal law passed in 1977 that prohibited federal funds from paying for abortion even if the procedure was necessary to save the life of the mother.

**identity politics** The existence of self-identified social groups, usually defined in opposition to the dominant society.

**indentured servant** Person who promised to work for a term of years (usually between two and seven) in exchange for passage to the New World.

**Indian Citizenship Act** Federal law, passed in 1924, that extended U.S. citizenship to Native Americans, including the right to vote.

**industrialization** A reorganization of the economy for the purpose of manufacturing.

**Jazz Age** The decade of the 1920s, when jazz and blues music, both based on African roots and primarily developed by African American musicians, became widely popular.

**Jim Crow laws** Statutes discriminating against nonwhite Americans, particularly in the South. The term specifically refers to regulations excluding Blacks from public facilities or compelling them to use ones separate from those allotted to whites.

**Ku Klux Klan (KKK)** An organization associated with the bitterest and most violent opponents of Reconstruction and Black freedom. Formed in Pulaski, Tennessee, in late 1865, Klan members devoted themselves to denying African Americans any legitimate role in the public sphere, stressing the superiority of white, Protestant, Anglo-Saxon citizens. Revived in the 1920s as an anti-immigrant, anti-Catholic, and anti-Jewish organization.

**labor movement** The movement led by unions to gain better working conditions and pay for workers, especially those in the working class. The relationship between labor organizers and female workers was often difficult.

**Ladies Association of Philadelphia** A women's benevolent society that successfully raised funds for the Continental Army during the Revolutionary War. The ability to act in public as members of societies like this one represented a new role for women at this period.

**League of Women Voters** Organization founded in 1920 to help women exercise their newly-won right to vote.

**LGBTQ** Acronym for lesbian, gay, bisexual, transgender, and queer that is commonly used to refer to the larger queer community.

**Louisiana Purchase** Sale of a huge chunk of North American land to the United States by France in 1803. It provided a vast area that Americans felt entitled to settle by virtue of that purchase.

**lynching** Mob violence, often resulting in death by hanging, shooting, or burning; it was especially prevalent in the 1890s South against African Americans, both male and female.

**matrilineal** A society in which social identity is based on kinship and descendancy from the mother.

**Middle Passage** The forced voyage of enslaved Africans to the New World, one leg of a triangular trade route linking Europe, Africa, and the Americas.

**miscegenation** Laws that prohibited marriage between people of different races in an attempt to preserve white supremacy, especially property ownership.

**Miss America Pageant** Beauty contest in which young, unmarried women from each state compete for a crown and the title "Miss America." Members of the Women's Liberation movement protested the pageant in 1968 by crowning a sheep and depositing girdles and bras, seen as items of oppression, in a trash can.

**moral suasion** The strategy of using persuasion (as opposed to legal coercion) to convince individuals to alter their behavior. In the antebellum years, moral suasion generally implied an appeal to religious values.

**Mormons** Term of derision used for members of the Church of Jesus Christ of Latter-day Saints, a religion founded by Joseph Smith, who preached a conservative theology of patriarchal authority.

**Morrill Land Grant Act** Federal government act passed in 1862 that prompted the growth of land-grant colleges and universities, which were mainly coeducational.

**mutual-aid societies** Organizations through which people of relatively meager means pooled their resources for emergencies. Usually, individuals paid small amounts in dues and were able to borrow large amounts in times of need. In the early nineteenth century, mutual-aid societies were especially common among workers in free African American communities.

**National American Woman Suffrage Association (NAWSA)** Organization founded in 1890, headed by Carrie Chapman Catt, that sought a constitutional amendment to give women the right to vote.

**National Association for the Advancement of Colored People (NAACP)** Civil rights organization founded in 1909 that was innovative in establishing legal action as a powerful basis in the fight for African American rights.

**National Association of Colored Women (NACW)** Organized in 1896, the NACW, made up largely of Black middle-class women, addressed the needs of Black neighborhoods, establishing hospitals, day nurseries, and kindergartens, and also attacked segregation and lynching. The organization's motto was "Lifting as We Climb."

**National Organization for Women (NOW)** An organization founded in 1966 that advocated an end to laws that discriminated against women, opportunity to work at any job, and equal pay for equal work.

**National Woman Suffrage Association** Organization founded in 1869 by Elizabeth Cady Stanton and Susan B. Anthony that promoted the right to vote for women. They refused to support ratification of the Fifteenth Amendment because it gave the vote to African American men while white women were still denied that right.

**New Deal** Collective name given to President Franklin Roosevelt's programs to fight the Great Depression, first articulated during his 1932 presidential campaign. He pledged to use federal power to ensure a more equitable distribution of income and rebuild the economy.

**New Woman** A term first applied to women in the 1890s who defied traditional middle-class and upper-class Victorian feminine ideals by emphasizing education, work outside the home, women's suffrage, and vigorous physical activity.

**Nineteenth Amendment (1920)** Constitutional amendment granting women the right to vote.

***Obergefell v. Hodges*** Supreme Court decision in 2015 holding that the Fourteenth Amendment guaranteed same-sex couples the right to marry.

**Occupy Wall Street** Protest movement active in 2011 that criticized predatory banks and corporations and the unequal distribution of wealth. It popularized the contrast between the 1% at the pinnacle of the economic structure and the remaining 99%.

**Oneida Community** A utopian community in upstate New York that endorsed collective ownership of property and communal child-raising and rejected monogamy.

**Overland Trail** The trail from the Missouri River to Oregon and California, begun in the early 1840s and only replaced with the completion of a transcontinental railroad in 1869.

**polygamy** A marriage custom of having more than one partner at the same time, for example, when a man has more than one wife.

**Populist Party** Party in the 1890s that opposed the Eastern economic elites and favoring government action to help producers in general and farmers in particular.

**Progressive Era** Time period from 1890 to 1920 when progressive social movements like the suffrage movement and the labor movement made great strides. Women of all classes found more ways to be accepted into the public sphere during this period.

**queer theory** Academic study that provides alternative readings of historical and literary texts through a queer lens.

**Reconstruction** The time period following the Civil War when the federal government attempted to rebuild the South after the devastation of war and situate the formerly enslaved into society as freed people.

**Republican motherhood** In the early Republic, mothers were tasked with the education of children, including instilling their sons with the qualities of virtue, piety, and patriotism they would need to be leaders of a democratic society. This new role gave women greater access to education and knowledge of current events.

***Roe v. Wade*** U.S. Supreme Court decision upholding a woman's constitutional right to terminate a pregnancy.

**Rosie the Riveter** An iconic Norman Rockwell painting of a muscular woman in coveralls, she came to represent the women who left the home for the workforce during World War II, despite the fact that many of the women doing this kind of work had long been in the industrial workforce.

**Second Great Awakening** Religious revivalist movement of the early nineteenth century that echoed the Great Awakening of the 1730s. The movement linked evangelical Christians on both sides of the Atlantic to exchange ideas and strategies that inspired a broad set of social, cultural, and intellectual changes.

**second-wave feminism** The revival of feminism after 1960 as a movement that fought for social and political equality. Major issues of the second wave were equal pay, access to birth control and safe abortions, and an end to sex-based discrimination.

**Seneca Falls convention** A prominent gathering on the subject of women's rights held at Seneca Falls, NY in 1848. The Declaration of Sentiments and resolutions adopted there addressed questions of women's rights, including the right to vote.

**separate but equal** In 1896, *Plessy v. Ferguson* declared segregation was constitutional as long as the different accommodations provided for Blacks and whites were equivalent. This doctrine would allow legalized segregation throughout the South until the Supreme Court overturned the edict in 1954 with *Brown v. Board of Education*.

**separate spheres** The concept that women's lives were supposed to revolve around the familial and private, while men were expected to have public lives focusing on work and politics.

**settlement house movement** Movement to create community centers in poor urban neighborhoods that would provide social services, recreation, and education to local residents. Settlement houses were run by college-educated women and men who lived in them.

**settler colonialism** A distinctive colonizing strategy (different from trade- or mission-based colonialism) whereby collections of immigrants from foreign places used their numbers to gain control of territory and resources from indigenous peoples.

**Seven Sisters** A series of women's colleges founded throughout the late nineteenth century that provided broader educational opportunities for women.

**Shakers** A religious group that built communities based on reciprocity between the sexes rather than patriarchal domination. Shakers promoted celibacy and expanded by adoption and conversion.

**sharecropping** The practice of a tenant farming an owner's land for a share of the crop, sold when the harvest came in. This became a common form of employment for formerly enslaved people in the post–Civil War South.

**Sheppard-Towner Federal Maternity and Infancy Act** Passed in 1921, it was the nation's first federally funded public health campaign. It provided federal funding for maternity and childcare, which helped to medicalize childbirth and reduce infant mortality.

**Stonewall Riot** Riot in 1969 that resulted from an attempted police raid on a gay bar in New York City, the Stonewall Inn. This was a spark for the gay liberation movement.

**suffrage** The right to vote in political elections. Women advocated for the right to vote from the mid-nineteenth century on and eventually secured the franchise via the Nineteenth Amendment in 1920.

**Trail of Tears** Cherokee name for the United States' forced removal of their people from the Southeast to other lands. In early 1838, few Cherokee had prepared for the trip; contaminated water, inadequate food, and disease killed many of those restricted in stockades, and many more perished on the 800-mile journey west.

**transcontinental railroad** Rail line linking East Coast cities with California. Its completion in 1869 made the West much more accessible to white settlers.

**transgender** The attribute of feeling that one's actual sex does not match the one they were assigned at birth and affirmatively embracing a new gender identity. Transgender people have received increasing recognition in recent years, including legal protections.

**Treaty of Guadalupe Hidalgo** Treaty between the United States and Mexico that ended the Mexican-American War, signed on February 2, 1848. In exchange for $15 million, Mexico ceded Texas to the United States, in addition to all of the land west of Texas stretching up to Oregon, including California.

**Treaty of Paris (1763)** The treaty ending the French and Indian War whose terms transformed eastern North America's political geography. France surrendered North America, swapping Canada for the return of Guadeloupe. France ceded Louisiana to Spain, and Spain traded Florida to the British to regain control of Havana. The British Empire claimed almost all of North America east of the Mississippi.

**Triangle Shirtwaist Company** Site of a raging fire in March 1911 that swept through its factory in New York City, killing 146 workers, mostly young women, and leading to a series of workplace reforms.

**two-spirit** Gender non-conforming individuals among Native American tribes, usually individuals assigned male at birth who took on female roles. They are present in most Native cultures.

**Underground Railroad** A network of people who maintained safe houses for escaped people and helped transport them to places where they could be free from enslavement.

**U.S. Children's Bureau** Federal government agency tasked with investigating and improving children's lives.

**voluntary associations** Charitable organizations founded as an outgrowth of the Second Great Awakening, particularly by women.

**Voting Rights Act (1965)** Congressional act that outlawed literacy tests to vote and gave the Justice Department the power directly to register voters in districts where discrimination existed.

**Wagner Labor Relations Act** Legislation enacted in 1935 that guaranteed workers' rights to bargain collectively with their employers, prohibited the firing of workers after a strike, and restricted other anti-union measures.

**Woman's Christian Temperance Union (WCTU)** The nation's largest female reform organization of the nineteenth century, formed in 1874, specifically dedicated to the banning of intoxicating beverages. The WCTU also sought the vote for women.

**Women's Joint Congressional Committee** A coalition of ten major women's organizations formed after women won the right to vote in 1920. The committee lobbied for women's issues at the federal level.

**women's liberation (or "women's lib")** One of the strands of second-wave feminism, primarily made up of women who had experience as activists from working with the Civil Rights and anti-Vietnam War movements. Their goal was to dismantle patriarchy, replacing it with non-racist, non-sexist institutions.

**Women's March (2017)** A march on Washington held to protest the inauguration of Donald Trump as president of the United States. The march was echoed in cities across the country and around the world and was the largest single-day protest in U.S. history.

**women's rights activism** The more traditional strand of second-wave feminism, whose supporters worked for legal changes like the Equal Pay Act and the addition of "sex" to the Civil

Rights Act. They were organized as the National Organization for Women, led by Betty Friedan.

**women's sphere** The mindset that women's roles should be limited to the private, domestic sphere, primarily focused on maintaining the home and raising and educating children. This diminished the role that women had played in the colonies before about 1750, and was a result of the growing division between public and private realms in colonial society.

**World's Columbian Exposition** A World's Fair that was designed to promote the industrial, economic, and cultural strength of the United States to the rest of the world. It took place in Chicago and opened in 1893.

# CREDITS

## CHAPTER 1

CO1 Library of Congress.

1.1 Library of Congress Prints and Photographs Division Washington, D.C. 20540 USA http://hdl.loc.gov/loc.pnp/pp.print.

1.2 Sarin Images/GRANGER.

1.3 GRANGER.

1.4 Colonial Williamsburg Foundation.

1.5 Library of Congress.

## CHAPTER 2

CO2 American Antiquarian Society.

2.1 Library of Congress.

2.2 Library of Congress.

2.3 Library of Congress.

2.4 GRANGER.

2.5 Sarin Images/GRANGER.

2.6 Wikimedia Commons/Journal of the Civil War Era.

## CHAPTER 3

CO3 © CORBIS/Corbis via Getty Images.

3.1 Library of Congress Prints and Photographs Division Washington, D.C. 20540 USA http://hdl.loc.gov/loc.pnp/pp.print.

3.2 Courtesy of the George Eastman Museum.

3.3 Library of Congress.

3.4 Historic Collection/Alamy Stock Photo.

3.5 Library of Congress.

3.6 Wikimedia Commons/Collection of the National Museum of African American History and Culture shared with the Library of Congress.

## CHAPTER 4

CO4 The Reading Room/Alamy Stock Photo.

4.1 Library of Congress.

4.2 Gado Images/Alamy Stock Photo.

4.3 Nebraska State Historical Society.

4.4 WS Collection/Alamy Stock Photo.

4.5a Courtesy of the Peabody Museum of Archaeology and Ethnology, Harvard University, 2004.29.5634.

4.5b Courtesy of the Peabody Museum of Archaeology and Ethnology, Harvard University, 2004.29.5635.

4.6 Schlesinger Library on the History of Women in America, Radcliffe Institute.

## CHAPTER 5

5.1 Library of Congress.

5.2 Library of Congress.

5.3 Wikimedia Commons.

5.4 Library of Congress.

5.5 Mass Historical Society.

5.6 Library of Congress.

## CHAPTER 6

CO6 Everett Collection Historical/Alamy Stock Photo.

6.1 Arizona Historical Society, PC 1000 Tucson Photo Collections, Portraits-Huerta-Castro Family, #6266.9

6.2 Everett Collection Historical/Alamy Stock Photo.

6.3 Library of Congress.

6.4 Library of Congress.

6.5 Japanese American National Museum (Gift of Dr. Sumi Shimatsu, 97.89.7.

6.6 Library of Congress Prints and Photographs Division Washington, D.C. 20540 USA.

## CHAPTER 7

CO7 Everett Collection Inc/Alamy Stock Photo.

7.1 AP Photo.

7.2 Bettmann/Getty images.

7.3 Collection of the Smithsonian National Museum of African American History and Culture.

7.4 Library of Congress.

7.5 Library of Congress Prints and Photographs Division Washington, D.C. 20540 USA http://hdl.loc.gov/loc.pnp/pp.print.

7.6 AP Photo/Michael Dwyer.

## CHAPTER 8

CO8 Dennis Brack/Alamy Stock Photo.

8.1 Library of Congress.

8.2 Office of Nancy Pelosi.

8.3 AP Photo.

8.4 JG Photography/Alamy Stock Photo.

8.5 Photo by Spencer Platt/Getty Images.

8.6 Photo by JIM WATSON/AFP via Getty Images.

# INDEX

Note: page numbers in italics refer to illustrations